Environmental Politics

Second edition

Britain, Europe and the
Global Environment

Robert Garner

Published in Great Britain by
MACMILLAN PRESS LTD
Houndmills, Basingstoke, Hampshire RG21 6XS and London
Companies and representatives throughout the world

A catalogue record for this book is available from the British Library.

ISBN 0–333–76309–2 hardcover
ISBN 0–333–76310–6 paperback

Published in the United States of America by
ST. MARTIN'S PRESS, INC.,
Scholarly and Reference Division,
175 Fifth Avenue, New York, N.Y. 10010

ISBN 0–312–23391–4

Library of Congress Cataloging-in-Publication Data
Garner, Robert, 1960–
Environmental politics: Britain, Europe, and the global environment/Robert
Garner.– 2nd ed.
p. cm. – (Contemporary political studies)
Includes bibliographical references and index.
ISBN 0–312–23391–4
1. Environmental policy. 2. Environmentalism. 3. Sustainable development.
I. Title II. Contemporary political studies (St. Martin's Press)

GE170.G38 2000
363.7–dc21

00–023936

This book is printed on paper suitable for recycling and made from fully managed and
sustained forest sources.

Copy-edited and typeset by Povey–Edmondson
Tavistock and Rochdale, England

10   9   8   7   6   5   4   3   2   1
09   08   07   06   05   04   03   02   01   00

Printed in Hong Kong

Contents

List of Tables and Figures

Tables

Figures

Abbreviations

ALF	Animal Liberation Front
AONB	Area of Outstanding Natural Beauty
BATNEEC	best available techniques not entailing excessive costs
BPEO	best practical environmental option
BPO	best practicable option
BSE	bovine spongiform encephalopathy
BTCV	British Trust for Conservation Volunteers
CA	Countryside Agency
CBD	Convention on Biological Diversity
CC	Countryside Commission
CFCs	chlorofluorocarbons
CITES	Convention on the International Trade in Endangered Species
CPRE	Council for the Protection of Rural England
CSD	Commission on Sustainable Development
DETR	Department of the Envronment, Transport and the Regions
DoE	Department of the Environment
DTI	Department of Trade and Industry
EA	Environment Agency
EU	European Union
GATT	General Agreement on Tariffs and Trade
GEF	Global Environment Facility
GNP	Gross National Product
HMIP	Her Majesty's Inspectorate of Pollution
IAPI	Industrial Air Pollution Inspectorate
ICBP	International Council for Bird Preservation
ICRW	International Convention for the Regulation of Whaling
IPC	integrated pollution control
IPCC	Intergovernmental Panel on Climate Change
IUCN	International Union for the Conservation of Nature and Natural Resources
IWC	International Whaling Commission

MIT	Massachusetts Institute of Technology
MAFF	Ministry of Agriculture, Fisheries and Food
MEP	Member of the European Parliament
NCC	Nature Conservancy Council
NFU	National Farmers Union
NGO	non-governmental organization
NRA	National Rivers Authority
OECD	Organization of Economic Cooperation and Development
PCBs	polychlorinated biphenyls
RCEP	Royal Commission on Environmental Pollution
RSNC	Royal Society for Nature Conservation
RSPB	Royal Society for the Protection of Birds
RSPCA	Royal Society for the Prevention of Cruelty to Animals
SEA	Single European Act
SSSI	Site of Special Scientific Interest
UNCED	United Nations Conference on Environment and Development
UNEP	United Nations Environment Programme
VAT	Value Added Tax
WTO	World Trade Organization
WWF	World Wide Fund for Nature

Preface

The function of this substantially rewritten and expanded second edition is to maintain the book's original purpose, to convey the scope of environmental politics by identifying and exploring its major dimensions and by indicating the range of published material in what is a rapidly expanding academic discipline. It is therefore intended primarily as an introductory text providing a framework for those taking undergraduate courses in environmental politics. It is hoped, too, that the material will be useful for students and teachers of political theory and public policy. Last, but not least, the aim is also to produce a book which is accessible enough to be of interest to the general reader.

Much has happened since the first edition was written, not least the election of a new Labour government in Britain claiming to be Greener than its predecessor, and further progress in the international arena, most notably the Kyoto agreement on climate change. Over the last few years, too, the environmental politics literature has mushroomed and, as a consequence, the bibliography of this second edition is much expanded. The basic structure of the book has been maintained although there has been an extensive rewrite. Some major alterations are worth noting. In particular, the chapter on political parties has been omitted and a chapter on the European Union added. In the former case, the material has been distributed to other, arguably more appropriate, parts of the book. In the latter, a separate chapter on the EU was deemed necessary because of its growing impact on the environmental policy of member states and the concomitant expansion of the literature focusing on it.

The additional chapter on the EU is but one illustration of the general trend in this volume towards a greater emphasis on the supranational dimension, which in turn is a reflection of the growing internationalization of politics in general and environmental politics in particular. While the national focus is still on Britain, there is greater emphasis on the supranational influences upon national environmental politics and policy. This shift is also illustrated by the reordering of the chapters with those focusing on Britain now appearing towards the end of the book.

xii *Preface*

Many debts have been incurred during the process of researching and writing the two editions of this book. I would like to thank Stephen Young, Wyn Grant, Andy Dobson and John Dryzek for their advice, encouragement and kindness. Two anonymous reviewers provided a great deal of useful comments, many of which have been acted on. Clare Grist was responsible for seeing the first edition through to publication and my new publisher, Steven Kennedy, provided much-needed enthusiasm, encouragement and patience as the second edition proceeded often more slowly than necessity required. Responsibility for the (undoubtedly many) omissions and mistakes remains, of course, with me. The book is dedicated to the memory of my father.

Leicester ROBERT GARNER

1

Introduction: the Political Dimensions of Environmentalism

Thirty years ago, the themes covered in this book would not have been included in a popular series providing introductory accounts of political issues and processes. This is not to say that people were not concerned about the environment then, since many of the major environmental groups in Britain and the United States were well established by the 1960s. It was not until the 1970s, however, that the environment became an important political issue and not until the latter half of the 1980s that it became a mainstream one. As a consequence, the study of environmental politics has discarded its Cinderella status.

Indeed, by the late 1980s, we seemed to be entering a new Green era, where environmental concern had become the height of fashion. In the developed world at least, opinion polls revealed mounting public concern for the state of the environment; consumers demanded environmentally friendly products, and producers, with varying degrees of honesty, sought to provide them; recycling centres and bottle banks flourished. In Britain, the then prime minister Margaret Thatcher discarded her initial scepticism and described the environment as 'one of the great challenges' of the late twentieth century and, moreover, that it was only safe in the hands of a Conservative government (McCormick, 1991, pp. 1–2). As if to confirm that Thatcher's political antennae were working effectively, the Green Party came from nowhere to win 15 per cent of the British vote in the 1989 European Parliament elections, pushing the newly formed Liberal Democrats into fourth place.

Since the late 1980s, the environment has slipped down the issue agenda a little, overtaken by dramatic political and economic events in Britain and elsewhere. It is now established, however, as a permanently important feature of political and academic discourse. Sovereign states are now locked into a supranational structure of institutions and processes, initially set in train by the United Nations Conference on the Human Environment convened in Stockholm in

1

1972 and built upon at the United Nations Conference on Environment and Development (UNCED) held in Rio twenty years later, which guarantees the continued participation of nations in the search for acceptable solutions to environmental problems.

The environment as a political issue

So, what is the stuff of environmental politics? An appropriate starting point is a definition. The common-sense definition of the term 'environment' – constituting our surroundings – would seem to be hopelessly broad, although it does reveal a sense of how all-pervasive the subject is. In practice, we can impose a limitation by focusing on the 'natural' environment, so that environmental politics becomes a study of the human impact on the natural environment. Some prefer to use the label 'Green politics'. 'Green' has been used since the 1950s to indicate concern for the environment and is now used in a blanket fashion by most casual observers. For others, the term Green is associated with the radical ideas and policies of Green political parties, to be distinguished from the more moderate and reformist character of many environmental organizations (see below).

To understand the *politics* of the environment, some knowledge of environmental problems is necessary, but in order to distinguish between the scientific and social-scientific study of the environment, we must go further than this. We must also seek to explain why it is that the environment has become a political issue, what its distinguishing characteristics are, what impact political decisions have had on the environment, why some decisions were taken rather than others and what political structures are best able to protect the environment. It is with these themes that this book is concerned.

The simple answer to the first of these questions is that the environment has become an important political issue because enough, or the right, people perceived there to be a problem that had to be tackled. This, of course, is to beg the question: why did this happen? A number of answers suggest themselves. We shall start by looking at the impact of environmental problems.

Environmental Degradation

Obviously, the raw material of the environmental debate is the deleterious effects of human activity on the planet, and Chapter 2 seeks to outline the nature and consequences of this activity. Information on environmental degradation is readily available, and one would be forgiven for concluding that the rise of the environment as an important political issue is related to lay observations and scientific evidence concerning such 'invisible' phenomena as global warming and ozone depletion. Indeed, one factor which ostensibly distinguishes the environment from many other issues is the extent of objective measurement involved. Thus, there is a crucially important technical core to the study of the environment, providing a key role for engineers, scientists and technicians (Weale, 1992, p. 10). Put simply, if there is a hole in the ozone layer and this threatens the stability of the global environment, then we need to do something about it. And if something needs to be done, then we need to decide what is causing it and do something about preventing it.

The growing sense of an objective environmental crisis, therefore, is an obvious reason for heightened concern. One can point here to the well-publicised environmental disasters of the past forty years or so – the mercury poisoning at Minamata Bay in Japan in 1959; the slag-heap slip at Aberfan in Wales which buried a school, with great loss of life, in 1966; the oil pollution caused by the stricken tankers *Torrey Canyon* (in 1967) and *Exxon Valdez* (in 1988); industrial accidents at Bhopal in India, which killed over 3000 people and injured many hundreds of thousands, and at Seveso in Italy; the near thing at the Three Mile Island nuclear facility in the USA in the late 1970s and the real thing at Chernobyl in the 1980s – to name but a few. One can point, too, to important books, conferences and scientific research – Rachel Carson's best selling *Silent Spring* (1962) which documented the effects on the countryside of pesticide use; the first pictures of the Earth taken from space in 1967 which emphasized the fragile and insignificant nature of the planet and its occupants; the *Limits to Growth* report (Meadows *et al.*, 1972); the previously mentioned Stockholm conference (proceedings published as Ward and Dubos, 1972); the Brundtland Report (World Commission on Environment and Development,1987); and various scientific papers relating to global warming and ozone depletion – which have had the effect of informing decision-makers and the wider public about environmental problems.

This evidence indicates not only that environmental problems have increased quantitatively, in the sense that the number of environmentally damaging incidents have risen markedly, but that there has also been a qualitative shift. Environmental problems are no longer perceived merely as localized concerns affecting relatively few people and having few long-term consequences. Instead, the central concern has become nothing less than human survival on a planet which, it is now recognized, cannot continue indefinitely to cope with the consumption of non-renewable resources or the absorption of waste products from industrial processes at the levels which it is presently asked to do. The following information tells its own story:

> Since 1900, the world's population has multiplied more than three times. Its economy has grown twentyfold. The consumption of fossil fuels has grown by a factor of 30, and industrial production by a factor of 50. Most of that growth, about four-fifths of it, occurred since 1950. Much of it is unsustainable. (MacNeil *et al.*, 1991, p. 3)

Of course, as Young (1993, p. 4) points out, environmental problems do manifest themselves at the local level, but 'what appear to be little local difficulties are the visible parts of much more complicated sets of inter-related problems', with regional, national and international aspects. Thus, for many people, the increasing volume of traffic and the building of more roads to meet rising demand, causes readily visible congestion and damage to the country-side. It also, though, causes less visible health problems and, even further removed, it contributes to acid rain, increases the level of carbon dioxide in the atmosphere thereby adding to the threat of global warming and, last but not least, uses up more of the world's precious oil reserves (Young, 1993, pp. 5–6).

These observations lead us to identify two further features which distinguish environmentalism from many other issues. In the first place, present practices will have long-term consequences affecting the fundamental interests of future generations. This, of course, raises practical questions about the representation of future generations in our decision-making arenas as well as philosophical questions concerning inter-generational justice (Weale, 1992, pp. 8–9).

Second, is the increasingly international character of environmental decision-making. Co-operation between states to achieve environmental objectives has a long history, but three post-war developments have markedly intensified the shift in focus. First, as Chapters 6 and 8 confirm, a great deal of environmental policy-making in Britain and other member states is now made in the context of the European Union. Secondly, the identification of global environmental problems has not only increased the urgency for nations to act in concert because they are potentially so serious, but it has also been recognized that they are problems that can *only* be dealt with by global co-operation. As List and Rittberger (1992, p. 108) point out: 'Ecological policy, like charity, begins at home, but, unlike the latter, stopping there is often immediately self-defeating.' Put simply, all countries stand to suffer from the depletion of the ozone layer but it is little use for one country, or a handful of countries, to act by banning the production of chlorofluorocarbons (CFCs) if other countries do not follow suit. Thirdly, there is the related problem of Third World development since one, if not *the*, main threat to the environment is the rapid industrialization of developing countries eager to replicate the material quality of life in the developed world.

This book recognizes the increasingly supranational character of environmentalism. The global nature of environmental problems is discussed in Chapter 2, Chapter 5 is devoted to a general examination of the character and effectiveness of international environmental regimes, and Chapter 6 focuses on the EU as a particularly important example of such a regime. Moreover, whilst Chapters 7, 8 and 9 are concerned with environmental politics and policy in Britain, supranational influences upon British theory and practice are not neglected.

The limits to an issue-based approach

We should not over-exaggerate the importance of objective environmental problems as an explanation for the existence of a *politics* of the environment. These objectively defined problems can, of course, be distinguished from a subjective awareness of, and concern for, such problems so that the existence of the former does not necessarily by itself explain why the environment has become an important issue. This is why the social sciences can make an important contribution to the environmental debate, and why it is not merely the preserve of scientists, technocrats or even philosophers, important though their contributions might be (Yearley, 1992, p. 49, pp. 184–5). This recognition explains why there has been a tendency for environmental science degree courses to be redefined as environmental studies (Young, 1990, p. 91). At one extreme, it has even been suggested that the objective conditions are not at all important in explaining the rise of a social problem such as the environment (Kitsuse and Spector, 1981).

As Chapter 2 illustrates, some of the standard explanations for the rising popularity of environmental protection, based on an affluence-induced post-material culture and a post-war occupational shift, do come close to denying the social importance of the increasing severity of environmental problems. While we might not want to ignore completely the explanatory capacity of objective environmental problems, the opposite extreme – that there is a simple relationship between identifying environmental problems, providing remedies for them and the generation of widespread popular support for their implementation – is equally simplistic.

There are a number of arguments which, at the very least, throw doubt upon the 'objective problem' explanation. First, many environmental problems are not directly observable or, in the case of natural resource depletion, not easy to visualize, and such problems are mediated through scientists – whose conclusions are rarely universally accepted within the scientific community – the media and pressure groups. Secondly, even though most people have indirect experience of environmental problems and disasters, many of these still remain distant affairs with few immediate effects. For example, even though we have been told that the Chernobyl nuclear accident has affected us, in terms of an increased incidence of cancer, the effects remain imperceptible and we can comfort ourselves with the somewhat complacent thought – encouraged, rightly or wrongly, by nuclear scientists with a vested interest in the continuation of the industry – that our nuclear safety record is such that a similar accident could not happen here (the relationship between scientific evaluation of risk and the 'real' world inhabited by the general public is discussed by Beck, 1992).

A final point is that, even when environmental problems are recognized, it does not automatically follow that remedial action will follow. The causes of a particular visible problem may be disputed and this may delay action. For example, the British government refused for a long time to accept that the damage caused to Scandinavian forests and rivers by acid rain was primarily caused by emissions from British power stations. The British government's reluctance was mainly a product of political expediency but there may also be genuine doubts as to the effects of particular practices as well as the causes of, and therefore the most appropriate remedies for, environmental problems. The unwillingness to act when there is doubt will be compounded where proposed solutions involve considerable sacrifices, as in the case of action to minimize the relatively little-understood phenomenon of global warming.

Reluctance to act may also be caused by the costs of solutions which people are unwilling to accept, coupled with a perception that a certain degree of environmental degradation can be accommodated. Even if this causes long-term problems, it may be decided that passing on these problems to future generations is preferable to making sacrifices now. To some degree, then, there are choices to be made in the environmental debate, and, as a consequence, it is a debate that is often more concerned with values, ethics and interests than with objective facts. This perception is confirmed by the changing nature of the case put by environmentalists. In the 1970s, their case was structured by warnings of imminent catastrophe, encouraging, as one stream of thought, a survivalist mentality where the objective imperatives – act now before it is too late – predominated (Hardin, 1968; Ehrlich, 1972; Goldsmith *et al*, 1972; Heilbroner, 1974; Meadows *et al*, 1972). More recently, however, radical Greens have put greater emphasis on the desirability, as opposed to the necessity, of change. Thus, a doom and gloom scenario has been discarded in favour of promoting a society which places a good quality environment above one which worships material consumption.

One can see the advantage of such a position. The Green case is, as Robyn Eckersley (1992, pp. 17–21) points out, driven above all by an 'emancipatory' ethos, since it is not just telling us that we have to give up our present material standard of living, leaving us to mourn our loss, but it is also telling us how our lives can be enriched by adopting a set of values and institutions which will make us happier and more fulfilled. This appeal to self-interest is coupled with an appeal to our altruistic nature, since a central feature of the radical Green approach is an ethical case for discarding an anthropocentric approach to the natural environment in favour of an ecocentric one which recognises the inherent value of nature.

Quite clearly, then, it is simplistic to equate the rise of the environment as a political issue with the mere existence of environmental problems. Convincing scientific evidence, particularly if backed up by clearly observed environmental deterioration, obviously makes a social-problem claim more robust, adding credibility to campaigns mounted by environmentalists (Yearley, 1992, p. 75). Of equal, if not greater, importance, though, are the social, economic and political processes involved in placing the environment near the top of the political agenda. Of prime importance is the role performed by the environmental movement in raising the profile of the issue and generating concern, justifiable or not. But this is to jump one step ahead of ourselves. The significant growth of the organized environmental movement in the 1970s and 1980s, and the greater public receptiveness to its campaigns, was itself the product of a shift in public attitudes which can, at least in part, be explained by important social and economic change. These issues are discussed particularly in Chapters 2 and 9.

The distinctive nature of the environment as an issue adds weight to the claim that public desire for its protection does reflect something more than a recognition of objective problems. For it might be argued that increased support for environmental protection represents a paradigm shift in post-war politics. In the first place, the emphasis on the empirical and normative limits to economic growth challenges the goal of every post-war government, whose major objective has been to find the best means of increasing material prosperity. Furthermore, as Weale (1992, p. 7) points out, the environment is a post-welfare state sector of public policy in that it 'does not use public spending as its primary policy instrument' because it is not concerned with arriving at the correct formula for distributing the fruits of economic growth. Indeed, as Beck (1992) has pointed out, the environment may be more correctly seen as a matter of being concerned with the distribution of the 'bads' or 'risks' of economic growth and human interference with the natural world. Perceptions of risk are central to the issue of nuclear power, as we have seen, but it is also a crucial factor in other high-profile issues such as BSE and biotechnology in general and genetically modified food in particular. Finally, although distributive issues are an important element of environmental politics, with environmental degradation impacting unevenly across different sections of society, a quality environment remains a public good and not a narrow sectional interest. Since the benefits of action to protect the environment will usually be widespread, distinctive problems of collective action bearing upon the behaviour of groups and individuals occur. These will be considered in the chapters that follow.

The political response

The relationship between public concern and the responsiveness of political institutions is critical to a study of environmental politics. It is clear that widely perceived 'problems', however much scientific expertize has been utilized to identify them, do not always result in positive and sustained political action. It is precisely for this reason that the social sciences are able to make a contribution to a study of the environment. Thus, Chapters 5, 6 and 8 examine the structure of environmental decision-making in Britain and internationally, focusing on the institutions responsible for making and enforcing policies which have an impact on the environment. The changing nature of British environmental policy is documented and its effectiveness assessed.

The character of environmental policy is the product of political processes which need to be explained. Despite the enormous growth of the environmental lobby in recent decades, successive British governments have not been noted, at least before the late 1980s, for their concern with the natural environment and still less for action to remedy environmental problems. Likewise, despite the recognition by governments throughout the world that environmental issues are politically important, progress towards effective international agreements has been slow. It is, of course, a flawed approach to explain these developments by reference to the attitudes of governmental actors alone, although such attitudes can play an important role in policy outcomes (Nordliner, 1981). Rather, environmental decision-making is, like other public-policy issue areas, a complex matter involving a wide variety of actors, interests and considerations.

Pollution as a technical problem, for instance, does not raise insurmountable difficulties, but it enters the realm of politics precisely because it is not merely a technical problem, but one which causes conflict between competing interests – for instance, motorists, oil companies and road builders versus cyclists, pedestrians and wildlife and, at a supranational level, the developed versus the developing world – which governments must seek to resolve. The way in which they do so will reflect the nature of power and representation in the political system: central concerns of the political scientist. The nature of the political processes involved in environmental policy-making is a recurrent theme in this book. Chapters 5 and 6 focus on the international arena, Chapter 7 examines the political impact of the environmental lobby and Chapter 9 outlines various approaches to decision-making and assesses their relevance to environmental policy-making.

A distinguishing feature of environmental policy-making is the potential for conflict between the many competing interests involved. This is primarily because environmental issues cross-cut a huge variety of governmental activities – transport, agriculture, trade and so on – and these separate policy arenas tend to provide a great deal of influence for development-oriented interests. As we will see, a truly sustainable policy requires the integration of environmental policy to ensure that problems are not merely displaced (from air to water or from one government department to another or, indeed, from present to future generations) but are genuinely resolved (Dryzek, 1987, pp. 10–13).

Approaches to environmentalism

It will have become apparent that the environmental debate revolves around competing normative and empirical claims. To make sense of these competing claims or discourses (Dryzek, 1997, pp. 7–12), it is useful to identify the constituent parts of reformist and radical perspectives (see Table 1.1). To avoid confusion, it should be pointed out that various terms have been utilized to distinguish these two positions. Dobson (1995) and Porritt (1984) refer to 'dark' and 'light' green approaches (only the former justifying the label 'Green'); Young (1993) and Hayward (1995) prefer to use the terms 'radical' and 'weak' or 'reformist' environmentalism; Naess (1973) coined the terms 'deep ecology' and 'shallow ecology'; Eckersley (1992) distinguishes between 'ecocentric' and 'anthropocentric' approaches, while to add to the confusion, both O'Riordan (1976) and Pearce *et al.* (1993) distinguish between 'ecocentric' and 'technocentric' approaches.

The term 'ecologism' is preferred by some radicals because it signifies the interrelationship between the human species and nature, and implies a non-hierarchical order of things displacing man from his dominant position – both key characteristics of the radical approach. Use of the label ecologism, however, can lead to confusion since the term ecology – first used by the scientist Ernst Haeckel in the 1850s – also describes a branch of biology which studies, in a neutral fashion, the relationship between living organisms and their environment (Heywood, 1992, p. 247).

The differences between the radical and reformist positions is more easily definable than the terminology would suggest. Each approach contains an economic, political and philosophical perspective. Put simply, the reformist position is human-centred, holding that protecting the environment is primarily for the benefit of humans. In addition, it suggests that environmental protection can be effectively incorporated within the political and economic structures of modern

Table 1.1   Reformist and radical approaches to environmentalism

Reformist	Radical
1. Modified sustainable economic growth/Ecological Modernization	1. Limits to, and undesirability of, economic growth.
2. Large role for technological development as a provider of solutions for environmental problems.	2. A distrust of scientific and technological fixes.
3. Environmental solutions can co-exist with existing social and political structures	3. Radical social and political change necessary: either authoritarian (for 'Survivalists') or decentralised and democratic political organization.
4. Anthropocentrism and a commitment to intragenerational and intergenerational equity.	4. Intrinsic value of nature or, at least, a weaker version of anthropocentrism; a commitment to social justice within human society and between humans and non-human nature

industrial society, without fundamentally threatening economic growth, material prosperity or liberal democracy.

For the reformists, then, economic growth and environmental protection are not necessarily incompatible objectives. Economic development must be sustainable; it must, in the words of one well-known definition, be 'development that meets the needs of the present without compromising the ability of future generations to meet their own needs' (World Commission on Environment and Development, 1987, p. 43). One way of defining environmental reformism is to describe it as the politics of catalytic converters, power-station scrubbers and bottle banks. It is therefore an optimistic approach, putting faith in the ability of science and technology to solve environmental problems without fundamentally challenging our institutional and value systems.

Many would regard this as the totality of what is involved in being Green or environmentally aware, but from the radical perspective at the other end of the spectrum, much more is required. Indeed, fundamental economic, social and political change – nothing less, that is, than the creation of a new kind of society with different institutions and values – is required both to deal with the severity of the crisis and to enable humans to live more satisfying and fulfilling lives and to provide nature in general with the respect it deserves. From this perspective, the reformist's tinkering with the structures of modern industrial society – providing a few palliatives to mitigate the worst effects of industrial society – is not enough to forestall environmental catastrophe and represents an inadequate and 'shallow' response to the environmental crisis.

A number of general points can be made about the approaches sketched above. In the first place, it is not being claimed here that this is the only, or even the most adequate, typology available. Barry (1994, 1999), among others, for instance, regards the polarisation endemic in the division between radical and reformist as unhelpful, not least because it tends to belittle, or direct attention away from, the important task of developing a theoretical perspective which can help us to understand the nature of environmental politics in the present, thus enabling us to chart a course which recognizes the many obstacles standing in front of sustainable development. Dryzek (1997) provides a more complex typology which helps to counter Barry's objection. By distinguishing between 'prosaic' and 'imaginative' discourses Dryzek offers us the possibility of preferring the much more sophisticated 'sustainability' model which, while remaining reformist, confronts directly some of the main radical objections to a more simplistic or 'prosaic' reformism.

The second general point is that the distinction between reformism and radicalism is over-simplistic, an inevitable and necessary feature of all typologies. In particular, it is possible to hold positions in both camps. An acceptance of the limits to growth thesis, for instance, does not preclude one from espousing an anthropocentric ethic. Similarly, there is nothing in principle incompatible with holding a belief in radical social and political change while at the same time accepting the role of technological innovation. Thirdly, the typology is incomplete. Even the reformist approach recognises that there is an environmental 'problem' requiring action. Both the radical and reformist approaches are challenged by a so-called 'Promethean' or 'cornucopian' approach which denies the existence of acute environmental problems and has 'unlimited confidence in the ability of humans and their technologies to overcome any problems presented to them' (Dryzek, 1997, p. 45). Although it was the dominant mode of thinking about the human relationship with the natural environment in the last century and for much of this, this discourse was, as Chapter 3 reveals, articulated as never before in response to the challenge it faced from environmentalists in the 1970s. Since then its fortunes have waxed and waned according primarily to the state of the economy (*ibid.*, pp. 45–60).

A great deal of attention in this book will be devoted to the reformist part of the spectrum, since this is the context of the 'real' world in which government responses to environmental problems are located and in which environmental groups must operate. No book on environmental issues, and still less one which focuses on environmental *politics*, though, can ignore the radical challenge to environmental reformism. This is in part because of its empirical claim that environmental catastrophe faces us unless we take radical steps to limit production and consumption levels. Equally, the radical approach offers a challenge to Western political thought since its claim is nothing less than that the Green approach to politics represents an entirely comprehensive and distinctive ideology, justifying a separate political party whose role is to articulate a programme of policies based on it. As a consequence, Chapters 3 and 4 consider the radical case in some detail.

2

The Environmental Crisis

One reason for the growing importance of the environment as a political issue, albeit not the only or even the principal one, is the existence and recognition of severe environmental degradation, and this chapter is mainly concerned with an exploration of the nature and scope of these environmental problems. Documenting the objective reality of environmental problems is much more straightforward, however, than explaining why the environment has emerged as an important social and political issue. In particular, we cannot just assume that the former accounts for the latter. Indeed, some social scientists have argued that social and political concern for the environment is a product of either cultural or structural changes which are entirely independent of alleged environmental decay. The chapter begins by reviewing this literature.

Explaining environmental concern

Adapting Martell (1994, ch. 4), it is possible to identify three possible types of explanations for the rise of the environment as an important social and political issue. First, there are those that see growing environmental concern as a by-product of cultural and structural factors happening independently of the actual objective state of the environment (reviewed in Lowe and Rudig, 1986, pp. 513–20). Second are those that place emphasis on the mediating influences of the environmental lobby, the media and scientists. Finally, there are those that focus on the existence of worsening environmental problems as the key trigger for concern. We might be led by our intuition to assert that objective environmental problems, and the way in which these issues are mediated through pressure groups and the media, are self-evidently important explanations of rising environmental concern. Advocates of cultural and structural

14

Table 2.1   Material and post-material value types in six Western European nations by age group, 1970.

Age group	65+	55–64	45–54	35–44	25–34	15–24
%						
Material	48	45	36	35	31	20a
Post-Material	3	7	8	12	14	25a

a The generation born after 1945.
Source: adapted from Inglehart (1990, p. 49).

explanations, however, would deny this 'common-sense' view of the world and, for this reason, we shall examine their claims in some detail.

Proponents of a cultural change focus on a shift in values which, it is argued, has produced as one of its consequences mounting concern for the environment. Ronald Inglehart (1977; 1986; 1990), the best known proponent of this type of explanation, charts the rise since 1945 of a section of the population expressing so-called post-material values (see Table 2.1). These, he argues, have arisen as a consequence of post-war affluence. As the welfare state and economic success have taken care of many people's material needs in the developed world, these people have increasingly turned their attention to meeting non-material goals, one of which is the desire to live and work in a pleasant environment. These values are particularly prevalent in the generations who have grown up since 1945 and so, although post-material values are not yet held by a majority of the adult population, there is every possibility that they will become predominant in years to come.

In support of the affluence explanation, the development of the environmental movement does indeed seem to be linked with the economic climate. Lowe and Goyder (1983, pp. 16–17) identify four periods – the 1890s, 1920s, the late 1950s and the early 1970s – when concern for the environment was particularly evident, and these do correspond with the end of periods of extensive economic expansion. This would also seem to explain why concern arose again towards the end of the 1980s as the economy was booming and dropped off in the early 1990s when recession arrived. As Worcester's research (1997, pp. 162–3) reveals, support for environmentalism is 'correlated negatively with the Economic Optimism Index, which measures

people's expectations of future economic prosperity', thereby confirming the view that 'people's concern for the environment rises
when they feel economically more secure'. Clearly, then, the economic
climate does have an effect on the issues people regard as salient.

The specific claims made by the post-material school are more
difficult to sustain. In the first place, it needs to be asked why the
satisfaction of material needs leads to post-materialism rather than
new material needs. Inglehart derives his ordering of values from
Maslow (1954) who argued that needs are pursued in an hierarchical
order according to the extent to which they are necessary for survival.
Once the basic physiological needs are met, he suggests, other higher-
order needs, such as love and esteem, come into play. It is by no
means clear, though, why this should be the case. For one thing, what
one generation regards as essential will differ from another. At one
time, televisions and motor vehicles were regarded as luxuries; now
they are common and not to own one through lack of resources is
regarded as a form of deprivation. In the future, computer ownership,
and access to the internet, will no doubt fall into this category
(Martell, 1994, p. 125).

A further criticism is that we could accept the evidence about post-
material values but deny that affluence has been the chief cause.
Jordan and Maloney's research (1997, p. 135), for instance, concur
with this, since they found that while the vast majority of Friends of
the Earth members exhibited post-material values, there was no
correlation between affluence and post-materialism. This brings us
to the competing explanations all of which could be held responsible
for the emergence of post-material values. The role of the environmental movement and the media in promoting post-material issues
might be responsible (Hansen, 1993; Martell, 1994, pp. 125–6; North,
1995, pp. 97–110). Alternatively, the shift in values may be a product
of the impact of the expansion of higher educational opportunities in
the post-Second World War period (Eckersley, 1989, p. 218). Finally,
structural changes in the class structure may have had an effect.

The structural interpretation is associated above all with Stephen
Cotgrove and Andrew Duff (1980; 1981), who argue that the rise of
environmentalism as an important issue reflects the ideological
disposition of a new social grouping which has emerged in the post-
war period. This new faction of the middle class consists of those who
work in the non-productive service sector – doctors, social workers,
teachers and so on – a sector that has grown extensively since 1945. It
is occupation as opposed to affluence, then, which, according to this

view, is crucial. Those working in new middle-class occupations are much more likely to espouse post-material values than the private sector working class and middle class because, it is argued, they are insulated from the dominant values of industrial society. Environmentalism, then, is 'an expression of the interests of those whose class position in the non-productive sector locates them at the periphery of the institutions and processes of industrial capitalist societies' (Cotgrove and Duff, 1980, pp. 340–1).

It is not being claimed here that environmentalism is an expression of class interests. Such a position is difficult to justify. Clearly, some environmental campaigns, particularly those that seek to prevent further development in leafy suburbs – the not in my back yard (NIMBY) syndrome – is motivated by self-interest (Lowe and Goyder, 1983, pp. 28–30). But this does not account for the post-materialism of the new middle class since those in white collar public sector jobs are far from being the most affluent part of the middle class. Indeed, psephological studies indicate that the new middle class are more likely to vote for the Liberal Democrats and Labour than for the Conservatives (Garner and Kelly, 1993, ch. 9). So, rather than deriving from need deprivation or class interests, the structural explanation suggests that changing values derive from ideals.

Persuasive though the structural explanation may sound, it has a number of problems. In the first place, the link between occupation and ideals is not entirely credible. As Lowe and Rudig (1986, p. 522) point out, why should those working in the public sector espouse the end of economic growth when it is precisely that which ensures the continued existence of the welfare state? Furthermore, while the social profile of the members of environmental groups does give some support to the structural explanation, with members of Friends of the Earth, the RSPB and the Conservation Society, for instance, being drawn disproportionately from the new middle class identified by Cotgrove and Duff, other groups, such as the Council for the Protection of Rural England (CPRE) draw their membership disproportionately from the more affluent middle and upper classes (Lowe *et al.* 1986, p. 115). In addition, the 'attentive public', consisting of those who are not members of any specific group but who express an interest in the issues raised by environmental groups, is much more evenly balanced socially (Lowe and Goyder, 1983, pp. 10–13; Porritt and Winner, 1988, p. 182). Finally, we can also make the point that it may be that the social characteristics of environmental activists simply reflects the greater propensity of the new middle class to join any voluntary organization as opposed to one with a specific environmental concern.

A more serious objection to the structural explanation is the difficulty of determining causality. Even Cotgrove and Duff (1980, p. 102) admit that: 'environmentalists try to choose occupations congruent with their ... post-material values'. If this is the case, the whole theory is devalued since post-material values can no longer be *explained* in terms of occupation. This, of course, takes us back to square one and our search for an explanation for the existence of the value shift! This does not mean that Cotgrove and Duff are prepared to accept the affluence argument of Inglehart after all, since their research still suggests that material conditions are not an accurate predictor of post-material values (*ibid.*, p. 106).

A final point here is that both the value and structural-based theories can be criticized on the grounds that they completely ignore the possibility that it is the deterioration of the environment, and those agents seeking to draw attention to it, which has played a key role in bringing the issue on to the political agenda. To 'effectively divorce ... environmental concern from ecological problems' (Lowe and Rudig, 1986, p. 518) is surely to lose sight of much that is important. To give one example, survey evidence demonstrates that concern for the environment manifests itself in different countries according to particular national and regional problems (see Martell, 1994, p. 134).

Environmental issues

The rest of this chapter is concerned with an exploration of the nature of environmental problems. The aim is not to provide a definitive or particularly technical account but rather a guide for those interested in the politics of the environment who have no background in science in general or environmental science in particular. We will be focusing, of course, on the effects of human (or anthropogenic) influences on the natural environment although it should be noted that natural phenomena – earthquakes, volcanoes, landslides, cyclones, droughts and so on – can have a devastating impact too (Pickering and Owen, 1994, ch. 8). As already indicated, a central feature of environmental politics is that the extent and consequences of the human impact on the natural environment is much disputed. From time to time, the account in this chapter refers to such empirical disputes and they are examined more thematically in Chapter 3.

The interdependence of environmental problems

Utilization of the Earth's natural resources stretches back many centuries (Goudie, 1989; Mannion, 1991), but the crucial turning point was the industrial revolution, which led to fundamental changes in manufacturing activities and resulted in far greater stresses on the natural environment. Industrial expansion resulted in rapid invest-ment-led technological innovation, unprecedented population growth and the large-scale movement of people from rural to urban areas and from towns to cities (Young, 1992, p. 11). Economic expansion has continued apace and received a further boost after 1945 when rising expectations demanded greater material prosperity, and a new financial system was designed to meet them (McCulloch, 1988b, p. 10).

Although convenient, it is somewhat artificial and misleading to consider different forms of environmental damage in isolation of others, since the problems are interdependent, a fact illustrated by the 'Limits to Growth' report discussed in Chapter 3. Thus, one parti-cular process has multi-faceted consequences, and actions to deal with one specific consequence often has knock-on effects causing unin-tended, and often undesirable, by-products. Both the inputs and the outputs of the industrial process cause environmental damage (Geor-gescu-Roegen, 1973). Raw materials are transformed into finished products by processes requiring energy. The inputs of raw materials and the energy sources required to transform them are usually non-renewable, leading to potential problems of resource depletion. More-over, the extraction and use of raw materials and energy sources may well cause pollution. The manufacturing process not only causes pollution but also land-use problems. In addition, by creating a large urban population, industrialism also requires an efficient, intensive and environmentally (and ethically) dubious farming sector to pro-vide adequate food supplies.

The end-products of the industrial process have to be transported by road, air or sea, and this has implications for energy consumption, pollution and the fate of the countryside (not to mention the species of flora and fauna residing there) parts of which may have to be destroyed to build the necessary transport infrastructure. Once these products have outlived their usefulness, they have to be disposed of. This again raises issues of land-use, water and air pollution, and the fate of the human and non-human species who inhabit the areas utilized.

Many of the products of the industrial process are damaging to the environment when in everyday use, and none more so than the symbol of the modern environmental crisis, the motor car. It is easy to see why the motor vehicle has become such a symbol. Above all, it helps to illustrate why many environmentalists argue that there are no small-scale, piecemeal solutions to the crisis. Producing motor vehicles uses valuable raw materials and energy; vehicles consume energy and pollute the environment while in use; they require roads to run on; they cause urban congestion, thereby reducing the quality of life for many; and, finally, they must be disposed of when no longer needed. Seen in this context, the solutions proposed and acted upon seem entirely inappropriate. While the use of lead-free petrol and the fitting of catalytic converters do stop some of the worst emissions, they do not deal with the other consequences of car use. While cars continue to be produced, they still consume energy and still require roads. What is more, they still emit carbon dioxide, the gas which is regarded as a primary cause of global warming. The only solution, therefore, would seem to be a drastic reduction of road vehicles rather than the production of more environmentally friendly ones.

Air and water pollution

The issue of pollution is in itself an enormous topic. To some extent, what is covered under the heading depends on the definition used. Albert Weale (1992, p. 3) for instance, defines it as 'the introduction into the environment of substances or emissions that either damage, or carry the risk of damaging, human health or well-being, the built environment or the natural environment'. This is a very broad definition and, for our purposes, it can be made more manageable by the introduction of three caveats. In the first place, following the earlier limitations imposed on the subject area, we can exclude the built environment. Secondly, it is appropriate to exclude the issue of climate change here also, since global warming and ozone depletion are such distinct issues, with such potentially devastating consequences, that they deserve to be considered separately. Thirdly, as intimated earlier, only anthropogenic pollution will be considered.

The existence of other materials in air and water does not necessarily cause environmental hazards. Problems are caused by the quantity of a substance or the nature of the impurity (Harvey and Hallett, 1977, p. 50). In the latter case, the nature of the impurity can be such that its introduction into the air or water can be devastating. Radioactive material and some pesticides fall into this category. In the former case, problems can arise either if the impurity cannot be diluted – the classic examples being oil spills and the chemicals implicated in the production of smogs – or if an additional small quantity of an already existing substance is introduced. In some cases, such as zinc and copper, a small amount of a substance is beneficial to living organisms but becomes toxic when this limit is exceeded (*ibid.*, p. 53). For some substances, such as mercury and lead, a moderate amount may be benign but is deadly in increased quantities. Finally, the introduction of large quantities of a naturally occurring substance (the classic example being the use of nitrogen fertilizers) can upset the natural balance and cause great environmental damage.

Mercury is a substance used in various manufacturing processes and excessive long-term exposure to it causes severe health problems including impaired vision, speech and movement. It was once used in the hat industry to cure felt and, before mercury poisoning was recognized, the symptoms were associated with madness – hence the Mad Hatter character in Lewis Carroll's *Alice in Wonderland* (Harvey and Hallett, 1977, p. 51). A primary source of lead is from car exhausts. Lead was first added to petrol in 1924 to improve engine performance but evidence that it can cause severe damage to the central nervous system led to the introduction of a tax incentive to encourage motorists to use lead-free petrol.

The substances discussed above constitute a fraction of the 25 harmful chemicals, gases and particulates which are regularly emitted into the atmosphere during various stages of the industrial process, ranging from arsenic – emitted through oil and coal combustion and glass manufacture and linked to lung and skin cancer – to manganese, emitted from power stations and during smelting and linked to Parkinson's disease (Simpson, 1990, p. 56). Of these, nine – most notably carbon dioxide and chlorofluorocarbons, or CFCs – are climate and atmosphere-modifying gases.

A high proportion of the total number of harmful substances are emitted from fossil-fuelled power stations and vehicle exhausts. In combination, these are responsible for so-called photochemical smogs and the phenomena of acid rain (McCormick, 1989). Smogs in the major cities of the world are commonplace. One of the best known was the infamous 'pea-souper' which engulfed London in December 1952. Lasting about five days, the smog was held to be responsible for almost 4000 deaths as people inhaled acidic water droplets. This was the necessary stimulus for the passage of the 1956 Clean Air Act, and the legislation, coupled with the widespread adoption of gas-fired central heating, helped to eradicate the pollution caused by the domestic burning of coal. Smogs still exist, however, but now they are largely the product of motor vehicle pollution. In December 1991, for instance, a severe smog occurred again over London with high recorded levels of nitrogen dioxide. In other parts of the world – particularly in huge conglomerates such as Mexico City, Los Angeles and Athens – the problem is far worse with smogs, and the consequential health problems, a regular occurrence (Pickering and Owen, 1994, pp. 107–8).

Acid rain has become an increasingly important issue since the 1980s, although the phenomenon has been known about since the middle of the nineteenth century. It is caused when certain chemicals combine with rainfall, turning the latter literally to acid. The principal culprit is sulphur dioxide (SO_2) although nitrogen oxides and hydrocarbons are also implicated. The most visible effect is the devastation caused to trees and water courses, vegetation becoming seriously affected because of the level of soil acidity. Acid rain is a problem which occurs throughout the world with the former Soviet Union and the United States being the biggest emitters of SO_2. In Europe, it is the Scandinavian countries which have borne the brunt of the damage, much of it deriving, due to prevailing air-flow patterns, from power station emissions from the United Kingdom (Schoon, 1990). By 1986, 13 per cent of all forest cover in Europe had been badly affected, an area equivalent to the size of the United Kingdom (Myers, 1989, p. 35; Pickering and Owen, 1994, ch. 4).

There is some good news on SO_2 emissions. Due to a variety of factors – international agreements, the recession, less reliance on coal-fired power stations and technological developments making for cleaner power stations and cars – SO_2 emissions actually fell in OECD countries by a quarter in the two decades from 1970. In the same period, however, nitrogen oxide emissions increased by 12 per cent (Weale, 1992, pp. 23, 25).

Over two thirds of the earth's surface is covered by water and, as it is essential to human life, protecting it against pollutants is crucially important. Initially, the most serious pollutant was human waste, but laws passed since the nineteenth century and in more recent times, especially at the instigation of the European Union (see Chapter 6), have resulted in rigorous water-quality standards (Pickering and Owen, 1994, pp. 137, 142).

Organic waste still, however, constitutes a problem. In many developing countries, water quality remains poor and diseases such as cholera and typhoid are common. In addition, the dumping of sewage sludge in the sea remains a problem for industrialized countries, which has only recently begun to be tackled (Pickering and Owen, 1994, pp. 136–44). Finally, there is the problem of the disposal of animal waste. In reasonable quantities, this can be used as fertilizer to enrich the soil, but the colossal amount of slurry produced often means that large quantities of nitrates, ammonia and bacteria are leached into streams and rivers. An additional problem is the use of large amounts of antibiotics which intensive animal farming often requires. Antibiotic residues get into water courses, with consequences that are not yet fully understood, and also into the food chain, thereby increasing human resistance to their use in medical interventions. (Mason and Singer, 1990).

In industrialized countries, the biggest water pollution problem now is not organic wastes but industrial and agricultural wastes, including radioactive chemicals, nitrates, heavy metals and oil. Pollution from these sources in British rivers has increased significantly in the past decade or so with the doubling of reported pollution incidents (Pickering and Owen, 1994, p. 137). The main problem areas are:

(1) nitrates and phosphates caused by the use and disposal of fertilizers and detergents;
(2) dangerous organic chemicals, most notably polychlorinated biphenyls (PCBs), involved in the manufacture of paints and plastics, and pesticides;
(3) heavy metals such as mercury, lead, arsenic and aluminium; and
(4) oil.

The main consequence of excessive use of nitrates and phosphates is that, when deposited in water, it produces an explosive growth of algae, which in turn dies and decays gradually depleting the water of oxygen (see *Guardian*, 6 January 1995). This kills the fish and seriously affects aquatic animal species. This process, known as eutrophication, is particularly common in the Great Lakes of the United States. Nitrates are a particular problem since the relatively recent shift towards intensive agriculture has resulted in chronic nitrate depletion, thus requiring a massive increase in artificial sources in the form of fertilizers. There are also some direct human health consequences from excessive amounts of nitrates in water. In particular, it is associated with a blood disease in very young children, the so-called 'blue baby' syndrome, and with stomach cancer (Harvey and Hallett, 1977, p. 32; Pickering and Owen, 1994, p. 145).

Dangerous organic chemicals can have a devastating impact on marine life with consequences for those higher up the food chain. PCB residues, for instance, have been found in polar bears (Pickering and Owen, 1994, p. 147). Equally, some pesticides are extremely dangerous to living organisms. The first generation of pesticides was introduced after the Second World War as part of the effort to maximize food production. These were based upon chlorinated hydrocarbons and included the now infamous dichoro-diphenyl-trichloro-ethane (DDT). This category of pesticides was comprehensively banned in the West from the 1970s onwards but their use continues in developing countries. Now, pesticides tend to contain less dangerous compounds, but they still cause ecological damage and their continued use may owe more to the power of the agrochemical industry (world sales of pesticides are thought to be around $50 billion a year) than to their intrinsic value. Insects can, of course, devastate crops and, in developing countries, the control of mosquitoes and locusts is vital for human health as well, malaria in those countries remaining a big killer. Nevertheless, there is a mass of evidence to suggest that the long-term use of pesticides results in resistant strains of insects and it may be that the future lies in 'integrated pest management systems'. This involves, among other things, the breeding of resistant plant varieties and the utilization of natural pest predators (Simpson, 1990, pp. 71–4).

Heavy metal residues in water pose severe health problems for humans. Mercury, lead, arsenic, tin, cadmium, cobalt, copper and manganese are all regularly used in industrial processes and are all linked to brain damage and, in the event of excessive exposure, death. A special mention should be made of aluminium, which is being increasingly linked with Alzheimer's disease. High levels of aluminium have been found in some drinking water supplies, but the most dramatic illustration occurred in 1989 in the Camelford area of Cornwall, when a lorry driver mistakenly dumped 20 tonnes of aluminium sulphate into a water tank which was then released to the mains supply. Local people subsequently reported illnesses ranging from diarrhoea to mouth and nose ulcers and some began to suffer from memory loss – a symptom of Alzheimer's disease (Pickering and Owen, 1994, pp. 148–50). The subsequent government inquiry, however, found no scientific evidence to support the residents' claims of a link between these conditions and the pollution (North, 1995, pp. 110–15).

Oil spills are one of the most visible signs of pollution, but the spectacular accidents widely reported in the media account for a relatively small amount of the total quantity of oil deposited in the sea, the rest coming from routine discharges from ships cleaning out their tanks, natural seepage, industrial effluents and the consequence of war, most notably the deliberate sabotaging of Kuwait's refineries by Iraq in the 1991 Gulf War. When the *Torrey Canyon* ran aground in 1967, it deposited 117 000 tonnes of oil off the coast of South West England, but even though it was enough to kill between 40 000 and 100 000 sea birds, the spill rather pales into insignificance when one contrasts it with the total annual spillage of about 3.6 million tonnes (Simpson, 1990, pp. 112–15).

It goes without saying that oil pollution can have a devastating impact on marine life. It kills fish by depriving them of oxygen, and birds and other sea mammals die, either because of the indirect effects of a reduction in fish stocks or directly through poisoning or because of the effects of oil on their buoyancy and insulation. There can be fewer distressing and emotive sights than a dying bird seeking desperately but hopelessly to clean itself. As a symbol of human disregard for the natural environment in the pursuit of material comfort, it cannot be bettered. In reality, some oil spills have little long-term damage on the ecosystem. Whether or not we should still regard the suffering and death of many thousands of animals and birds in such circumstances with equanimity is a philosophical question to which we shall return in Chapter 3.

Global atmospheric change

As if the long-standing problems of pollution discussed above are not bad enough, in recent years evidence has arisen that human activities have damaged the environment in much more sinister ways. We refer here to ozone depletion and global warming. They are more sinister developments for a number of reasons. In the first place, both are invisible phenomena and affect life only indirectly. The scientific community disagrees over the extent and likely consequences of both phenomena. The problem here, of course, is that should we wait until a scientific consensus about causes, scope and consequences emerges (which is unlikely), it may be too late to take any effective action. Secondly, both ozone depletion and global warming are truly world-wide problems. Up to now, the developed world has caused the lion's share of the problems and fairness suggests that it ought therefore to bear the bulk of the costs of dealing with them. The biggest future threat, however, comes from the prospect of increasing industrial development in the Third World. As a consequence, only effective global action can hope to deal satisfactorily with them. Such global co-operation, as Chapter 5 will illustrate, is not easy to achieve. Finally, of course, the consequences of failure are profound because, if the scientists are right, we do not have the option of continuing with present practices.

The ozone layer first became an issue in 1977 when the British Antarctic Survey discovered a significant depletion in the strato-sphere, but it took another decade for this finding to be confirmed independently (Pickering and Owen, 1994, pp. 67–8). By the 1980s, the threat posed by ozone-depleting chemicals was generally accepted, as evidence of substantial thinning over the polar regions, and the existence of large quantities of ozone-depleting chemicals over major cities, was discovered. As a result, action was taken (see Chapter 5).

Ozone (O^3) is a naturally occurring and highly reactive gas made up of oxygen atoms. In the stratosphere, between 20–30 kilometres above the Earth's surface, a band of ozone exists which operates to exclude ultra-violet radiation from the sun. This radiation is extre-mely damaging to living organisms and it is predicted that the consequences of a reduction in the ozone layer, allowing more radiation to reach the Earth, will be an increased incidence of skin cancer, an increased risk of crop failure and, some scientists have suggested, global warming (the following is based on the excellent account in Yearley, 1992, pp. 12–16; see also Booth, 1994; Elliot, 1998, pp. 53–4; Gribben, 1988).

The phenomenon of ozone depletion is rare, in environmental terms, for its uni-causal nature. Although compounds such as carbon dioxide and methyl bromide have been implicated, as have changes in sea-surface temperatures, by far and away the main culprit is held to be chlorofluorocarbons (CFCs). CFCs are a product of the industrial age, developed early this century for use in aerosols, as coolants in refrigerators and in air-conditioning systems, foam-filled furniture, fast-food packaging and as cleansing agents in the electronics industry. CFCs do not break down easily and reach the stratosphere largely intact. High-energy radiation does, however, cause CFCs to break up and the chlorine then released destroys the ozone.

The damage caused by CFCs has been addressed by governments and, although the agreements reached are far from perfect, it would not be premature to say that a potential crisis has been averted (see Chapter 5). It is equally fair comment to add, though, that it is a relatively easy problem to solve. Not only is it possible to identify a single major cause of ozone depletion, but, in addition, substitutes for CFCs are readily available and relatively inexpensive. Crucially, solutions to the problem do not involve significant cuts in industrial production. The same fortuitous set of circumstances does not apply to the phenomenon known as global warming.

Global warming was first observed in the nineteenth century. It refers literally to an increase in the temperature of the Earth and is widely thought to be a product of the changing balance of oxygen and carbon dioxide (CO_2) in the atmosphere; other so-called greenhouse gases making a smaller contribution to global warming are methane, nitrous oxide and tropospheric ozone. Like the glass in a greenhouse, CO_2 acts as an insulator and the more of it there is, the more difficult it is for the sun's warmth to escape. The process of photosynthesis, whereby plants absorb CO_2 and release oxygen, helps to ensure that a balance is maintained. Human activities, however, have put increasing stresses on this natural mechanism. Population growth, thus increasing the demand for oxygen, has been one factor at work, but the major problem derives from the additional CO_2 in the atmosphere. This has been caused partly by deforestation, reducing the availability of natural 'sinks' for CO_2 – thereby making the preservation of the rain forests a crucial issue. Most important of all, however, is the additional CO_2 released through the burning of fossil fuels. In the absence of human activity, the carbon in fossil fuels would remain unused, out of circulation under the Earth's surface, but fossil fuels, in the form of coal, oil and natural gas, are the mainstay of industrial society and their use has dramatically increased. It is estimated that the total annual emissions of CO_2 have increased from 1.5 million tonnes as recently as 1950 to almost six billion tonnes in the 1990s, and it is further predicted that CO_2 concentrations will double by the year 2050 unless action is taken (Simpson, 1990, p. 58; Pickering and Owen, 1994, p. 72).

It is argued that the effects of global warming are considerable although there is still a heated debate in the scientific community about the extent of increases in global temperatures, the predicted rise of sea levels, the link between greenhouse gases and the global climate and even whether global warming, even if it does exist, is necessarily a bad thing (Pickering and Owen, 1994, pp. 88–91; North, 1995, pp. 67–72; Elliot, 1998, pp. 60–4; Connelly and Smith, 1999, p. 120; see also Beckerman, 1992, for an optimistic view). Most scientists would concur, however, that the evidence seems to point to a potentially severe problem. The 13 warmest years since record keeping began in 1866 have occurred since 1979, and four of these have occurred since 1990 (L. R. Brown, 1998, p. 10). Rising sea levels are regarded as a key consequence, caused by an increase in the volume of sea water as the polar ice caps melt, and the expanding of warmer oceans. Since the early 1970s, ice and snow cover has decreased by about 8 per cent and recent evidence shows an increase in plant growth in the Antarctic. The result of rising sea levels will be flooding, initially of low-lying areas. In addition, increases in temperatures will affect vegetation and agriculture and, of course, there is a limit to the amount of heat which living organisms can cope with. Scientists in the Intergovernmental Panel on Climate Change (see Chapter 5) have estimated that a 'no action' scenario would lead, by 2050, to a situation where there are 'about 22 million additional people at risk from hunger because of climate change (over and above that expected because of population change), about 23 million additional people at risk from coastal flooding, and 110 million additional people living in countries with extreme water stress' (*Guardian*, 2 December 1997).

The lack of precise evidence about the causes and consequences of global warming, and the extent of the sacrifices that will have to be made in order to deal with it, have hindered attempts at containing the problem. Beckerman (1992, p. 260) argues that the costs of dealing with global warming outweigh the benefits. 'Whatever one does with the estimates', he writes, 'they are unlikely to demonstrate that the present state of scientific knowledge justifies great trouble and expense to cut CO^2 emissions by very large amounts.' Nevertheless, if the finger is to be pointed at CO_2 emissions, the solutions are clear-cut. One is to use other sources of energy, including nuclear power (which, whatever else may be said about it, does not involve the use of fossil fuels) and 'Green' alternatives based on wind, water, waves and so on. Another is to use existing sources of energy more efficiently through better insulation of homes and workplaces and restrictions on car use. Finally, as indicated above, the conservation of forests, and particularly the tropical rain forests, is also crucial.

The preservation of the rain forests illustrates well the interdependence of environmental problems. Not only do they provide habitats for a huge variety of animal and plant species, as well as protect against soil erosion and the silting of rivers and lakes, they also perform a vital function as 'sinks' for carbon dioxide. Far from being conserved, however, the rain forests are being cut down at an alarming rate, with one estimate suggesting that half of the world's tropical forests were cleared in the 1980s alone (cited in Simpson, 1990, p. 134).

The problem is not just that forests are felled for timber, but they are often cleared to create agricultural land. The burning of the felled trees not only releases further CO_2 into the atmosphere, thus intensifying the global warming problem, but can also cause severe pollution, and thereby health problems, as witnessed in the forest fires in Indonesia and elsewhere. Describing the situation and offering a simplistic technical solution is, as always, to overlook the social and political context (Crace, 1997; Vidal, 1997; P. Brown, 1997 and 1998). Here, the clearing of the rain forests takes us into often intractable issues concerning Third World development and the thorny questions concerning the West's responsibility for environmental degradation and the moral legitimacy of asking already poor nations to make further sacrifices for our benefit (issues discussed further in Chapters 3 and 5).

Biodiversity

The number of plant, non-human animal and insect species with which we share the planet is startling. Indeed, such is the incredible variety of life on Earth and the difficulty of determining the numbers, we simply do not know how many species there are (May, 1989). Excluding plants and vegetation, estimates of the total number of living species vary from between 5 to 30 million. Only about 1.5 million have so far been identified. It is probable, therefore, that some species have disappeared (perhaps recently) without us knowing they ever existed. What we do know is that in the last 2000 years, humans have exterminated about 3 per cent of the world's mammal species, one half of these losses occurring since 1900 (Regenstein, 1985). The crucial point to make here is that human activity is responsible for extinction rates that would appear to have accelerated way beyond their 'natural' level (Tuxill, 1999, p. 97).

Despite the signing of the Convention on Biological Diversity at the UNCED in 1992, there appears to be little improvement in extinction rates. The International Union for the Conservation of Nature's (see Chapter 5) latest Red Data Book published in 1996 indicates, for instance, that 4 per cent of bird and 11 per cent of mammal species are in immediate danger of extinction and a further 16 per cent of bird and 28 per cent of mammal species are either threatened or nearing threatened status (cited in Tuxill and Bright, 1998, pp. 43–55; see also *Guardian*, 10 December 1996). The Harvard entomologist Edward O. Wilson estimates, conservatively, that three species are being extinguished every hour (*Guardian*, 18 February 1995).

There are many threats to living species, some of them natural, but many of them deriving from human activity. Hunting, for instance, has seriously eroded the numbers of many species of whales and poaching has done likewise for African elephants and rhinos. The greatest threat, though, is not caused by deliberate direct attacks on non-human species but by the destruction of the habitats on which they depend. For example, agricultural practices have led to the removal of hedgerows, the draining of wetlands and the pollution of water courses – all vital habitats to one species or another. Similarly, over-fishing may cause birds and marine mammals to starve and, as was intimated earlier, the destruction of the rain forests causes immense damage to biodiversity since although the tropical forests cover only 6 per cent of the Earth's land surface, they contain at least 50 per cent of all the Earth's species. Tropical forest depletion is thus far and away the main cause of species extinction (Myers, 1989, p. 27). As a consequence, then, of the uneven distribution of the Earth's biodiversity, the issue (as with environmental protection in general) is inextricably linked with the relationship between North and South and the latter's desire to develop.

Clearly, then, excessive species extinction does occur as a result of human activities. The question to ask is: does it matter? The first answer is to say that it matters because nature has inherent value which we ought to respect. We will return to this moral question in Chapter 3. More pertinent for the present discussion is the anthropocentric dimension – that protecting biodiversity matters because it is beneficial to us. Here we are on safer ground because, in many instances, this is clearly the case (Pearce *et al.*, 1993, pp. 98–100;

Abramovitz, 1997, pp. 95–114), although balancing the interests of endangered species with those of indigenous human populations in the developing countries is not easy (see Chapter 3).

There is, first, the aesthetic pleasure we receive from experiencing the majesty and beauty of non-human nature. More instrumentally, many plant and animal species are economically valuable to us, in terms, for instance, of tourism and food. There is an economic disincentive to hunting whales to extinction, for instance, since, with effective conservation measures, stocks can be made to last longer. Indeed, the International Whaling Commission (IWC) was set up with precisely this intention, although in recent years it has been used for different purposes by those with a principled opposition to whaling (see Chapter 3).

Genetic variety is also important from a medical, agricultural and industrial perspective (Tuxill, 1999). Many commonplace medicines derive from natural sources – aspirin, the contraceptive pill and cancer treating agents, to name but a few – and there is every reason to think that future discoveries may greatly benefit humans and other animals. Biodiversity has made these contributions with scientific investigations into only one per cent of plant species and a far smaller proportion of animal species (Myers, 1989, pp. 30–2). Maintaining the diversity of the gene pool is also crucial in guarding against disease which could otherwise eradicate plant species which are vital as sources of food for humans and other animals. Finally, there is the more general point that the workings of nature are so little understood that by destroying species, we simply do not know the full consequences of our actions. This brings us back to the interdependence of the natural world, that damage to one part of an ecosystem can have unsuspected knock-on effects, a point that was graphically illustrated by Rachel Carson's (1962) classic work on the effects of pesticides (see also Lear, 1998).

One issue related to biodiversity is the role of zoos. Zoos have increasingly emphasized their conservation role in place of, or in addition to, their educational and entertainment functions. Some zoos, without doubt, perform an important conservation function, although their role is no substitute for protecting habitats. Too many, however, have no real conservation function and in some the treatment of animals leaves a great deal to be desired. From an animal rights perspective (see Chapter 3), zoos are morally illegitimate whatever contribution they make to conservation, since to keep animals in captivity is, in the case of many species at least, to seriously infringe their rights (see Bostock, 1993).

Resource depletion

Continuing with the interdependency theme, the emphasis on economic growth, powered by the use of fossil fuels, not only leads to pollution and atmospheric changes, but also raises questions about resource depletion. As we have seen, one of the key features of the radical Green position is the assertion that there are limits to growth and this position is held, at least in part, because growth is predicated on the use of non-renewable resources.

Statistics on the use and life-span of non-renewable resources are all too revealing. For example, it is estimated that humans use the same amount of fossil fuels in one year that it took nature one million years to create and, taking inflation into account, energy expenditure is now twenty times greater than it was about 150 years ago (Pickering and Owen, 1994, p. 183). These raw figures disguise the shift from a primary reliance on coal by the end of the nineteenth century, to a reliance on oil which now constitutes over a third of the world's energy supply. Oil, of course, is not only a fuel but also, among other things, the raw material for fertilizers, pesticides and the plastics industry (Harvey and Hallett, 1977, pp. 39–41). Utilization of these non-renewable resources has taken a heavy toll. Estimates of available supplies differ, and a great deal depends upon what is meant by 'recoverable' reserves and future estimates of population size and demand. Taking these factors into account, proven recoverable reserves of oil and gas are expected to last just over 50 years and coal over 200 years (Dasgupta, 1989, pp. 121–2).

There is then an obvious need to focus attention on the conservation of energy and the development of energy alternatives, particularly given the desire for economic development in the Third World. One answer is in nuclear power which at present constitutes only about 15 per cent of the global energy supply (but over a quarter of Britain's energy sources and as much as three quarters in France). Environmentalists take a dim view of the nuclear option but it does, at least superficially, seem to answer most of the problems, as it provides energy without the problem of carbon dioxide emissions (for a generally positive account see North, 1995, pp. 80–90). Of course, this is not the whole story. There are significant difficulties involved in the disposal of nuclear waste; high capital costs are involved in setting up and running nuclear power stations and there is the ever present danger of accidents which, as Chernobyl demonstrated, can easily turn into catastrophes (Porritt, 1984, pp. 173–4; Pickering and Owen, 1994, pp. 71–4).

There are many alternative sources of renewable energy: hydro-electric power, wind power, tidal energy, solar energy, geothermal energy and biomass forms of energy. Each has its negative aspects in terms of cost or effects on the environment and, whatever else might be said, it remains the case that a great deal more research is necessary to make any one of them viable (North, 1995, pp. 119–21). There are other barriers too, such as the great vested interests involved in the production, marketing and retailing of fossil fuels. In addition, the large subsidies given to the nuclear industry, largely for political reasons (see Chapter 9), has created a significantly uneven playing field which makes it extremely difficult for advocates of renewable energy sources to compete effectively.

The bulk of this chapter has been concerned with sketching out the major environmental problems facing the global community. They are formidable and have increased over the past two decades or so. By themselves, these problems constitute a possible explanation for the rise of social and political concern about the environment, but, as we saw, there are those who would challenge the view that there is an automatic link between the identification and popular dissemination of information documenting these problems and the rise of concern about them. The rest of this book seeks to explore the social and political processes operating around environmental issues. We start, in Chapters 3 and 4, by examining the attempt to develop a set of moral and political principles which, Greens hope, can provide an ideological battering ram for change.

Further reading

The debate about the rise of environmentalism is summarised in Martell (1994). The chief protagonists are Inglehart (1977 and 1990) and Cotgrove and Duff (1980 and 1981). Reference should also be made to Lowe and Rudig (1986) for a critique of cultural and structural explanations. There are a number of texts written by scientists and social scientists which provide an overview of environmental problems. Two useful book-length studies are Pickering and Owen (1994), a more or less neutral account, and North (1995) which contains masses of information but is geared towards persuading the reader that environmental problems are not as bad as many environmentalists would have us believe. Mannion (1991) traces environmental problems historically, Friday and Laskey (1989) provide a worthwhile collection of articles and there is also much useful information in Harvey and Hallett (1977), Simpson (1990), Porritt (1984) and Yearley (1992, ch. 1).

An increasing number of studies of particular environmental problems have emerged. The most notable are McCormick (1989) on acid rain, Mason and Singer (1990) on factory farming, Gribben (1988) and Booth (1994) on ozone depletion, Paterson (1996) on global warming, Ehrlich (1972) on population and Regenstein (1985) on endangered species. Finally, for up-to-date and accurate information, the long-running annual *State of the World* series published by the Worldwatch Institute is hard to beat.

3

Environmental Thought: Economic and Philosophical Dimensions

The emergence of environmental problems, and the corresponding rise of an environmental protection movement, has been accompanied by the development of ideas which seek, on the one hand, to justify our preoccupation with environmental issues and, on the other, to lead us to the most appropriate solutions for the problems identified. As indicated earlier, the major dichotomy in environmental thought can be crudely defined as being between radicals and reformists – between, that is, exponents of the dark Green or ecocentric position on the one hand, and exponents of the light green or technocentric position on the other. The next two chapters seek to explore the constituent elements of these competing perspectives. The economic and philosophical underpinnings are considered in this chapter while the relationship between Green thinking and mainstream political thought is the subject matter of Chapter 4.

Ecology and economy

Radical and reformists differ firstly over their approach to the economy. The former see economic growth as incompatible with environmental objectives. Their challenge to the ethos of economic growth and material consumption consists, in part, of an empirical claim; that there are natural limits to growth and that unless production and consumption levels and population size are reduced to sustainable levels, economic collapse will result. It is better then to manage this reduction, be prepared and act on it, or risk being overwhelmed by a crisis which will have unpredictable consequences. Edward Goldsmith's *Blueprint for Survival* (a text, originally published as an edition of the Ecologist Magazine owned by Goldsmith, which is often regarded as the definitive statement of

Green ideas, at least in Britain) commented that continued economic growth will end 'either against our will, in a succession of famines, epidemics, social crises and wars; or because we want it to ... in a series of thoughtful, humane and measured changes' (1972, p. 15).

The limits to growth

The empirical claim received its impetus from what is now a classic study, published in book form as the *Limits to Growth* in 1972 (Meadows *et al.* 1972). The research for the book was undertaken by academics at the Massachusetts Institute of Technology (MIT) who were commissioned by a group of industrialists, economists and civil servants, led by an Italian management consultant Aurelio Peccei, operating in a group called the Club of Rome (for historical background see Hajer, 1997, pp. 80–4). The researchers at MIT used computer modelling techniques to examine the interdependencies between a number of environmental variables – industrialization, resource depletion, pollution, food production and population – computing the likely result of changes in individual variables (the results of the research are outlined in Martell, 1994, pp. 24–40; and Dobson, 1995, ch.3).

The conclusions of this study, setting the agenda for the survivalist stream of thought evident in the 1970s, were quickly grasped by environmentalists as evidence of the catastrophic fate that awaited us unless changes to existing levels of production and consumption were made (for an overview of survivalist literature see McCormick, 1992, ch.4; Dryzek, 1997, pp. 23–44). Seven different computer runs were suggested, the first assuming continued growth in all of the variables at present trends and the others assuming solutions to one or more of the problems. Two key conclusions were reached. First, the report argued that, because of the interdependence of the phenomena being investigated, there are no viable technological fixes available to solve the environmental consequences of growth. Only a significant reduction in economic activity will suffice. Secondly, it was also suggested that the environmental problems identified (resource depletion, pollution and so on) are increasing in an exponential, as opposed to a linear, fashion, and as a result, the crisis point will creep up on us much more quickly than expected (Meadows *et al.*, 1972, pp. 27–9).

The 'standard run' resulted in industrial collapse early in the next century due to resource depletion, but even when, in the second run, a doubling of resource availability was assumed as a result of techno-logical developments, increased industrial output produced unsus-tainable pollution levels and eventual resource depletion. Even when solutions to both pollution and resource depletion were fed into the model, collapse was still predicted due to food shortages caused by an increasing population and the appropriation of arable land by industry. Solutions to this problem, the report suggested, are equally futile since they have knock-on effects. Diverting capital to agricul-ture causes a drop in industrial output and even if a solution to food shortages could be found which did not have this effect, the result would be unsustainable population growth, pollution and resource depletion.

Seen from the perspective of the 1990s, the Limits to Growth thesis seems unduly pessimistic and, as we shall see below, the radical case is not based solely on the empirical claim that far-reaching social, economic and political change will inevitably occur whether by design or as a consequence of the collapse of industrial society (the report was updated in Meadows *et al.*, 1992). The MIT team's work has been criticized on a number of grounds (for a review see Martell, 1994, pp. 33–40). In the first place, it is claimed that the computer model was too simplistic, omitting variables which might have produced very different results, and seriously underestimating the capacity of humans to develop technological solutions to environmental pro-blems. The impression created was therefore too deterministic and pessimistic. Further, it has been claimed that the conclusions of the research reflected the class interests and ideological bias of the authors, since the conclusions were based on assumptions influenced by an ideological predisposition towards post-material values, which were in turn the product of the comfortable middle-class lives of the authors. A related criticism was the total absence of any recognition that economic growth in developing countries may be more desirable than in the rich North, thus giving the impression that the poorest peoples in the world should be asked to pay for the excesses of the rich developed world.

The most ferocious attack on the Limits to Growth report, and subsequent Green arguments based on it, came from a group of scholars who, in the absence of a more appropriate label, can be described as 'cornucopians' or 'Prometheans' after the character in Greek mythology who stole fire from the gods (Beckerman, 1974, 1995; Maddox, 1972; Myers and Simon, 1994; Simon, 1981; Simon and Kahn, 1984; for an overview see Dryzek, 1997, pp. 45–60). The

Prometheans attempt to belittle the Green case by providing indicators which, they argue, illustrate the infinite capacity of the Earth to cope with human exploitation and the ingenuity of humans to solve problems that arise. They point, for instance, to the declining price of natural resources which is exactly the opposite of what ought to happen if, as Greens argue, they have become more scarce. As a corollary, it is argued that, should scarcity become a problem, prices will rise thus protecting remaining stocks and providing an incentive for finding substitutes. Growing food supplies, improving air and water quality as well as longer life expectancy are also invoked to indicate the increasing quality of life for most people.

The Promethean arguments were particularly influential in the United States in the 1980s and were used as part of the backlash against the Green movement symbolized by the Reagan presidency (Rowell, 1996). As we will see below, however, the dominant challenge to the limits to growth and survivalist schools of thought comes from those who accept there is a problem. For most, the arguments of the Prometheans are just too optimistic and even reckless (Dryzek, 1997, pp. 57–60). Economic forecasting, on which they base much of their case, is an inexact science and we take risks by assuming that new sources of existing natural resources or adequate substitutes will be discovered. The costs of seeking to focus on reducing unsustainable economic activity, it might be suggested, outweigh the potential consequences of trusting to chance.

Science and technology

As we have seen, the limits to growth school has little faith in the ability of science and technology to aid the development of a sustainable society. The attitude of radical Greens, in general, to science might be characterized as ambivalence (Barry, 1999, pp. 29–31, 67–9, 202–6). On the one hand, it is recognized that science has played an important role in the identification of environmental problems, which has, in turn, put pressure on governments to act. The development of the science of ecology, too, by emphasizing the interdependence of nature, has done much to promote the idea that the human species is just as likely to suffer from environmental damage as any other. Ecology itself was greatly influenced by the work of Charles Darwin. Central to Darwin's work, of course, was the idea of the common origin of species which has revolutionary implications since it undermines the ideology which puts humans on a pedestal, as separate from nature and therefore entitled to dominant it (Pepper, 1986, pp. 100–3; see also Rachels, 1990).

Radical Greens also recognize that faith in science and technology can lead to a reliance on technical fixes. This encourages the idea that we can continue to deplete non-renewable resources and to pollute because, in the end, science will come up with solutions. For the radicals, this is far too complacent, and only a fundamental shift in values, and more appropriate social and political institutions, will provide genuine answers to the environmental crisis. A reliance on technical fixes, then, is to leave the resolution of environmental problems to 'experts' which, in turn, has the effect of depoliticizing environmental issues thereby preventing normative dimensions emerging.

In addition, the radical Green perspective stresses the point that the ideology of science has itself contributed to environmental problems. As David Pepper (1986, pp. 37–52) thoroughly documents, beginning in the sixteenth century the scientific revolution replaced the Medieval belief in God as the creator of the world with scientific rationalism. There was a strong emphasis within Christian belief upon the human stewardship role. Thus, if God was the creator of nature, humans should respect it as a divine creation and not seek to exploit it. The central feature of the scientific revolution, on the other hand, was the separation of humans from nature and the belief that the former could understand and tame the latter. From this, it is a short route to the position, rejected by radical Greens, that the world was made for human use; that it only has meaning and value in relation to our needs.

The normative case against economic growth

Whatever the validity of the responses to the limits to growth school of thought, whether from the Promethean camp or from the reformist sustainable development strand discussed below, it is important to recognize that the radical case is not based solely on the empirical claims concerning the possibility of sustainable growth. It also opposes the reformist position by challenging, in a number of ways, the desirability of economic growth, whether this growth is sustainable or not. The first argument here is that ending the perpetual search for economic growth and material prosperity is an intrinsic good because it leads to richer and more fulfilling lives. Schumacher (1973, p. 26) expressed this view well when he wrote that 'prosperity ... is attainable only by cultivating such drives of human nature as greed and envy, which destroys intelligence, happiness, serenity and thereby the peacefulness of man'.

What should we make of this claim? At first glance, to accept a less materially comfortable lifestyle – fewer labour-saving devices, fewer, if any, cars, less travel, and so on – does not seem particularly inviting. Greens would reply, though, that, divested of a desire for material acquisitions, people will find fulfilment in presently neglected aspects of life: in intellectual pursuits, in finding themselves spiritually, in enjoying work for its own sake and not for the monetary rewards and in developing non-dependent and therefore more satisfying relationships with others.

As Martell (1994, pp. 48–50) points out, however, there are problems with this. In the first place, who is to say that the pursuit of material possessions is not intrinsically satisfying for at least some people? Indeed, most of us could attest to the pleasures that material acquisitions have given us at some point in our lives, and, no doubt too, many of those without a materially comfortable standard of living throughout the world would attest equally to their feelings of disadvantage. Moreover, there is a strong case for saying that a certain level of material comfort is a prerequisite for the development of an individual's spiritual and intellectual life, since many material acquisitions free people from the everyday tasks of physical survival. As we saw, one of the key explanations for the emergence of the environment as an important political concern is growing post-war affluence, which has enabled people to direct their attention to quality of life issues.

A number of other arguments can be employed in support of the radical Green case against economic growth. First, there is the view that economic growth, by continually providing more for everyone, obviates the need for radical redistributive policies. It serves, therefore, as a legitimizing mechanism for inequality. A related objection to economic growth is Fred Hirsch's (1977) analysis of the 'positional economy'. The argument here is that economic growth increases demand for positional goods: uncongested roads, well-paid jobs, exotic holidays and so on, whose supply cannot be increased to meet rising demand. Economic growth, therefore, fails to bring satisfaction since there are social limits to its enjoyment. The obvious method of dealing with this problem is to increase the price of positional goods, thereby reducing the benefits for many that might, superficially, have accrued from economic growth.

Another objection to economic growth involves its relationship to liberal democratic principles. It is commonly believed that governments, since the Second World War, have pursued a growth strategy as a direct response to the rising materialistic demands of the electorate. An alternative view is that political elites pursue such a strategy and encourage citizens to want material gains, in order to increase their own political power. Economic growth, according to this analysis, is not only environmentally destructive but is also inimical to the democratic health of a society. If this is correct, liberal democratic principles, involving the tolerance of dissent and the preservation of property rights against the state, are well fitted to restrain economic growth (Lauber, 1978). Linked to this is the argument that the more individuals become passive consumers, the less they will be active citizens. Indeed, the dominant empirical and, for some, normative model of democracy in the post-war period has been the so-called 'economic' variety whereby elections become simply a means by which political elites, behaving like producers in a market economy, compete with each other to offer benefits to a largely passive, consumerist, electorate (Lively, 1975, pp. 88–108).

Sustainable development, ecological modernization and environmental politics

An indication of the strides environmentalism has made in the past few decades is that the dismissive Promethean response to the claims of radical Greens is no longer the norm. Instead, a more common response is an appreciation of the need to tackle environmental problems, but coupled with an insistence that they can be dealt with without the extensive action recommended by radical Greens. The pivotal feature of the limits to growth approach is the assumption of an automatic trade-off between environmental protection and economic growth, so that an emphasis on one necessitates neglecting the other. The reformist's position has become increasingly centred on a denial of this assumption. Instead, it is argued that the key challenge for environmentalists is to demonstrate that sustainable growth is possible; that an emphasis on environmental protection is not incompatible with economic growth and may even enhance it.

The insistence that the relationship between environmental protection and economic growth is not a zero-sum game provides one popular defining feature of the concept of sustainable development.

This term is sufficiently vague to have many competing definitions, serving the interests or ideological positions of those who espouse them (Dryzek, 1997, pp. 124–8; Elliot, 1998, pp. 184–9). For example, from a radical Green perspective, sustainable development can only be meaningful if development is not synonymous with economic growth (Richardson, 1997, p. 49). In popular parlance, however, the term has been taken to symbolize the attempt to achieve growth that is sustainable, thereby locating the concept squarely in the reformist camp.

Sustainable development is above all associated with the Brundt-land Report and the attempt to reconcile Third World development with environmental protection (World Commission on Environment and Development, 1987). At the level of the developed nation state, however, an attempt has been made to put flesh on a reformist version of sustainable development through the articulation of what has come to be known as 'ecological modernization' (Weale, 1992, pp. 66–92; Dryzek, 1997, pp. 137–52; Hajer, 1997; Barry, 1999, pp. 113–18). It has been suggested that the ideological acceptance of ecological modernization by decision-makers in some European countries, notably Germany, during the 1980s enabled them to take action on environmental problems without fearing an economic backlash. Since it was accepted that the economic consequences would not be severe, governments were also able to be proactive and take action even when the causes and consequences of environmental problems were not entirely clear. By contrast, Britain's environmental record can be at least partly explained by decision-makers' failure to recognize the force of ecological modernization (Hajer, 1997, pp. 104–74).

The ecological modernization position revolves around a number of distinct, but related, arguments. In the first place, it is argued that economic growth is not synonymous with the increased use of non-renewable resources. What is important, therefore, is not in reducing economic growth (measured in terms of Gross National Product (GNP)) but in making sure that growth is sustainable. For David Pearce (1993, p. 4) this means: 'making sure that substitute resources are made available as non-renewable resources become physically scarce and . . . ensuring that the environmental impacts of using those resources are kept within the Earth's carrying capacity to assimilate those impacts'.

This sustainability is to be achieved in part at least through technological developments. To give one example, although Britain's

GNP has risen by over 30 per cent in the last two decades, the amount of energy used has stayed about the same (Pearce, 1993, pp. 22–3). Not only does environmental protection fail to hinder economic growth according to this view but it can also be a source for future growth. This, it is argued, will be achieved through the production of low pollution goods – 'clean' cars, CFC-free aerosols and so on, which consumers are increasingly demanding. In addition, pollution-control technology itself has the potential to become an important source of economic wealth. As a consequence of greater environmental awareness among consumers and investors, companies are being forced to behave in more environmentally responsible ways.

A further claim of the ecological modernization position is that the trade-off theory overlooks the fact that, although failure to act on environmental problems now may save costs for present generations, these costs do not disappear but are transferred to future generations. In 1990 alone, the cost of pollution abatement in Britain has been estimated at £7.3 billion, over 1 per cent of GNP (Pearce, 1993, p. 38). Similarly, it is argued, the trade-off theory too often assumes that whatever reduces the profits of manufacturing concerns (as tighter environmental measures would do at least initially) will result in an overall reduction in a nation's economic prosperity. This, though, is not necessarily the case since it does not take into account the problem of 'externalities', a phrase that crops up regularly in the environmental literature (Goodin, 1992a, pp. 100–4). In the absence of any environmental regulations, factory owners can take the decision to discharge the waste their factories produces into the air and water, thereby reducing costs. For an individual businessman or businesswoman, this may well be a rational decision. Air and water are public goods, external to the profit and loss account. However, the clean-up costs have not disappeared; they are simply transferred to someone else.

Now, it may well be that those who are affected by this pollution are prepared to put up with it in return for the economic benefits the factory provides. It may be, alternatively, that the community decides that they should clean up the pollution and/or insist on the implementation of more stringent environmental regulations so that the externalities are 'internalized' as a cost borne by the factory owner. One of the regular complaints made by environmentalists is that the GNP measure of national prosperity is too narrow and should be replaced by a broader indicator of national well-being, which includes the quality of the environment (Sagoff, 1988; see also *Guardian*,

14 December 1994; Connelly and Smith, 1999, pp. 149–52). In the context of ecological modernization, though, the key point is that even if we limit our indicator of national prosperity to straightforward economic factors, allowing factories to pollute indiscriminately will still produce costs since the factories' pollution will damage the economic position of others too. It may, for instance, damage the tourist or the fishing industry and it may compromise the health of the people affected, thus diminishing the quality of the workforce and thereby reducing the competitiveness of the economy overall. For example, the costs of acid rain to the economy in terms of the market price of the timber destroyed and the health costs amount to between £1.3 and £3.3 billion a year. Likewise, the estimated costs of unsustainable transport policies in terms of road congestion, road damage, and health costs amounted to between £22.9 and £25.7 billion in 1991 alone (Pearce, 1993, p. 59; pp. 152–8; see also Huby, 1998, pp. 102–10).

The ecological modernization position seems to offer a viable theoretical framework which can be utilized both as a device to persuade governments to act and as a means of judging how sustainable their response is. Advocates of the limits to growth position may still say, of course, that environmentally responsible growth is still no substitute for low or zero growth. At the very least, we can say in response that in the real world such a scenario, particularly in the developing world, is flying in the face of reality. Whether sustainable growth is possible in the long-term is an open question. It is clear, though, that we have more time to deal with the problem than some of the more alarmist accounts in the 1970s led us to believe.

Nature and value

The rest of this chapter is concerned with the philosophical, or, to be more precise, ethical, underpinnings of environmental thought. The most distinct principle of the radical Green perspective relates to a particular view of the relationship between people and nature. Radical Greens typically reject an anthropocentric or human-centred ethic. An anthropocentric ethic argues that the human species is morally superior to non-human parts of nature. Non-human animals may be granted intrinsic value, in the sense that we recognise that they have important interests which matter to them, but while these interests have to be taken into account, human interests take precedence. However, the rest of nature (including living but not as far as we know sentient parts of nature such as plants and trees, and inanimate objects such as rocks, stones, rivers and mountains) only has extrinsic value. That is, according to the anthropocentric position, non-human nature (or at least non-sentient parts of it) has value but only to the extent that it is of use to us (Passmore, 1980).

Critics of anthropocentrism seek to extend the moral universe. Some focus on extending the moral status of non-human animals (see below), while other, life-centred or biocentric thinkers (Taylor, 1986), want to include all living things within the category of entities that can be accorded moral standing or moral considerability. Finally, the ecocentric position seeks to extend the moral universe the furthest by insisting that the whole of nature has intrinsic value in the sense that 'non-human beings are not simply of value as a means to human ends' (O'Neil, 1993, p. 10). The inspiration for this ecocentric position is widely accredited to the American writer Aldo Leopold and later from the philosopher Arne Naess (Leopold, 1949; Naess, 1973).

Two features of the ecocentric position are worth noting at this point. First, its characteristics not only apply to the relationship between humans and the rest of the natural world but also impact on how we should behave towards each other. This is drawn out nicely by Eckersley (1992, p. 56) who points out that 'a perspective that seeks emancipation writ large is one that *necessarily* supports social justice in the human community'. Secondly, those radical Greens who adopt a non-anthropocentric (life-centred or ecocentric) ethic argue that it is indispensable, since establishing the inherent or intrinsic value of entities other than humans gives them a *prima facia* expectation of respectful treatment. The expected consequence of the acceptance of a non-anthropocentric ethic is that unsustainable exploitation of the entities granted intrinsic value becomes less likely even if humans stand to gain by it.

Evaluating ecocentrism

Space prohibits us from doing much more than to touch on the major themes of the debates within environmental philosophy. The vast majority of us would agree that humans have intrinsic value and the moral standing that many think accompanies it. We know from our own experience that we can be harmed directly in a way which matters to us. That is not to say that all humans in all circumstances should be treated in the same way, but it does mean that our interests should be taken into account when our actions are evaluated. More problematic is the question of our obligations to future generations, those who are not yet born.

Most of us would probably answer that we do owe obligations to future generations but some awkward questions remain (the issue is discussed in Attfield, 1983; Connelly and Smith, 1999, pp. 26–31; Hayward, 1995, pp. 140–2; Martell, 1994, pp. 80–5). In particular, although it is clear that what we do to the environment now will affect future generations, does that mean we should take their interests into account, even if by so doing the interests of some humans living now are harmed? This relationship, between inter- and intra-generational justice, is problematic, and relates particularly to the environmental demands the West is now pressing upon the developing world (discussed in Chapter 5). The concept of sustainable development, vague though the term is as an operational principle, would seem to provide a possible answer here, reconciling the needs for present development with a recognition that this development should not deprive future generations of the opportunity to have a similar quality of life to which we aspire.

The question of future generations is, of course, still an anthropo-centric one. Particularly acute difficulties arise when we seek to justify extending moral standing beyond the human species and even beyond non-human animals. One crucial, and much commented upon, difficulty relates to the moral significance of sentience, or the capacity to experience pain and pleasure. While sentience can, and has, been utilized to extend moral considerability or moral standing to non-human animals, how can we accord moral standing to non-sentient nature when it is obvious that rocks, trees or mountains cannot be harmed in the same way as sentient animals? Raymond Frey (1983, pp. 154–5) puts the problem succinctly by contrasting the terms 'being harmed' and 'being wronged'. We can quite sensibly talk about non-sentient nature being harmed just as I can talk about harming my television set by kicking it! But it does not seem sensible to talk about wronging non-sentient nature. Thus, polluting a river is to harm it but since the river only has extrinsic value for those sentient beings who benefit from it, it is only they who can be wronged by polluting the river. At the risk of labouring the point, Peter Singer (1983, p. 123) expresses the same doubts when he states: 'There is a genuine difficulty in understanding how chopping down a tree can matter *to the tree* if the tree can feel nothing' (see also Wissenburg, 1993).

According to this interpretation, then, sentience is the benchmark for moral standing, and a life-centred or ecocentric ethic is invalid.

There have been some ingenious attempts to provide a solution to the sentience criteria problem outlined above. The first point to make is that it is perhaps easier to envisage assigning moral standing to living parts of nature, whether sentient or not, than it is to accord it to the whole of nature, inanimate as well as living. The arguments of biocentrics such as Taylor (1986) is that living things can have interests even though they are not aware of them. For some environmental thinkers, living things are characterized by the property of 'autopoiesis' which refers to self-production or self-renewal, characteristics which living things possess but which can also be applied to ecosystems or species as well (Eckersley, 1992, pp. 60–1).

It might be argued that, intuitively, we do recognize the intrinsic value of living things because of their capacities. Robin Attfield (1983), engaging in a thought experiment, suggests we consider a nuclear war which wiped everyone out except one (dying) man and a healthy tree. Would it be right for the dying man to chop down this tree? A negative answer would reveal some acceptance of a value for the tree independent of its use for humans (see also Stone, 1974). The problem with the justification for the life-based ethic, however, is that it is not clear how the emphasis on interests sets living things apart from inanimate objects (Hayward, 1995, p. 67). It is, after all, still in the interests of a television set not to be kicked even if it is not aware of it. Ecocentrics, of course, do not want to stop at living things.

Assigning moral standing to the whole of nature, and not just living parts of it, would seem to be more difficult still. One well-known approach is the development of an ecological consciousness which requires a change from a position based on a 'code of conduct' to one based on a 'state of being' (terms used by Warwick Fox quoted in Dobson, 1995, pp. 56–61). In other words, authors in this tradition, such as Fox (1995), Rodman (1983) and Matthews (1991) reject the rationalistic moral extensionist project in favour of a psychological approach which documents the need for a wider view of the self (a 'transpersonal ecology' in Fox's words, an 'ecological sensibility' in Rodman's and an 'ecological self' in Matthew's). That is, only if we are able to see that we are not separate from nature but part of it, and enriched by it, will we identify with it and appreciate the need to protect it. Protecting nature, therefore, becomes protecting ourselves.

It has not been lost on some environmental thinkers (see Hayward, 1995, p. 71) that the arguments of Fox and others may, ironically, not take us beyond anthropocentrism and, indeed, can be taken to be a defence of anthropocentrism. This is because these arguments seem to amount to saying that: if I am part of the environment, it is in my interests to try and protect it. If so, this would seem to be little different from a moderate anthropocentrism, and therefore open to the objection (explored below) that protecting the environment remains contingent on it being in human interests to do so, which, of course, it might not. Moreover, as Dobson (1995, pp. 60–1) points out, little attention has been directed to the issue of how this new consciousness is to be generated. Deep ecologists deny that reasoned argument can fulfil this task and only 'rhetorical strategies that reach beyond reason to passion' (Dryzek, 1997, p. 166) will ultimately suffice. Asking humans to 'think like a mountain' or howl like wolves, however, are not likely to take us very far. But without an effective means of showing how and why people should relate to nature, and see themselves as part of it, the force of the deep ecology position is minimised.

An enlightened anthopocentrism?

One might reject an ecocentric ethic on the grounds that, by relegating humans from the centre of the moral universe, it is undesirable. Even if we accept the moral desirability of an ecocentric ethic, however, the difficulty of establishing such a position academically, coupled with the inevitable problems of persuading decision-makers and the general public of its validity, makes it worthwhile asking whether the achievement of Green objectives necessitates, politically and strategically, such a case being made in the first place. It is clearly the case that anthropocentrism need not necessarily be synonymous with the exploitation and degradation of nature. Eckersley (1992, pp. 33–47), although an advocate of an ecocentric ethic, for instance, does recognize that there is an anthropocentric continuum on which different strands can be placed according to the weight they place on the exploitation of nature (see also Fox, 1995, p. 160). Thus, the resource conservation type emphasizes conserving natural resources to enable their continued exploitation, whereas human welfare ecology focuses on the human benefits deriving from a clean and unpolluted environment and preservationism stresses the aesthetic value of preserving wilderness areas from development.

   While Eckersley still regards ecocentrism as preferable to even the more environmentally enlightened anthropocentric approaches, an increasing number of scholars have argued that such moral extension-ism is not an essential part of a radical Green position. Goodin (1992a, pp. 26–41), for example, seeks to argue that the value of nature consists in its very naturalness and that we derive satisfaction from knowing there are forces of nature operating independently of us and with a history of their own. Goodin recognizes that this remains anthropocentric because the value of nature still derives from the satisfaction *we* get from it and not from something internal to it. Nevertheless, he insists that there can be a gradation of views from anthropocentrism to ecocentrism and that his position is towards the ecocentric end. His green theory of value, therefore, entails the proposition that nature must have value 'in relation to us' but that this is different from saying that nature only has value 'for us'.

Dobson (1995, pp. 61–71), Vincent (1993, pp. 254–5), Barry (1999, chs. 2 and 3), Hayward (1994 and 1998) and Norton (1991) all concur with Goodin's espousal of an enlightened anthropocentrism. Dobson distinguishes between weak and strong versions of anthropocentrism while Vincent develops a continuum bounded by a 'light anthropocentrism' and a 'hard-nosed exploitative anthropocentrism'. Dobson's weak or light version is 'human centred' because only humans can place value on things but this is different, he argues, from the illegitimate strong, exploitative or 'human instrumental' version which involves seeing the non-human world purely as a means to human ends. Much the same reasoning is behind Hayward's distinction between 'human chauvinism' and enlightened self-interest. Finally, Barry (1999) seeks to show that 'a self-reflexive ... as opposed to an "arrogant" ... anthropocentrism can secure many of the policy objectives of ecocentrism' (p. 8) without the need to enter into deep ecology's '"fundamentalist" complexion which is a hindrance to convincing non-believers to support its political aims' (p. 27). For these authors, then, an enlightened anthropocentrism provides the necessary protection for nature required by the radical Green position.

The problem with these defences of anthropocentrism is that they still involve nature's value being seen in terms of human benefits. While it is quite correct to say that these benefits can be conceived in terms of the protection of the natural world, this is a subjective account and, as such, is vulnerable to competing human claims which may be exploitative. As Michael Saward points out, 'although Tasmanian mountains may be inspiring and uplifting, the New York skyline may be no less so' (Saward, 1993b, pp. 5–10). So, if Goodin tells me I should not cut down trees because he derives satisfaction from knowing that they are there, I may respond by simply saying that I disagree! That is to say, without an argument to the effect that I should not cut down trees because to do so is to wrong them, then his green theory of value would appear to have no particular advantage over mine, particularly if I can point to the advantages that will accrue to humans as a result of cutting the trees down.

Of course, there *are* strong human prudential grounds for protecting the environment. However, it may be possible to drive a considerable distance down the road of environmental degradation before human survival is put at stake. Radical Greens want the brakes put on long before this point is reached, but it is unclear that an anthropocentric approach is the best means of achieving this ambitious objective. Warwick Fox (1995, p. 186) nicely sums up the problem of relying on an anthropocentric ethic when he writes that:

> The upshot of this is that even if one wins the battle in regard to preserving this area or that species, one is contributing to losing the ecological war by reinforcing the cultural perception that what is valuable in the non-human world is what is useful to humans. If the next battle in which one is engaged concerns an area or a species that is relatively 'useless' to humans then this battle becomes that much harder to win.

Against these arguments challenging the validity of enlightened versions of anthropocentrism, however, is the point that the acceptance of an ecocentric ethic does not guarantee that, in the event of a clash, the interests of nature will take precedence over those of humans. This is because an ecocentric ethic only establishes that non-human nature has moral standing, that it is worthy of moral consideration. In other words, it does not tell us that we should protect nature, only that we should consider its interests before deciding on a course of action. There is a crucial distinction, therefore, between moral standing and moral equality or between an entity being morally considerable and the degree of moral significance it possesses (Elliot, 1995 p. 13). This becomes particularly apparent when we turn to consider the relationship between our own species and non-human animals.

Animals and morality

A sub-set of environmental thought is the relationship between humans and non-human animals. Here, much attention has been paid in recent years to the development of a radical position which grants to non-human animals a higher moral status than the one afforded by the traditional animal welfare view. The radical position is popularly described as animal rights although, for reasons that will be explained, this label is somewhat misleading.

The origins of concern for animals, on the one hand, and the environment, on the other, derive from very different roots. Indeed, it is very noticeable how far apart the animal protection movement and the environmental movement still remain organizationally and ideologically. The current animal protection movement derives from the humane societies of the nineteenth century which were closely interlinked with other Victorian social reform movements concerned with slavery, child labour, women's emancipation and so on (Garner, 1993a, ch.2). The environmental movement, on the other hand, emerged to conserve the countryside as an amenity (see Chapter 7).

Humans, animals and nature

In increasing order of radicalism, it is possible to identify four main positions when discussing the relationship between humans, non-human animals and nature (adapted from Garner, 1993a, ch.1):

1. A *pure anthropocentric position* (associated, above all, with the French philosopher, Rene Descartes) which sees non-human animals as little more than machines. As such, humans owe no moral obligations to animals, although we may have indirect duties to them by virtue of our direct obligations to their human owners.

2. The *moral orthodoxy position* which regards humans as morally superior to animals but recognizes that, as sentient beings, we owe some moral obligations to them in terms of not inflicting unnecessary suffering. This is the standard way in which animals are treated in many European countries and North America. That is, it is an offence in many countries to inflict suffering on an animal for fun or in anger, but it is not an offence to inflict suffering in the pursuit of medical knowledge in the laboratory or in the raising of an animal for food. Note here, too, that there is no mention of life and death as such. What is at issue in the moral orthodoxy is the degree and purpose of suffering inflicted. Killing an animal, providing it is conducted painlessly or humanely, is not an issue.

3. A *radical challenge to the moral orthodoxy position*. Here, it is possible to distinguish between accounts based on the granting of rights to animals (most notably, associated with Regan, 1988) and accounts based on utilitarianism, often distinguished by the term animal liberation (Singer, 1990). Although there are significant differences between these two positions (see Garner, 1993a, ch.1), both regard animals as much more important morally than the conventional view allows.

4. An *ecocentric position* which, as we have seen, seeks to incorporate the whole of nature, including non-human animals, into the moral community.

Points of agreement and conflict

There is one comparison that can be made between the radical animal rights/liberation view and the ecocentric view. This is that they both seek to argue that the moral universe must incorporate all sentient life, thus removing humans from the moral pedestal. The points of conflict, though, are equally significant. In the first place, ecocentrism wants to incorporate the whole of nature within the moral community, a position which, as we have seen, is very difficult to sustain. Secondly, as we saw earlier, there is a tendency in Green thinking to emphasize the moral value of whole ecosystems or species rather than the individuals within them, and a tendency, too, to complain about the lack of ecological sophistication in the animal rights movement (Callicott, 1995). This conflict was nicely illustrated when British animal rights activists released factory-farmed mink into the countryside in 1998. This act was widely condemned by the conservationist community for its potential impact on the local ecosystem. For animal rights activists, however, this was irrelevant since the liberation of the animals took precedence, whatever the consequences (*Daily Telegraph*, 10 August 1998).

It is clear that the focus of the animal rights position is on individual animals. For ecocentrics, on the other hand, it is not so clear to whom or what moral standing is being accorded. Is it to individuals, to species, to ecosystems or to the concept of diversity itself? The classic statement of the ecocentric position was provided by Aldo Leopold who, in a well known passage, wrote: 'A thing is right when it tends to preserve the integrity, stability and beauty of the biotic community. It is wrong when it tends otherwise' (Leopold,

1949, p. 217). The problem here is that, if value is to be given to collectivities, as is usually suggested by ecocentrics, we are committing ourselves to a position which may require us to sacrifice the interests of individuals (including human individuals) in order to maintain the 'stability' of the whole. This holism puts radical Greens at odds with the individualistic focus of animal rightists. Tom Regan (1988, p. 362), for instance, describes Leopold's position as 'environmental fascism'.

This focus on whole species or ecosystems is, then, anathema from an animal rights perspective. Thus, imagine a choice between saving the last few remaining members of an endangered species and, say, 20 000 from a common species. For the animal rightist, the survival of the 20 000 must come first since more individuals will be saved. The fact that the other animals are members of an endangered species is irrelevant (Regan, 1988, pp. 359–61). Radical Greens, and environmentalists in the reformist camp, on the other hand, are inclined to say that the endangered species must come first since it is the survival of species that matters and not individual animals.

The focus on collectivities causes problems for ecocentrics when they seek to distinguish morally between the various parts of the biotic community. A position which might be called biotic egalitarianism is clearly inadequate. To cope with this, the moral relevance of sentiency has been utilized. Thus, Warwick Fox (1984, p. 199) states that:

> the central intuition of deep ecology does not entail the view that intrinsic value is spread evenly across the membership of the biotic community. Moreover, in situations of genuine value-conflict, justice is better served by not subscribing to the view of ecological egalitarianism. Cows do scream louder than carrots.

The concern with sentience allows radical Greens to object to factory farming because of the animal suffering involved. In general, though, the differences identified between environmentalists of radical and reformist hues, on the one hand, and animal rights advocates on the other does have profound practical ramifications, and not just in the area of wildlife conservation (on which see below). Environmentalists in general have had very little to say about the ethics of our treatment of domesticated farm or laboratory animals, and being a radical Green does not necessitate being a vegetarian, let alone a vegan, which is obligatory from an animal rights perspective (see Garner, 1994). Indifference is one thing, but for some Greens, domesticated animals, in so far as they damage the 'integrity' of ecosystems, can also be regarded in a negative light. In a much-quoted passage, John Muir, the nineteenth century American environmentalist, described domestic sheep as 'hooved locusts' (quoted in Callicott, 1995. p. 49), and, in a modern version, John Baird Callicott has written that: 'From the perspective of the land ethic a herd of cattle, sheep, or pigs is as much or more a ruinous blight on the landscape as a fleet of four-wheel-drive off-road vehicles' (*ibid.*, p. 50). This hostility explains why there is not a great deal of co-operation between environmental groups and animal protection groups which, from a strategic perspective at least, is unfortunate (see Ryder, 1992, for an attempt to bring the two sides together).

The politics and ethics of wildlife conservation – a case study

It might be assumed that environmental ethics, while interesting, remains peripheral to the world of practical politics where the luxury of the finer points of philosophical enquiry cannot be afforded. This assumption is an error. To illustrate this, the rest of the chapter provides a case study of wildlife conservation, where it will be seen that ethical issues, relating to the relationship between humans and non-human animals and between humans in the developed and developing worlds, are crucial to an understanding of the issues and to the development of effective and just solutions (see Clayton, 1998 who provides an attempt to relate competing ethical positions to the particular case of whales trapped under ice in Alaska).

The preoccupation with endangered species

The first point to note is that, of all the issues relating to non-human animals, there is a preoccupation – in both legislative and public interest terms – with wild animals and, in particular, with endangered species. This is the case with domestic legislation where, in countries such as Britain and the United States, the laws relating to endangered species are much more stringent than those relating to domesticated animals (Garner, 1998). At the international level, too, the emphasis is on the protection of endangered species and, in more modern parlance, the preservation of biodiversity (see Chapter 5).

The focus on species of endangered wild animals can be explained by reference to the wide variety of interests served by it. We might want to protect wild animals because we recognize their intrinsic value which requires that we treat them with respect. We might value a particular species, too, for the role it plays in maintaining the balance of an ecosystem. Accompanying these non-anthropocentric reasons for preserving species, though, are a variety of justifications for protecting wildlife which centre on the human interests served by it. Thus, we might appreciate the aesthetic beauty of at least some species, or we might recognize their economic value – in terms of tourism or as a source of economic profit – or medicinal value. To see how these competing justifications, based on competing ethical positions, operate in the contemporary politics of wildlife conservation, we will focus on the particular issue of whaling, before considering in general the so-called 'sustainable use' debate which has played a dominant role in wildlife conservation discourse and reveals a great deal about the ethical assumptions at work.

Whaling

The politics of whaling is only explicable in terms of the competing ethical perspectives involved. Whales serve a wide variety of commercial purposes and they have been hunted since the sixteenth century (Allaby, 1986, pp. 146–7). By the twentieth century, it was recognized that some control had to be exercised over whaling in order to preserve stocks and this led to the concluding of the International Convention for the Regulation of Whaling (ICRW) in 1946. This set up a standing body, the International Whaling Commission (IWC), which calculates annual sustainable quotas for each species, which are then discussed and applied by a meeting of the parties to the treaty. If the numbers of any particular whale species were calculated to be low enough, a complete ban could be imposed. The crucial point is that the ICRW was set up purely for a specific anthropocentric motive, the continuation of hunting.

As a device to conserve whales, the ICRW has been largely unsuccessful. As an agreement between sovereign states, whaling nations are not obliged to join and, although most have, this is primarily because the ICRW sought to encourage the widest possible membership (see Chapter 5). In reality, whale species have tended to be protected only once they have been hunted to the point of extinction. Thus, of the 14 'great' whales, all but the small minke have been exploited to danger levels. Most symbolically of all, the blue whale – the largest mammal ever to have existed on earth equivalent in size to 25 adult elephants – was not protected until 1963, by which time its numbers had dwindled to between 200 and

2000 (*Guardian*, 13 July 1990). There is no precise way of determining how many whales in any particular species exist and thus what the quota should be. In consequence, political expediency has played a significant part in the IWC's deliberations. It is in the commercial interests of whaling nations to continue exploiting whale stocks to the point of extinction since they can then use the profits to invest in other projects (Cherfas, 1988, pp. 200–3). On ecological and aesthetic grounds, of course, it is a different matter.

Since 1986, a moratorium on commercial whaling has been in place, although whaling for scientific purposes continues (see Chapter 5). Ostensibly, the moratorium was instituted because whale stocks had declined to such a degree that the continued viability of whaling was in question. In reality, non-whaling nations such as Britain and the United States, who have come to dominate the ICRW, forced through the moratorium, and have voted to retain it ever since, for other, non-economic, reasons. These governments are reacting to the anti-whaling sentiments of their citizens, who, in turn, have been influenced by the campaigning of the environmental movement. To some extent, undoubtedly, the opposition to whaling is based on the perception that whales have intrinsic value and, therefore, they have interests which ought to be protected, but it is also based on the aesthetic value of the mammals which, of course, is equally anthropocentric as the economic justification for conservation. With growing evidence that some whale stocks are now sufficiently large to justify a resumption in hunting, the conflict – between the original intention of the treaty as a means of managing whaling to increase its life-span, and the animal cruelty and aesthetic justifications for continuing the moratorium – have come to a head (see Chapter 5).

Sustainable use and the African elephant

The competing ethical principles identified in the case of whaling also exist in the debate about protecting African game and, in particular, the elephant. To a considerable degree, wildlife conservation depends on the ability to control the trade in endangered species. To this end, the Convention on the International Trade in Endangered Species (CITES) treaty was concluded in Washington DC in 1973. The parties to the CITES treaty have been preoccupied with the fate of African game and, in particular, with the elephant. Up to the 1980s, the elephant population was declining rapidly, primarily as a result of poaching. As a result, the commercial trade in elephant products was prohibited by the CITES treaty, thus making the profitable ivory trade illegal. This decision provides the context for a crucial strategic and ideological debate in wildlife conservation, revealing a complex web of ethical assumptions (Garner, 1993a, ch.6). Two major camps have emerged. On the one hand, there are those who argue that there should be a complete ban on the trade in ivory (and other products derived from elephants and rhinos) and on the other are those who advocate a policy of 'sustainable use', whereby a restricted sustainable trade should be permitted.

There are strategic and ideological dimensions to this debate. In terms of strategy, it is argued by the sustainable use advocates that the only effective way to prevent poaching is to allow the exploitation of wildlife by the mostly poor rural people who have to coexist with African game reserves. Only then will they see wildlife conservation as a source of income as opposed to a threat to their mainly agricultural livelihoods, and only then will they cease to turn a blind eye to poaching or cease to engage in it themselves. Even parts of the conservation community have accepted this strategic case for sustainable use. The opponents of this strategy, however, argue that it will necessitate the reopening of the ivory trade and the consequent difficulties of determining 'legitimate' from poached ivory. They would point to the period, between 1985–9, when a restricted trade in elephant ivory was in operation, and its failure to prevent or even reduce the incidence of poaching. In addition, although the strategy of complete prohibition will require some culling of elephants as their numbers increase, this regulated and managed culling activity is preferable to the arbitrary nature of poaching where the strongest and youngest members of the herd are just as likely to be killed as the old and the sick. Finally, there are other methods, and in particular eco-tourism, of enabling indigenous people to benefit from wildlife, a practice which the Kenya Wildlife Service has long adopted (*Guardian*, 28 April 1999). Killing, therefore, is not the only option.

The pressure to adopt a sustainable use strategy has been intense, and has resulted in a limited reopening of the ivory trade. This decision was all the more likely as soon as it was accepted that elephant numbers have increased, particularly in Southern African countries. In 1997, parties to CITES agreed (by 76 votes to 21) to permit Namibia, Botswana and Zimbabwe to resume, from March 1999, marketing ivory. Only a relatively small amount of existing stockpiles can be sold; Japan is to be the sole trading partner and mechanisms must be in place to counter the emergence of a black market. Despite the limited nature of the trade resumption, many conservationists regard this as the thin end of the wedge and, in addition, question whether there are stringent enough safeguards to prevent the re-emergence of wide scale poaching (*Guardian*, 19 March 1999).

Mere numbers, however, are only part of the debate, since there is a crucial ethical dimension too. As an ideology, sustainable use is based on the ethical principle that wildlife conservation should not take precedence over the interests of humans. Clearly, the protection of endangered species *can* seriously effect the interests of humans, whether they be those who make their living out of whaling or those whose land is threatened by the incursion of elephants. For advocates of animal rights, of course, the exploitation of wildlife, whether endangered or not, is illegitimate, and there is no doubt that the influence of animal rightists (and animal welfarists appalled by the suffering inflicted on animals by poachers, trappers and whalers) on the conservation community has increased. This has made it difficult for groups like the World Wide Fund for Nature to support sustainable use even if they think it is strategically and morally justified. One can just imagine the howls of protest from members should they find out that the organization they pay to protect the elephant is, in actual fact, conniving in having some of them killed.

As with the whale, there is a mixture of human and non-human centred justifications for protecting elephants and other species. The effect is that the protection of such species, heavily promoted by Western governments and conservationists, often results in sacrificing the interests of Third World peoples who stand to gain by exploiting them. This by itself is morally dubious but we must add to it the developed world's propensity to exploit animals when they find it valuable to do so, even to the point of overriding statutes designed to protect endangered wild animals, as in the case of the British government's decision to continue gassing badgers suspected of carrying the tuberculosis virus. In such circumstances, the moral case for allowing Third World peoples to exploit wildlife, irrespective of the consequences for endangered species, would appear to be unanswerable (Garner, 1994).

We have considered in this chapter the economic and philosophical dimensions to the debate between radical and reformist environmentalists. Not surprisingly, the radical approach has had relatively little impact on the way in which the environmental debate has been couched in the mainstream political arena. However, the challenge it provides has hastened the attempt to develop a viable reformism. Irrespective of the validity of the bleak prognosis of the limits to growth school, the ecological modernization position offers environmentalists far greater opportunity to influence decision-makers. Similarly, given that it is extremely difficult to find arguments which can support an ecocentric ethic, environmental protection would seem to be dependent on the strength of human-prudential grounds. There are compelling reasons to suggest that these grounds *are* strong and varied enough for us to afford to jettison, or at least not be too preoccupied about, the need to show that the whole of nature does have moral standing.

Further reading

There are now a number of introductory accounts of Green ideas. Dobson (1995) has become the standard text but Dryzek (1997) and Eckersley (1992) are also very thorough and Martell (1994) provides an invaluable summary and a useful critical commentary. Useful articles providing overviews of the debate are Vincent (1993), Barry (1994) and Young (1992). More difficult, but ultimately rewarding, is Goodin's book (1992a) which, despite its title, develops a particular point of view and assumes some knowledge.

On environmentalism and the economy, the *Limits to Growth* report (Meadows *et al.*, 1972) is essential and has been updated (Meadows *et al.*, 1992). The ecological modernization position is explored in Hajer (1997), Weale (1992) and Pearce (1993). It is important to read classic ecocentric works. The most important are Leopold (1949), Naess (1973), Goldsmith *et al.* (1972) and Fox (1995). A useful anthology of key writings is Dobson (1991) and Dryzek and Schlosberg (1998). Finally, a summary of the animal rights debate can be found in Garner (1993a), and the two major philosophical works are Singer (1990) and Regan (1988).

4

Greens and the Western Political Tradition

In Chapter 3 we examined the economic and philosophical dimensions of the radical and reformist versions of environmentalism. In this chapter, we focus on the political dimension, and ask, in particular, whether there is anything distinctive about the political prescriptions environmentalists make. To prejudge much of what is to come, it is important to note that environmental reformists see the protection of the environment as essentially just another policy issue which the political system has to cope with. For them, although environmental issues may cause peculiar problems which require some institutional tinkering, no fundamental reordering of the political system is required and no particular set of political arrangements is defended. Seen in such a way, environmentalism is suitable for single-issue pressure groups and for absorption by the mainstream political parties. On the other hand, radical Greens claim to be putting forward a self-contained, coherent set of principles which cannot merely be tacked on to an existing set of policies or incorporated within an established system of thought. In order to assess this claim, this chapter examines the relationship between radical Green thinking and the major ideologies and concepts associated with Western political thought.

Ecology and political ideologies

A glance at the literature reveals that virtually all ideological traditions claim to be able to incorporate a concern for the environment. Can this be so? That is, can the environmental claims of ideologies as diverse as conservatism, liberalism, socialism, feminism and anarchism be equally consistent with the protection of the environment? If not, is there a particular ideological tradition which is better able to incorporate the demands of environmentalists or does Green thinking represent a distinct position, not reducible to the political prescriptions of other ideologies? By examining the main ideological traditions in turn, we may be able to provide answers to these questions.

Conservatism

There are surprising similarities between conservative thought enshrined, in particular, in the work of the eighteenth-century writer and politician Edmund Burke, and themes that regularly appear in Green writing (Smith, 1998, pp. 57–61). Greens, like conservatives, are sceptical of the Enlightenment tradition's emphasis on the human capacity to comprehend a complex, interconnected world. Greens, like conservatives, therefore, are persuaded to leave things as they are. Preservation and conservation are, then, terms equally applicable to the conservative and the Green thinker. For conservatives, as for Greens, the appropriate image of a social reformer is a gardener, seeking to prune and trim, rather than an engineer seeking to restructure society according to a rationally thought-out plan. These links between Green and conservative ideas enable John Gray (1993, p. 176), from a conservative perspective, to applaud Green theory, which he argues is 'an invaluable corrective to the Whiggish, anthropocentric, technological optimism by which all the modern political religions are animated and which has, in the form of neo-liberalism, even infected most of what passes today as conservatism'.

There is, on the other hand, much in the conservative tradition which is inconsistent with Green thinking. The image of social reformer as 'gardener', for instance, sits rather uneasily with the radical Green critique of 'nature as garden' with its anthropocentric overtones, and the dark Green celebration of wilderness which implies a 'hands-off' approach (Dobson, 1995, p. 49). Furthermore, conservatism does not have anything to say about the limits to growth, at least beyond a general nostalgia for a pre-industrial past, nor does it seek to extend moral standing beyond humans. Moreover, the radical Green emphasis on radical social and economic change, and the interminable plans of a new society which appear in Green literature, also sits uneasily with the cautious approach of conservatism (Martell, 1994, p. 141).

Fascism/authoritarianism

In the past, the extreme Right has shown an interest in environmentalism. Anna Bramwell (1989) has documented the early interest in ecology by the Far Right and, indeed, the interest in the Far Right by ecologists. Elements of the National Socialist party in Germany, for example, were interested in ecological issues from the 1920s and, having gained power, the Nazis were environmentally active, setting up nature reserves and experimenting with alternative forms of energy among other things. There are ideological similarities between ecologism and fascism. As Hay (1988, p. 23), points out: 'Use of biological metaphors, stress on the organic community and the individual's need to merge with it, elevation of ritual, intuition and the mystical, and distrust of the rational' are all elements that can be found in both Green writing and fascist ideology. However, it is wrong to take the association too far. As Andrew Vincent (1993, p. 266) comments: 'Because national socialists used socialist methods or favoured ancient German traditions does not mean that either socialism or conservatism are eternally besmirched. The same qualification holds for ecology'.

When critics label Green thinking as fascist they are more often than not referring to the authoritarian strain that does exist in some Green writing. This authoritarian strand, particularly prevalent in the 1970s, emphasizes the need for drastic coercive solutions, particularly in the areas of reducing consumption and cutting population size, thought necessary to deal with the severity of the environmental crisis (Hardin, 1968; Heilbroner, 1974; Ophuls, 1973). These accounts tend to be based on a Hobbesian model of Man as ultimately selfish and individualistic, requiring an authoritarian state (the Leviathan) to keep order.

One well known exponent of an authoritarian solution is Garrett Hardin whose articles *The tragedy of the commons* and *Living on a lifeboat* (1968, 1977) are among the best-known environmental writings. His thesis is that, left to their own devices, people will always despoil the commons through greed and naivety and therefore access to it should be limited by a strong state to those who are best able to look after it. 'Freedom in a commons', therefore, 'brings ruin to all' (Hardin, 1968, p. 1244).

While most environmentalists would agree with Hardin that environmental damage does come about in the ways he suggests, most would not accept his prescriptions (see Hays, 1988, pp. 23–4; Hayward, 1995, pp. 148–51). This is particularly the case with his extremely illiberal views on the Third World, where, in the so-called lifeboat ethic parable, he argues, in a Malthusian idiom, that the West (in the lifeboat) should not give a helping hand to the Third World (drowning in the water) since to do so would encourage population growth and greater demands upon natural resources, and so ultimately lead to everyone drowning. Hardin and other like-minded individuals, most notably Paul Ehrlich (1972), formed an organization called the Environmental Fund in the 1970s which, among other things, campaigns against food aid to the developing world.

Two basic criticisms of Hardin's eco-authoritarianism can be made. In the first place, it might be suggested that his 'Tragedy of the commons' describes not a commons regime but an open access regime with no rules or codes of conduct designed to prevent unsustainable exploitation. Further, his 'lifeboat ethic' has been criticized for its unjustified pro-developed world stance. As Paehlke (1989, pp. 65–6) points out: 'Why does Hardin not suggest a more sensible scheme, one advocating the eviction of North Americans from the lifeboat? It would cost far fewer persons and would achieve for the species considerably more time to bring about stabilisation than would avoidable starvation in the so-called Third World'.

The authoritarian theme is very much the exception in environmental literature, and was a particular product of the doom-laden 1970s where survival was the major concern; hence the title of Ophuls' work *Leviathan or Oblivion* (1973). To be fair, though, many exponents of the authoritarian position adopt it with a heavy heart, stressing, with some justification, that coercion now is essential to avoid the much greater amount that will be necessary later to deal with even greater environmental degradation (Martell, 1994, p. 146). A final point is that concern about population increases does remain central to environmentalism but this concern is not synonymous with authoritarianism as a wide variety of non-coercive measures have been recommended.

Liberalism

There are some ways in which the liberal tradition might be regarded as an influence on Green thinking. The inclusion of non-humans within the ethical community, for instance, might be regarded as taking the liberal language of individual rights and obligations to its logical conclusion (Martell, 1994, p. 141; Eckersley, 1995, 1996). Certainly, as we have seen, contemporary advocates of animal rights and liberation do invoke the liberal tradition of rights and utility to justify their position. It is true that both J.S. Mill and Jeremy Bentham recognized that non-human animals, as sentient beings, were entitled to moral consideration, although neither were prepared to say (as consistency, at least for Bentham, demanded they ought) that non-human animals should have a moral status equivalent to humans (Clarke and Linzey, 1990, pp. 135–40).

On a number of dimensions, however, liberalism and ecology are at odds. First, the ecocentric and holistic core of Green thinking puts it at odds not only with the failure of liberalism to countenance going beyond sentience as the grounding for moral standing (and most liberal thought is unashamedly anthropocentric), but also with liberal individualism. Moreover, as Hayward (1995, p. 145) argues, moral arguments might be better couched in terms of responsibilities rather than rights since 'the consistent pursuit of the full range of human rights, for all human beings, would be ecologically unsustainable'.

In terms of economics, there is a debate about the compatibility of the free market and environmentalism (Eckersley, 1993; Vincent, 1993, p. 267; Wissenberg, 1993), and market solutions to environmental problems have been suggested (see Chapter 8). However, even if there is a case for a market approach, it is a reformist strategy designed to alleviate the worst excesses of economic growth rather than to challenge this growth head-on. As such, it is not consistent with the limits to growth core of radical Green thinking. Even from a reformist perspective, 'concern with the environment immediately raises the possibility of interfering with private choices' (Smith, 1998, p. 51) and therefore challenges the liberty which liberals so prize.

Despite contemporary attempts to rescue it, it should not be forgotten too that liberalism was originally inextricably linked with a productivist ethos. It reached its ascendancy in the nineteenth century, an era when economic growth, technological optimism and a belief in the ability of humans to master the environment were guiding principles (Gamble, 1981, ch.1). One exception was J.S. Mill, who put the case for ecological diversity and a stationary state economy, but he remains very much an isolated figure in the liberal tradition (Eckersley, 1992, p. 23).

Marxism and socialism

Greens have rarely raided the liberal tradition for ideas but ideological links between Greens and the Left are much more evident (see Weston, 1986). This is partly because there have been political alliances between Greens and socialists, particularly in Germany, and partly because Marxism and socialism offer the kind of state or community intervention and regulation which most Greens think is necessary to deal with environmental problems. This is not to say that the relationship has been an untroubled one. Many Greens have denied there is an ideological link between their doctrine and socialism, pointing out that the real distinction on ecological grounds is not between capitalism and socialism but between capitalist or socialist industrialism on the one hand and the Green approach on the other. According to this view, it is the 'super-ideology' of industrialism which causes environmental degradation and not a particular form of ownership. As Porritt (1984, p. 43) points out: 'The politics of the Industrial Age, left, right and centre, is like a three-lane motorway, with different vehicles in different lanes, but *all* heading in the same direction'. As some members of the British Greens put it, socialism represents 'fair shares in extinction' (quoted in Dobson, 1995, p. 168).

There is some justification in the claim made by some Greens that socialism is no more ecologically sound than capitalism. In the first place, industrialism in the former Communist regimes of Eastern Europe caused extensive environmental problems (see Gray, 1993, pp. 125–33; Smith, 1998, pp. 73–5). Of course, socialists can retort by saying these regimes were not really socialist at all or that environmentally damaging industrialism was necessary because of the threat posed by hostile capitalist enemies (Pepper, 1986, pp. 172–3; Yearley, 1992, p. 105). What we can say is that, in these countries, the means of production were state-controlled and that state-directed industrialism was not environmentally benign.

Secondly, at a theoretical level, orthodox Marxism (or at least the way in which orthodox Marxism is usually perceived) is arguably inconsistent with Green thinking, since it is 'ultimately wedded to the same expansionary ethos and anthropocentric framework as liberalism' (Eckersley, 1992, p. 24). It is anthropocentric because Marx, just as Locke and Hobbes had done before him, regarded the non-human world exclusively in terms of its use for humans, holding that it only acquired value when being worked on by humans (*ibid.*, p. 25). Even a modern eco-socialist such as David Pepper (1993b, pp. 436–42) accepts that socialism is not ecocentric in orientation and, indeed, he celebrates the fact since ecocentrism, he argues, is often translated into, at worst, anti-humanism and at best a disregard for the human condition – the Gaia hypothesis of Lovelock (1979) being a prime example of the latter.

Of course, this Green critique of socialism will depend upon whether we accept ecocentrism as a central part of Green thought, which, as we saw, is not an assertion all environmental thinkers would agree with. If we reject ecocentrism as an essential Green principle, then the Green credentials of Marxism and socialism might be rescued. This is particularly the case if we accept the reinterpretation of the writings of Marx and Engels conducted by scholars such as Parsons (1978) and Benton (1993). Particular attention here is devoted to Marx's early work in which human interaction with the natural environment is regarded as important for spiritual and aesthetic development, as much as it is for meeting material needs (Martell, 1994, p. 149). The problem here is the difficulty of weighing the importance of these earlier writings, as compared with the more exploitative anthropocentrism of Marx and Engels' later prose.

While it might be possible to reconcile Marx's anthropocentrism with Green thought, it is less easy to argue away the productivist foundation of socialism and Marxism. For Marx, it was not the forces of production (the raw materials, technology and labour power that constitutes the productive process) but the capitalist relations of production which provided the obstacle to social and political change. Indeed, the technological developments forthcoming under the capitalist social epoch were the pre-condition for a future socialist society (Eckersley, 1992, pp. 77–82). Unreconstructed Marxists still regard environmentalism as a peripheral issue, of concern to the middle class who are simply defending their selfish interests and preventing the working class from benefiting from society's productive potential (Enzensberger, 1974).

Some contemporary Marxists have sought to adapt the doctrine in order to take account of modern concern for the environment (Williams, 1986; Redclift, 1984). Here, the focus has been on demonstrating the culpability of the capitalist system of production rather than industrialism *per se*. Thus, the competitive character of the capitalist system, the need to continually persuade us that we want new goods, and the resulting wastefulness and inefficiency, provide the real reason for environmental degradation. Conversely, under a system of common ownership, production can be organized more effectively and science and technology can be brought to bear in order to provide solutions to environmental problems.

Clearly, with its anthropocentric basis, its orientation towards growth (although toned down somewhat in most modern eco-socialist writing) and its faith in technological fixes, even this reformulated Marxism does not come up to scratch from a radical Green perspective. Nevertheless, there is a great deal in the Marxist, and more general non-Marxian socialist tradition, which Greens can agree with and perhaps even learn from, and there is a growing body of literature which seeks to draw out these features (see, for instance, Gorz, 1982; Pepper, 1993a) Here, we can point to the vision of small-scale participatory democracies found in the writings of socialists such as Charles Fourier, William Morris and G.D.H. Cole (Hayward, 1995, pp. 177–8); the emphasis on egalitarianism both within Western societies and between rich and poor countries; and the socialist analysis of political power, which provides Greens with a useful account of how vested interests often stand in the way of environmental improvements, and how environmental protection may be in the interests of the working class, who can be mobilized to promote this objective.

Beyond left and right

It has been claimed that Green thinking is more in accord with ideologies such as feminism and anarchism than with the mainstream traditions of Western thought. There is certainly an extensive and ever-increasing eco-feminist literature (for an overview see Mellor, 1997) and it is equally the case that there are growing links between the women's movement and the environment. At a practical level, it is very noticeable that a large proportion of environmental and animal rights activists, although not movement leaders, are women (Garner, 1993a, ch.2; Jordan and Maloney, 1997, pp. 108–10), although note Seager (1993) who suggests that the environmental movement's domination by men and masculine values reduces its effectiveness.

The basis of the eco-feminist position is the idea that women, rather than men, have a greater affinity to environmental protection (see Griffin, 1978; Merchant, 1980; Mellor, 1992). There are two main strands to this argument. The first relates to women's nurturing role (derived from their reproductive function), which provides for a set of values (of caring and compassion) more conducive to an identification with the natural world – the so-called 'essentialist' position.

These values, it is suggested, are inferior to masculine values in Western patriarchal societies and, as a consequence, there is an emphasis on the domination, control, and ultimate despoilation, of nature. Secondly, it is argued that women can identify with the environment since they have a mind-set adjusted to oppression – the so-called 'materialist' position, hence the title of Collard's (1988) book *Rape of the Wild* (for a feminist account of animal rights along these lines see Adams, 1990; see also Regan, 1991, ch. 5). According to this argument, then, there is an identity of interests between the ending of male exploitation and the ending of human exploitation of the natural environment.

Both approaches are challengeable. In the first place, the simplistic portrayal of different male and female values is questionable, and even if it were possible to attach labels such as tough and aggressive to males and maternal and compassionate to females, it is by no means clear that these are innate as opposed to being a product of the social division of labour (Eckersley, 1992, p. 66; see also Evans, 1993). Secondly, women are not the only oppressed group in society and, in addition, it is not clear that patriarchy and anthropocentrism are synonymous since, as Eckersley (1992, p. 68) points out, many traditional patriarchal societies did not despoil their natural environment.

There is also a strong affinity between anarchist thought and much Green political theorizing. Dobson, for instance, argues, in the first edition of his text, that the 'anarchist solution' is 'the closest approximation ... to the centre of gravity of a Green sustainable society' (Dobson, 1990, p. 83; see also Atkinson, 1991, p. 8 and Carter, 1993). Anarchism is concerned with justifying stateless, decentralized, and self-sufficient communes where people live in harmony with each other (Heywood, 1992, pp. 259–60).

Although the ecological imperative was not the major focus of classic anarchist thought, there are obvious parallels between the anarchist vision and the Green account of a post-industrial society. For example, 'on about twenty major points' there is agreement between Peter Kropotkin's *Field, Factories and Workshops* (written in 1899) and the *Blueprint for Survival*, although there is no acknowledgement, and Kropotkin himself was influenced by other anarchists such as Godwin and Proudhon (Pepper, 1986, pp. 188–93).

The best known eco-anarchist is the American Murray Bookchin (1962; 1971), although he is by no means the only author to adopt an anarchist approach to Green political thought (see Schumacher, 1973; Sale, 1984; Bahro, 1986). In a series of books, Bookchin has developed a comprehensive anarchist account (described as 'social ecology') with ecological principles at the forefront (see Eckersley, 1992, pp. 146–60). He suggests that social hierarchy, based on class, race and gender, is the major cause of environmental degradation since domination over non-human nature follows from human domination over other humans.

Whether or not one accepts Bookchin's particular brand of eco-anarchism, all of the varieties are based on the fundamental principles of decentralization and self-sufficiency. As such, they are all subject to the critique, examined in detail below, which questions the ability of such small communities to deal with the international and global nature of environmental problems. Because of this, a number of Green writers have suggested that it is by no means clear that a radical Green position can accept anarchist solutions.

Decentralization, democracy and ecology

Radical Greens place considerable emphasis on decentralization, local self-government and egalitarianism as the key operating principles of the sustainable society (see Goldsmith, 1972; Schumacher, 1973; Sale, 1980; Goodin, 1992a, pp. 147–56). Perhaps the best-known version is Kirkpatrick Sale's advocacy of bio-regions, whereby self-sufficient and autonomous communities are 'determined by natural rather than human dictates, distinguishable from other areas by attributes of flora, fauna, water, climate, soils and land forms' (Sale, 1984, p. 168).

The idea of small-scale communities, facilitating participatory democracy, has had a long shelf-life in Western political thought. It is associated, above all, with the practice of the Greek city-states and the later work of such luminaries as Thomas More, Jean-Jacques Rousseau, G.D.H. Cole as well as anarchist thinkers such as Godwin and Kropotkin (Pateman, 1970; Eckersley, 1992, p. 160). In addition, there is a considerable literature on the general desirability and viability of this form of social and political organization (see Bachrach, 1969). Our remit, in an assessment of the Green advocacy of decentralization and democracy, though, is much more limited. That is, the question we need to ask is: what contribution can the existence of a decentralized, egalitarian and participatory democracy make to the realization of Green objectives?

Greens would point, first, to the direct environmental benefits of decentralization. Thus, small, autonomous communities will require self-sufficiency, therefore ending the environmental damage caused by the national and international market in goods and large-scale industrial production. In addition, such communities (particularly in the case of Sale's bio-regions) will foster a greater appreciation of nature's value, beauty and power. Secondly, there is the argument that a decentralized, participatory and egalitarian society is one that recognizes each person's value as an important and respected member of the community. Each person is entitled to participate equally in the making of laws, is not divided from others through unequally distributed material possessions and feels part of a cohesive community – all characteristics lacking in large and impersonal societies (Martell, 1994, pp. 51–3). As Goldsmith (1972, p. 51) argues: 'It is probable that only in the small community can a man or woman be an individual. In today's large agglomerations, he is merely an isolate'. In a similar vein, Porritt (1984, p. 87) states that a large-scale industrial society takes 'away our dignity, makes us passive recipients rather than active participants, makes us dependent rather than self-reliant, alienates us from the work we do and the people we live with'.

Much of the second point above relates to the relationship between Green thinking and democracy, which is discussed in some detail below. What we have to consider here is the extent to which the decentralized small-scale community (whether democratic or not) preferred by many radical Greens, is the most appropriate means of solving environmental problems. It should be noted that two of the best-known academic accounts of Green political thought, written by authors generally supportive of the radical Green position, doubt whether the small-scale autonomous community is the best model, as does Martell, in his sympathetic commentary on the Green case (Eckersley, 1992, pp. 176–8; Goodin, 1992a, pp. 146–68; Martell, 1994, pp. 54–61; see also Ryle, 1988, p. 66).

Robert Goodin, in particular, is determined to distance himself from the decentralization model. He attempts to achieve this by distinguishing between what he calls a 'green theory of value', which seeks to tell us why environmental protection is a desirable objective, and a 'green theory of agency', which is concerned with 'the nature of the mechanisms by which its recommendations *(put simply, protecting the environment)* are to be given practical meaning' (Goodin, 1992a, p. 113, emphasis in original). The latter, he argues, is not a central part of the Green case and any particular theory of agency should be accepted or rejected according to the extent to which it helps to promote Green objectives enshrined in the theory of value.

Now, Goodin's primary target here are the various life-style changes and consciousness-raising approaches which Greens are wont to espouse. By distinguishing between value and agency, he is able to recommend turning 'a blind eye' to some of the 'crazier views' or 'green heresies' since these are part of a theory of agency and not value (*ibid.*, pp. 16–17). Strategically, of course, Goodin may be correct here but for our purposes it is important to note that he also rejects the decentralization model on the same grounds, that it does not provide a means of achieving the objectives enshrined in the green theory of value (*ibid.*, pp. 147–66).

The central problem which Goodin, and other critics, point to is the inability of autonomous communities to cope with the co-ordination that would be required to deal with environmental problems which, as we have seen, are transnational or even global in scope. Greens might answer this charge in two ways. In the first place, they might argue that the decentralized communities advocated would be much more environmentally aware and would appreciate the need to act collectively to solve environmental problems. 'Think globally, act locally' is a phrase commonly used by environmentalists to emphasize their dual concern.

It is not clear, however, why decentralized communities would be more environmentally aware. It may be the case that people in large urban areas are more environmentally enlightened. After all, it should be noted that some of the worst environmental damage has been caused by farmers in small rural communities. Even if it were to prove generally true, there would still be no mechanism whereby the occasional despoiler could be brought into line with other communities. This could prove fatal since those communities making an effort to protect the environment may well conclude that it is not worth their while continuing to pay the cost whilst other 'free riders' are getting the benefits without contributing. Finally, as Martell (1994, p. 160) emphasizes, co-ordination is not just about the exercise of authority. Even if all of the communities were willing to behave responsibly, there would still be a need for a body to co-ordinate their activities, identifying problems and initiating a response.

The second answer to the criticism is to point out that radical Greens are not opposed to co-ordination, the need for which appears in much of the Green literature (Goodin, 1992a, pp. 151–2; Martell,

1994, p. 56). The problem is they are not particularly coherent. At most, they are prepared to accept that larger co-ordinating bodies should be informal networks rather than permanent unified structures, and certainly nothing like a nation state. The question remains, however, whether this would be sufficient. So, whichever way we look at it, there appears to be a strong case for an institutionalized enforcement and co-ordination body not dissimilar to the nation state or even a larger entity, equivalent to, say, the European Union.

Most Greens would argue that one of the benefits of decentralization is that it allows for greater participation by citizens in decision-making. Democracy and decentralization, however, are not necessarily synonymous, since one can envisage élite rule at a sub-state level just as one can envisage degrees of democracy at the state or supra-state level. Indeed, given the problems with decentralization we encountered above, it might be argued that the 'democratic transformation' of the state, rather than its abolition, is more important for Greens (Barry, 1999, p. 79). If this is so, however, we then have to ask whether there is any necessary link between democracy and Green thinking.

Following Hayward (1995, p. 174) the relationship between ecology and democracy can be 'one of indifference . . . one of incompatibility or . . . one of necessary connection'. In terms of incompatibility, we have seen that there are those who have argued that the ecological crisis requires authoritarian solutions. This school of thought, as we also saw, was particularly prevalent in the 1970s and was associated with the survivalist mentality that followed the predictions of imminent ecological catastrophe. Even if we accept that democracy is not conducive to the resolution of environmental problems, an assertion which is disputed – in as far as these predictions have proved to be overly pessimistic – it might be suggested that we can now afford the luxury of democracy.

Another, subtly different, ecological critique of democracy is the argument that democracy actually encourages unecological policies, as opposed to being unable to deal with pre-existing ecological problems. Democracy, according to this view, 'represents the unleashing of desires, of demands that cannot be satisfied and which have to be authoritatively restrained' (Barry, 1999, p. 196). This critique only applies, however, if we adopt a narrow definition of democracy as merely a means to the end of utility maximization, which may, in turn, be as much to do with the nature of acquisitive capitalist societies than democracy itself (Barry, 1999, pp. 197–8).

Another dimension of this critique of democracy is the suggestion that the resolution of environmental problems require the will of experts to prevail, and their role can sometimes be undermined or devalued by democratic decisions which pander to the often misguided views of the masses and the popular press. This argument has been employed regularly to justify, for example, the secrecy of the British pollution control regime (see Chapter 8). One case, often quoted as an example of an ecologically dubious action being taken as a result of popular pressure, was the fate of the Shell-owned Brent Spar oil loading buoy (*Sunday Times*, 10 September 1995; Dickson and McCulloch, 1996; Bennie, 1998). The company had originally decided to sink the platform in the North Atlantic but, due to enormous (but in some people's eyes ultimately misguided) public pressure led by Greenpeace, who later admitted that it had made some factually inaccurate claims, the platform was towed ashore in July 1995 and eventually put to use as a quay for ferries.

While not wishing to deny the importance of experts, however, environmental decision-making is concerned with competing interests and values at least as much as it is about technical resolutions to problems. As a consequence, it is important to ensure that all interests are represented in the decision-making arena. Moreover, as the employment of maverick scientists by fossil-fuel industries illustrates, it is naive to assume that 'experts' are always entirely divorced from the battle between competing interests.

Denying that there is an antagonistic relationship between democracy and ecology is one thing, demonstrating that there is a *necessary* connection between the two is quite another. In other words, are there any positive reasons from an environmental perspective why democracy should be favoured? A number of commentators have argued that the relationship is, at most, only a contingent one. In a much quoted passage, Goodin (1992a, p. 168) says that: 'To advocate democracy is to advocate procedures, to advocate environmentalism is to advocate substantive outcomes: what guarantee can we have that the former procedures will yield the latter sorts of outcomes' (see also Saward, 1993b)?

There are a number of reasons why democracy might facilitate environmentally-beneficial outcomes. First, the legitimacy attached to democracy might make it easier to persuade individuals to accept the sacrifices that might be necessary on environmental grounds. In addition, it might also be the case that so-called 'discursive' democracy involving extensive deliberation will produce the most enlightened and sophisticated decisions and, in so far as one assumes that protecting the environment is an enlightened and sophisticated thing to do, a positive relationship can be identified (Dryzek, 1990; Barry, 1999, pp. 214–20). One reason why an enlightened decision might be reached by democratic procedures is that the impact of vested interests, who may stand to benefit from ecological degradation, is reduced.

The problem with these types of environmental justifications for democracy is precisely that they are contingent. The operative word is 'might'. If, that is, it can be shown that democracy does not perform the functions claimed for it, as a means to the end of the achievement of environmental objectives, then democracy must be forfeited. We need to ask if there is anything about democracy that is inextricably related to Green thinking, such that the existence of the former is an essential characteristic of the latter.

One answer is to suggest that sustainability would always be advocated in a democracy because without human survival no democracy can exist. As Dobson (1996, pp. 136–9) points out, though, any form of government is dependent on human survival and so 'a sustainable society is as much a generalisable interest for authoritarians as it is for democrats'. In a similar vein, Saward (1996), in a rather half-hearted attempt to amend his earlier denial of the essential link between ecology and democracy, suggests that if adequate health care is seen as a democratic right, then, in so much as environmental degradation damages health, democracy does necessitate environmental protection. Of course, this argument depends on the challengeable inclusion of health care as a key democratic right.

Undoubtedly the most convincing tie between ecology and democracy is the argument that only a democratic society can provide the respect which ecology insists is due to individuals. Like the normative claims concerning the limits to growth we considered in Chapter 3, radical Green thinking is based on the assumption that the preferred social and political organization must be capable of producing more satisfied and fulfilled individuals in control of their own lives, not only as an end in itself but also as a means of making the sacrifice of material consumption worthwhile. Only a participatory democracy, it is suggested, can perform this function, thereby providing the social and political boundaries of a Green society. This is what Eckersley (1996, p. 223) is getting at when she writes that: 'authoritarianism is ruled out at the level of green principle (rather than on purely instrumental grounds) in the same way that it is ruled out according to basic liberal principles: it fundamentally infringes the rights of humans to choose their own destiny'.

Conclusion: a distinct ideology?

Our relatively brief exploration of Green political thought reveals that it draws its ideas from a wide variety of political traditions. As David Pepper rightly observes, Green thinking still remains in a 'rather muddled political state' (Pepper, 1986, p. 204). Nevertheless, we should not ask too much of Green political thought. As Hayward (1995, p. 199) sensibly suggests, we should not seek 'absolute novelty in conceptualizing society and politics' from Green thinking, but rather 'a thoroughgoing critique of dominant conceptions of the political in the light of ecological considerations'.

In order to assess Green thinking more coherently, we can, following Martell (1994, ch.5), ask two questions. First, is there anything distinctive about Green political theory which offers a challenge to mainstream political thinking? Here, the answer must be 'yes'. As Eckersley (1992, p. 2) points out: 'The questions raised by environmental philosophers have exposed a number of significant blind spots in modern political theory'. Two blind spots are particularly important. First, the emphasis on the limits to growth adds a new dimension which political thought must take account of (and to a certain extent has) when arguing for particular social and political arrangements.

Further, Green thinking challenges the anthropocentrism of mainstream Western political thought. As Heywood (1992, p. 245) points out, traditional ideologies 'merely promise different ways of exploiting nature for the convenience and benefit of humankind'. By contrast, a Green theory of justice requires us to consider the relationship, not only between humans currently living in different parts of the world, but also between those now living and future generations, and, last but not least, between humans and the rest of nature (Dobson, 1998). The adoption of an ecocentric ethic, involving the extension of inherent value beyond the human species to incorporate non-human nature, is clearly a distinct departure in political thought and requires fundamental changes in the way we think about social, legal and political institutions and practices. Even if, like some Greens, we are unwilling to accept the validity of an ecocentric ethic, the development of an enlightened anthropocentrism still challenges the Western tradition of political thought which has largely ignored, or been hostile to, questions concerning the moral standing of non-humans.

Our second question is to ask to what extent there are clear ecological reasons or justifications for particular kinds of social and political arrangements. Here, the answer is not so clear-cut. Some writers sympathetic to the Green cause, argue that ecology is consistent with a wide variety of political structures (Ryle, 1988) while others lean towards the view that particular social and political arrangements are more appropriate than others. Clearly, both cannot be right. The answer might be that both are wrong: that while there are a number of political structures capable of fulfilling Green objectives, the choice is not completely open (Martell, 1994, p. 160). From the analysis in this chapter, for instance, we would rule out decentralized solutions in favour of state-based ones capable of dealing with difficult environmental problems. But this state-based solution must not be authoritarian because such regimes do not give to humans the respect they deserve. It should be remembered that humans are part of nature and should not be treated with any less respect than the non-human natural world which Greens seek to protect.

Further reading

The relationship between ecology and mainstream political thought is covered in Eckersley (1992), Hayward (1995), Martell (1994, ch.5), Dobson (1995), Hay (1988) and Smith (1998). On particular ideologies, John Gray (1993) identifies links between conservatism and environmentalism, Pepper (1993a) has produced the definitive overview of eco-socialism, and eco-feminism is best approached through Mellor (1997). Goodin's (1992a) critique of decentralization is essential. There is a burgeoning literature on the relationship between ecology and democracy. There is much in the collections edited by Matthews (1995) and Doherty and de Geus (1996), and serious students of this topic cannot afford to ignore John Dryzek's work (1987 and 1990) which attempts to link ecological principles with the need for greater democratization.

5

The International Politics of the Environment

The modern politics of the environment is increasingly being fought out at the international level. Indeed, the historical chronology of the environment can be characterized by reference to the international gatherings at Stockholm in 1972, Rio in 1992 and Kyoto in 1997 as well as the influential, and impeccably internationalist, Brundtland Report published in 1987 (see Brenton, 1994 and Elliot, 1998, ch. 1). What Britain or any other sovereign state does in environmental terms then, is, at present to a great extent, dependant upon agreements reached at the supranational level. Equally importantly, it is widely recognized that the most critical environmental problems can only be tackled internationally. Of crucial importance in the global politics of the environment is the relationship between the developed and the developing world and this theme is discussed in a separate section as well as providing the backdrop to much of the material in this chapter.

International agreements concerning the environment are not new phenomena. It has long been appreciated that pollution is no respecter of national boundaries and requires co-operation between states to deal with it. Equally, animals, and particularly birds, do not respect national boundaries and so wildlife conservation agreements are required to prevent a particular species being protected in one country while being vigorously exploited in another. Further, live animals, and products derived from them, are now an important element of international trade and only supranational action can effectively constrain such trade if it represents a threat to a particular species or involves – as does, for instance, the trade in exotic birds – the infliction of a considerable degree of suffering (Boardman, 1981, p. 4).

In the last 20 or 30 years, however, there has been an increasing recognition that environmental problems necessitate supranational solutions and, concomitantly, the study of environmental issues within the academic field of international relations has become much more important too (Vogler, 1996). This international emphasis is partly a product of the general rise of social and political interest in the environment, which, in turn, can be at least partly explained by the severity of environmental problems.

Of greater importance is the fact that environmental issues are peculiarly international in scope. It can be readily admitted that some areas of environmental damage do not have a transnational character but international agreements may still be necessary or desirable in the interests of trade competitiveness. Thus, one obstacle to the development of stringent national environmental laws is the pressure that is likely to be applied by business organizations, which see themselves being economically disadvantaged since they have to pay the costs of environmental protection while their competitors in other countries do not. As we shall see in Chapter 6, one of the major justifications for the European Union's initial intervention in environmental matters was precisely on the grounds of harmonizing national laws rather than any specific interest in environmental protection *per se* (Simpson, 1990, p. 29).

More often than not, though, traditional environmental problems have always had direct supranational consequences. Moreover, the international dimension of environmentalism has become more prominent because of the identification of genuinely global problems, such as global warming and ozone depletion, in the 1980s. Only global co-operation can hope to solve these problems. What were originally national or regional problems have, with the threat to the ozone layer and the climate added to the equation, taken on a global character. Deforestation, for instance, has long been identified as an environmental problem, but whereas the destruction of the rain forests was once a regional concern, affecting the stability of rainfall and river patterns and anchoring the soil, the contribution that deforestation (it is now recognized) makes to climate change, transforms it in to an issue of global significance. Similarly, the massive increase in road transport has many local, regional and national effects but, as an important source of CO_2 emissions, it is also now inextricably linked with climate change and the international attempts to deal with it.

The global economy and development

Underpinning the international politics of the environment is the issue of the global economy in general and the relationship between the developed North and the developing South in particular (Miller, 1995). The potential for environmental damage due to Third World development is all too clear and therefore the active participation of Southern countries in international agreements is essential. Since the economic development of Third World countries is, in some ways, both inevitable and desirable (Hurrell, 1992, p. 39), there is a need to search for sustainable means of achieving this growth. This principle was originally put on the United Nations (UN) agenda in the 1970s and highlighted by the Brundtland Report, commissioned by the UN Secretary General in 1983 and published in 1987, which famously defined sustainable development as being about meeting 'the needs of the present without compromising the ability of future generations to meet their own needs' (World Commission on Environment and Development, 1987, p. 8).

It is easy to see why a credible environmental strategy must incorporate the developing world. For example, at present, the developed world utilizes about 70 per cent of the world's energy supplies and yet constitutes only about 5 per cent of the world's population (Pickering and Owen, 1994, p. 185; Simpson, 1990, p. 8). It is futile to imagine that economic growth will not take place at a significant rate in the developing world and this growth could be catastrophic for the world's ecology. Extra stresses are likely to be caused, in addition, by population growth. A common estimate is that the world's population may reach 10.5 billion by 2050 (over double its present figure) and the vast majority of this increase will take place in the developing world (Pickering and Owen, 1994, pp. 282–3).

A major concern of economic growth in the developing world is a massive increase in greenhouse gases; another is the depletion of non-renewable resources. A further fear is that the increase in population and urbanization will put stresses on the food production sector and the threat of shortages will encourage ever intensive agricultural practices causing further environmental damage. Under threat too are some of the most species-rich regions on the planet, and just as increases in pollution have consequences for the developed world, so does a decline in biodiversity (see Chapter 2). The vast majority of the world's most species-rich habitat can be found in developing coun- tries. Over half of all the species so far identified, for example, can be found in the tropical rain forests (Elliot, 1998, pp. 73–4). By contrast, only about 3 per cent of the global total of recorded species can be found in the UK (Pearce *et al.*, 1993, p. 102). The active involvement of developing countries in the protection of biodiversity is a more urgent task than, say, action to reduce greenhouse gas emissions. In the latter case, developed countries can take action to reduce their own CO_2 emissions while seeking the long-term participation of developing countries as their economic development proceeds. No such luxury is present in the case of biodiversity where immediate and irreversible damage is being done. If biodiversity is to be protected effectively, therefore, the immediate and active involvement of developing countries is required.

At this point of the discussion, mention also ought to be made of the ethical dimension. Sustainable development is not only strategically astute, given that there may be little that the North can do about the fact of economic development in the South, but it would also appear to be the morally right position to take in the sense of an imperative to alleviate the poverty and deprivation many people in the developing countries endure. Even though there is a strong justification for environmental protection on the grounds that we owe moral obligations to future generations, therefore, it is equally the case that we also owe them to people now living (Shue, 1992). One of the major criticisms of environmentalists is that they are essentially engaged in a selfish class-based exercise seeking to deprive the less affluent peoples of the world the standard of living they themselves enjoy (Martell, 1994, p. 39). On the other hand, an essential idea behind the principle of sustainable development is that without taking environmental considerations into account, economic growth cannot be sustained for very long (Thacher, 1992, p. 188). Seen in this way, the choice is not a completely stark one between present and future generations.

The general attitude of the developing countries is that the developed world is largely responsible for environmental degradation and should put its own house in order before the South acts. Even then, action will be dependent upon significant financial aid from the North to ensure that the South's development aims are not compromised. There are signs, however, of a split among developing countries. This was particularly apparent during the talks on climate change held in Buenos Aires in 1998 where Argentina (and more reticently, Mexico) appeared prepared to agree to greenhouse gas emission targets with China, while other developing countries remained opposed to such a move. The attitude of the developed world has also been divided. The United States government (along with Australia) has been reluctant to commit itself to stringent environmental measures unless the South participates, while many other developed countries have been willing to take the lead.

The stubborn attitude of the developing countries has been supported by many environmentalists who have been loud in their criticism of the North's exploitation of the Third World (See, for instance, Porritt, 1984, pp. 96–8; pp. 188–90). Indeed, there is a school of thought which argues that environmental degradation in developing countries is in large part a product of their dependence on the West (the following account of this position is based on the discussion in Yearley, 1992, pp. 149–81).

Dependency on investment from the developed world, for instance, often leads Third World countries to relax environmental standards in order to attract multinational companies, which can then avoid the more rigorous standards applied in their home countries (in addition to taking advantage of cheap labour and the availability of raw materials). Likewise, some Third World countries, particularly in West Africa, are willing to accept the income generated by the dumping of hazardous wastes which no developed country will accept. The consequence of this drive for income is often excessive pollution and sometimes, as in the disaster at the Union Carbide pesticide plant in Bhopal, an immediate and devastating impact on human life and health.

Agricultural development in the Third World, too, is designed to meet the demands of the developed world. As a consequence, the needs of local people are ignored, many not being able to afford to buy the food produced, and the imported intensive methods employed cause environmental damage. Thus, forests are cleared for cattle grazing and environmental regulations are relaxed so that many products banned in the developed world are used. An additional factor is the loans which developing countries have incurred to industrialize. In the past, it was rare for environmental conditions to be attached to loans and too often the capital was used to invest in large projects, such as dams, which had dire environmental consequences. The environmental consequences of dependency worsened with the onset of the debt crisis in the 1980s. As world trade slumped, developing countries found it increasingly difficult to repay the interest on the massive debts they had been encouraged to take out by the banks. As a consequence, in a desperate attempt to find the resources to meet their financial commitments, concern for the environment became an even lower priority.

Not surprisingly, given the discussion above, it has proven very difficult for the developed North to persuade the developing South to actively participate in international agreements designed to promote sustainable development. The interrelated issues of environment and development provided the backdrop, for instance, to the United Nations Conference on Environment and Development (the Earth Summit) held in Rio de Janeiro in June 1992. Given the contrasting interests involved, it is not surprising that conflict was endemic at the Rio Summit and the preceding negotiations. While developed countries were more interested in talking about the pressing environmental issues, developing countries were more interested in development questions and, in particular, action on (what they perceived to be) the unfair world economic system (Thomas, 1992, p. 257). As a result, any action to tackle global warming and other environmental problems by the South was to be conditional upon financial assistance from the North. For its part, as the biggest producer of CO_2 emissions (about 23 per cent of the world total from 4 per cent of the world's population), the United States was adamant that unless developing countries were prepared to, at the very least, indicate a future commitment to cut their own emissions, they would be unable to support a binding treaty because of the loss of economic competitiveness that would occur.

At Rio, legally binding agreements drawn up following extensive prior negotiations were eventually signed on climate change and biological diversity (see Brenton, 1994, pp. 163–95, for the former and pp. 197–206 for the latter). The Bush administration in the United States refused to sign either convention however, although this decision was reversed when Clinton succeeded to the presidency. Moreover, the developing countries were able to sign the Climate Change Convention because the agreement – a reduction in three greenhouse gases (CO_2, CH^4 and nitrous oxide) to their 1990 levels by the end of the century – applies only to developed countries. Further, cuts for post 2000 were agreed to by developed countries at the follow-up meeting held in Kyoto in December 1997, but again developing countries were not included and the United States was again extremely reluctant to commit to an agreement and only did so at the last minute (see below).

The Convention on Biological Diversity (CBD), although actively involving developing countries, has had a limited impact. The provisions look encouraging enough. Most significantly, the CBD, in order to provide incentives for developing countries to protect their biodiversity, confirms sovereignty rights over genetic resources and upholds the principle that developing countries have a legitimate claim to a proportion of any future profits made from the exploitation of biodiversity – a clause which led the United States to reject the Convention. Provision was also made for financial aid for the maintenance of biodiversity, to be distributed through the Global Environment Facility (see below). In addition to this, signatories are expected to develop their own national strategies for biodiversity, to provide inventories of biological diversity and to monitor biological resources (Elliot, 1998, pp. 77–80).

Little new funding to enable developing countries to preserve biodiversity, however, has been forthcoming. Moreover, the CBD has also been criticized for its general vagueness, and, in particular, for its lack of timetables and targets. The first round for the reporting of national biodiversity strategies was in January 1998 but less than half of those who signed the CBD met this deadline. Two key problems are apparent. First, although protected areas are often designated, they are under-resourced and understaffed. Secondly, there has been a failure to ensure that concern for biodiversity becomes an important component in a range of policy sectors such as trade, agriculture and forestry. Some progress has been made here but too often short-term economic requirements take precedence. In particular, it is difficult to see how biodiversity can be protected effectively without the concluding of a global forest convention (Humphreys, 1996). On a more positive note, although there have been few state-led initiatives, the general principle of sovereignty rights and a fair exchange for the fruits of biodiversity enshrined in the CBD has facilitated a number of so-called 'bioprospecting' agreements. Here, companies, usually pharmaceutical, agree to provide a payment to the biodiversity holders and a (very small) proportion of any future profits in return for having access to potentially valuable resources. There are now at least a dozen such schemes operating worldwide (Tuxill, 1999, p. 112).

The character of international environmental regimes

Agreements between sovereign states take two main forms. First, there is so-called 'soft law' which consists of agreements that fall short of formal treaties, and therefore do not have binding legal effect on the participants. These can occur in a number of forms such as the enunciation of general principles, the adoption of internationally recognized guidelines and the setting of standards by international technical bodies (Susskind and Ozawa, 1992, p. 154). One example is the *World Conservation Strategy* jointly presented by the International Union for the Conservation of Nature and Natural Resources (IUCN) and the World Wide Fund for Nature (WWF) (see below). Although having no legally binding force, the document serves not only as a guide for the parties entering into conservation treaty negotiations, but also as a 'battering ram' for change by indicating the urgency for action. Soft law, therefore, is often the option adopted when sovereign states cannot agree on binding commitments and also often serves as a first step towards such a binding treaty.

Agreements between nations in the form of treaties constitute the most common form of supranational environmental action. The most common form of treaty-making on environmental issues involves the use of conventions and protocols. As Susskind and Ozawa (1992, pp. 144–5) demonstrate, this approach involves several stages. First, before a treaty or convention is signed, it is necessary for a problem to be identified and acknowledged by the nations who can do most to tackle it. The role of the international scientific community here can be crucial (see below). Once enough nations are convinced, negotiations can begin on a convention. At this stage, general principles and objectives only are established and sometimes, in addition, the administrative machinery is set in place in the form of a secretariat whose function is to arrange for meetings of the parties and monitor the workings of the convention. Following this, there is then an often extensive period when the convention is ratified by the signatories, and only when a specified number of states have done so will the treaty come into force. At this point, thought will be directed towards specific objectives, which will appear in protocols negotiated between the parties to the original convention and possibly other countries too.

Agreements designed to tackle the global problems of climate change and ozone depletion have followed the convention protocol model. The original Framework Convention on Climate Change was signed at the Rio Summit in 1992 and this has been followed by protocols agreed at Kyoto in 1997 and Buenos Aires a year later. Attempts to deal with ozone depletion, too, provide one of the best examples of an environmental treaty following the same route (Benedick, 1991; Haigh, 1992, pp. 241–6; Brenton, 1994, pp. 134–45; Porter and Brown, 1996, pp. 72–7; Elliot, 1998, pp. 53–60). In the early 1980s, the United Nations Environment Programme (see below) provided the impetus for countries to negotiate a convention on the reduction of CFCs. The Vienna Convention, setting forth the general principle that controls on CFC production should be introduced, was eventually signed in 1985 and adopted by 21 states and the EU. This was followed, in September 1987, by more specific measures in the Montreal Protocol (signed by the original Vienna Convention countries plus 6 other states) which came into force on January 1 1989. The Protocol froze CFC production at 1986 levels followed by a 50 per cent reduction by the turn of the century. By the end of the 1980s, however, new scientific evidence revealed more severe ozone depletion than had previously been realized and, at a conference organized by the British government in March 1989, the EU, the USA and Canada agreed to the phasing out of the most dangerous CFCs by the year 2000. A further 20 countries signed the so-called London Amendment bringing the total number to 59, although three years later only just over half of these had ratified the revised version of the Montreal Protocol. Finally, in 1992, the timetable for phasing out CFCs was brought forward to 1996 in a further meeting of the parties in Copenhagen.

Actors in global environmental politics

A number of different actors can be identified as participants in international environmental politics.

Nation states

For some international relations scholars, nation states are by far the most important actors in international politics (see below). Even though there may be disagreement over the extent of their role, an adequate account of international politics cannot ignore the impact of sovereign states. Following Porter and Brown (1996, pp. 32–41), we can see that sovereign states can play one of four roles in the process of negotiating an international treaty. A 'lead' state is one which is highly committed to the objectives of a particular treaty and will try to ensure that other countries sign up to it too; a 'support' state is one which is prepared to go along with a treaty but is not willing to play a leading role; a 'swing' state is one which can be persuaded of the benefits of a treaty; and, finally, a 'veto' state is opposed to the objectives of a treaty and will try to block it.

From this, it is apparent that the success of a treaty will depend to a great extent on converting veto and swing states into supporters, and to do so may require making significant concessions. A good example of this occurred in the negotiations for a climate change treaty. In the run-up to the Kyoto meeting on climate change in 1997, the United States was extremely reluctant to agree to further cuts in CO_2 emissions. Indeed, the negotiating position of the US was a willingness to stabilize CO_2 emissions at 1990 levels somewhere between 2008–12 (in other words, a repeat of the target agreed to at Rio to be achieved up to 12 years late), followed by a willingness to make cuts by 2017. Eventually, though, the United States delegation fell in line and agreed to a 7 per cent cut of 1990 CO_2 emissions between 2008–12. Clinton, however, did not sign the protocol until November 1998, and it still has to secure the support of at least two thirds of the Senate before the treaty is finally ratified by the United States.

A key reason for the about-turn of the US was the granting of a concession in the form of an acceptance that the US be allowed to engage in so-called emission trading. Very simply, the basic principle of such trading (described as buying 'hot air') is that one country buys the unused portion of another country's emission allocation and counts it as part of its own contribution. So, for example, the economic decline of the old Soviet bloc means that their CO_2 emissions have plummeted. In such circumstances, the United States could give hard currency to, say, Russia, and in return the former can take the unused portion of Russia's CO_2 allocation (Brown and Cowe, 1997). Other countries, in particular China and India from the G77 bloc of developing countries, argued that to allow this would let the US off the hook and they threatened to veto any agreement which included emission trading. In order to get an agreement, the exact details of the emission trading that would be allowed were left for further negotiations, and these were continued, without resolution, at the following meeting of the parties, in Buenos Aires in November 1998.

Offering concessions does not necessarily weaken a treaty. In the above example, for instance, trading in emissions *can* play a part in contributing to an overall reduction in CO_2 emissions, since it provides a financial incentive for countries to cut their emissions below the required amount. There is a considerable incentive for the British government therefore to meet its 20 per cent CO_2 emissions reduction target since it is likely that it will be able to sell its unused portion (*Guardian*, 27 October 1998). Moreover, there is also the potential for technology transfer whereby more advanced countries can export technology, such as more efficient power stations, or plant new forests which act as a 'sink' for CO_2, in return for a carbon credit. This can lead to future environmental benefits, particularly if it involves developing countries. However, it is easy to see how such a system can be exploited. For example, if the US was allowed to 'buy' existing CO_2 savings from Russia (and count this as part of their own allocation) this would not contribute to an overall reduction since CO_2 emissions in Russia have declined from their 1990 level anyway, not because of the rigour of Russia's environmental policy, but because the manufacturing sector had gone into steep decline.

The negotiating position of a nation state will be dependent upon domestic and international factors (Porter and Brown, 1996, pp. 33–40). For instance, national governments have to take into account economic interests that might be threatened by environmental treaties. Japan and Norway, for instance, have been reluctant to agree to the continuation of the moratorium on commercial whaling. Likewise, for much of the 1980s the British government was unwilling to support a treaty designed to combat acid rain because of the economic costs involved in reducing SO_2 emissions from power stations, particularly given that the environmental effects were felt most severely outside of Britain's borders.

There is no doubt too that the reluctance of the Clinton administration to sign a climate change treaty was at least partly a product of the constraints provided by an extremely powerful lobby of fossil fuel industries organized within the so-called Global Climate Coalition. This lobby – containing almost every major US and European oil, gas, coal, automobile, chemical, airline, electricity and plastic company – mounted an expensive advertising campaign seeking to persuade the American public, and the American Congress, that the scientific claims about global warming are severely exaggerated and that any agreement at Kyoto would result in job losses and higher energy prices (Beder, Brown and Vidal, 1997). Similarly, members of the Organization of the Petroleum Exporting Countries, acting in concert with the Global Climate Coalition, were responsible for blocking progress at the 1998 climate change meeting in Buenos Aires, Argentina by insisting on compensation for lost revenue due to the reduced use of oil (*Guardian*, 12 November 1998). There are signs, however, that industrial opposition to a rigorous climate change treaty has begun to weaken, as corporations such as Shell and BP have distanced themselves from the Global Climate Coalition.

This change of heart is partly a public relations device, but it is also a product of industry's recognition that there is money to be made in the carbon trading market created by the climate change talks in Kyoto and Buenos Aires (*Guardian*, 11 March 1998; 18 November 1998).

As well as limiting what a particular government is prepared to offer in the international arena, domestic factors may also increase the likelihood of a positive response to a particular treaty. The strength of the environmental movement in any particular country will have an impact, and this in turn will probably be linked to public opinion in general. In Britain, for instance, the Thatcher government became much more interested in environmental issues in the late 1980s and this was, partly at least, a response to mounting public concern about the state of the environment, in general, and a surprisingly good performance by the Green Party in the 1989 European elections (see Chapters 7 and 9). Similarly, the lead role of the United States in the creation of an ozone convention can be explained at least partly by the fact that its industry was already in the process of developing alternatives to CFCs (Brenton, 1994, p. 139).

From time to time, domestic political factors will be outweighed by wider international political and diplomatic considerations. Damage to a state's international reputation or image, for instance, may lead it to accept a treaty despite misgivings about its content. International criticism was clearly one reason, for example, why the United States relented at Kyoto. Similarly, the ability to exercise sanctions against a state reluctant to agree to an environmental measure can provide a crucial bargaining tool. A classic case of this was the dispute between the United States and Mexico in the early 1990s when the former banned the import of tuna caught by the latter's fishermen on the grounds that the fishing methods used (prohibited in the United States) led to the death of large numbers of dolphins. Despite a Mexican appeal to the GATT (now the World Trade Organization), the ban remained in place and resulted in the adoption of a more sustainable fishing policy by the United State's neighbour (Porter and Brown, 1996, pp. 133–4).

International organizations

It is important to recognize that nation states are not the only, or even the most important, actors in the supranational arena. There are, for instance, a range of international organizations whose activities have a significant bearing on the character of international environmental politics. Some of these have a specific environmental function. Within the United Nations, for instance, there are two such organizations: the United Nations Environment Programme (UNEP), and the Commission for Sustainable Development (CSD).

UNEP was established in 1972 following the UN Conference on the Human Environment in Stockholm. The aim was that the UN should become 'the principal centre for international environmental co-operation' (Thacher, 1992, p. 186; see also McCormick, 1992, ch. 6; Elliot, 1998, pp. 108–12). In reality, the UNEP's primary role has been in environmental assessment activities (monitoring, research and information exchange), particularly through its global assessment programme 'Earthwatch', rather than actually doing something about the problems it identifies (Thacher, 1992, p. 187). The one crowning achievement of the UNEP was its role in placing the link between environment and development on the political agenda, the fruits of which were seen in the Brundtland Report (World Commission on Environment and Development, 1987) and the organization of the Rio Summit. However, UNEP remains, in Brenton's telling phrase, 'no more than a minnow in the piranha-filled UN pond' (1994, p. 50), with limited funding and a peripheral geographic location – Narobi.

Agreement to set up a CSD within the UN was made at the Rio Summit in 1992. Its intended role is to gather information on the implementation of the so-called 'Agenda 21' (a 800 page document established at Rio, setting out environmental tasks for the next century) to which signatories are supposed to adhere. Each signatory of the Rio Declaration agreed to provide to the CSD a national plan indicating how it will implement Agenda 21. In terms of climate change, for instance, each signatory has to provide information on the volume of CO_2 emissions, the range of 'sinks' for CO_2 (primarily forest and water coverage) and policies introduced to limit such emissions. One valuable purpose of these reporting mechanisms is that they enable concerned individuals and organizations to put pressure on governments who have poor environmental records. Moreover, there is the possibility of information exchange whereby governments can discern which policies are most effective in achieving environmental objectives (Paterson, 1992, pp. 271–2). Since it is designed to monitor the activities of the entire UN environment system, however, the CSD clearly has a 'herculean task' (Hurrell, 1992, p. 277; see also Connelly and Smith, 1999, pp. 211–16).

Another important international organization with a specific environmental remit is the International Union for the Conservation of Nature and Natural Resources (known as the World Conservation Union). Founded in 1948, the IUCN is a unique organization in that membership is open to governments and their agencies as well as non-governmental organizations (NGOs) and by the 1980s it boasted a membership of more than 50 states, 100 agencies and 400 NGOs (Boardman, 1981, pp. 88–91). Although it has no executive powers, IUCN reports are regarded as authoritative and influential (see below). Finally, in this section, mention should also be made of international scientific bodies who provide the expert advice on which many participants in treaty negotiations depend. Such 'epistemic communities' are regarded as important influences on the character of treaty making (Weale, 1992, ch. 7). The classic example is the Intergovernmental Panel on Climate Change (IPCC) set up in 1988 which, by repeatedly emphasizing the link between CO_2 emissions and global warming, has played a crucial role in persuading nations to agree to cuts in greenhouse gas emissions (Boehmer-Christiansen, 1996; Paterson, 1996). Worth mentioning too is the World Meteorological Organization which has also facilitated scientific research and conferences on climate change.

The second type of international organization consists of those whose activities, while not directly focused on the environment, may nevertheless impact on the environment from time to time. Organizations in this category include, perhaps most significantly, the World Bank. Investment decisions by the World Bank can have enormous environmental implications. Attaching environmental conditions for loans given to developing countries – as it is pressurised by NGOs to do – can have a determining role in promoting sustainable development (Piddington, 1992). Likewise, a failure to do so can have severe environmental consequences (see *Guardian*, 9 January 1995, 13 November 1998; Rich, 1994).

The World Bank now has a direct environmental function as the administrator of the Global Environment Facility (GEF). Originally created in 1990, the GEF was designated at Rio as the interim organization through which funds can be distributed from developed to developing countries (Paterson, 1992, p. 271; see also Hurrell, 1992, pp. 274–7; Porter and Brown, 1996, pp. 141–4). The North sought to use the GEF partly because of its technical competence but also because of a desire to retain control of funding decisions (the World Bank being dominated by developed countries). Needless to say, the

South preferred a new international body over which the developing countries would have considerably more influence (Hurrell, 1992, pp. 274–5; Elliot, 1998, pp. 198–204).

In addition to the World Bank, a variety of other organizations are responsible for decisions that have a positive or negative impact on the environment. Here, two additional United Nations bodies, the UN Food and Agriculture Organization and the UN Development Programme are relevant. Mention should also be made of the International Maritime Organization, the Organization for Economic Co-operation and Development, the International Monetary Fund, and even the Catholic Church, whose opposition to contraception and abortion has important ramifications for population size in the developing world. Of particular importance, finally, is the World Trade Organization (WTO). Formerly (before 1995) known as the General Agreement on Tarrifs and Trade, the WTO's promotion of free trade has, for some scholars, been generally detrimental to the environment (see below and Elliot, 1998, pp. 207–14).

The third category of international organizations is regional groupings of states. Of greatest importance here is the European Union (EU). The European Union is a unique international organization because of the degree of authority it has over its member states. Since its foundation in 1957 the EU has dabbled with environmental issues, but it was not until the 1970s that it began to seriously focus on the environment, and not until the Single European Act in 1986 that it had any legal competence to do so. Because of the EU's authority, its increasing propensity to issue environmental measures, and the large impact they have had on Britain, its role is considered in more detail in Chapter 6.

NGOs

Increasingly important on the international stage is the role of NGOs (see Elliot, 1998, pp. 131–44). Their presence at international treaty negotiations and, in particular, at the large set-piece environmental summits has become a familiar feature of such events. The term NGO is normally used to refer to environmental groups, although it should be remembered that there are other non-state groups (and particularly those concerned with defending an economic interest) who arguably, as we indicated above, have more impact on the character of international environmental regimes (Brenton, 1994, pp. 146–50; Porter and Brown, 1996, pp. 59–65; Rowell, 1996; Elliot, 1998, 123–9;

Guardian, 30 April 1997; 7 May 1998). Another important introductory point is that although supranational decision-making has become more pronounced, there is still plenty of scope for environmental groups to lobby at the national and sub-national levels (see Chapter 7). Not only can NGOs influence the negotiating position of national governments, they can also monitor the degree to which a government has implemented the provisions of a treaty.

Bearing these points in mind, it is possible to identify a number of different types of environmental NGOs operating in the international arena. In the first place, we can make a distinction between, on the one hand, those groups existing only in one country but which also lobby other governments and international organizations and, on the other, those groups with branches in other countries. In the former category can be included, most notably, the Royal Society for the Protection of Birds (RSPB) which set up an international office in 1979, employs a full-time Brussels lobbyist (McCormick, 1991, p. 134) and is an affiliated member of the International Council for Bird Preservation (ICBP), formed in 1922 to represent national bird-protection organizations.

In the latter category come organizations such as Greenpeace, Friends of the Earth and the WWF which, as well as having branches in a number of countries, have also set up their own Brussels offices. WWF (originally called the World Wildlife Fund) was set up in 1961 as a result of a British initiative involving, most importantly, Max Nicholson and Peter Scott (McCormick, 1992, pp. 41–3). It plays a crucial international lobbying role and also provides a great deal of financial resources for conservation projects throughout the world (Boardman, 1981, pp. 78–86; McCormick, 1991, p. 33). The existence of these kinds of federal organizations can be important in representational terms. Attendance at the meetings of the International Whaling Commission, for instance, is open only to those NGOs that have offices in more than three countries (Lyster, 1985, p. 23).

A further category of environmental NGOs consists of umbrella organizations which exist only to lobby at an international level (Long, 1998). The European Environmental Bureau, for example, liaises with the European Union on behalf of national environmental groups (Lowe and Goyder, 1983, ch. 10; McCormick, 1992, pp. 101–2, pp. 181–2). Founded in December 1974, the Bureau now represents about 100 groups from all of the member states, including over 20 from Britain (Lowe and Flynn, 1989, p. 272). Two further examples are the previously mentioned ICBP and Eurogroup for Animal

Welfare. The latter, which was set up by the Royal Society for the Prevention of Cruelty to Animals (RSPCA) in 1980, exists to represent national animal protection groups as well as providing the secretariat for the Intergroup on Animal Welfare consisting of MEPs (Garner, 1993a, p. 40). A final example of an umbrella organization which environmental NGOs can join is the previously mentioned IUCN. While not having any legal authority, the World Conservation Union does have influence. The joint IUCN/WWF reports *The World Conservation Strategy* (1980) and *Caring for the Earth: A strategy for sustainable living* (1991), for instance, are regarded as important guides to conservation issues and strategies by both governments and NGOs.

The environment and approaches to international relations

Any assessment of the effectiveness of international environmental regimes is, to a large extent, dependent on perceptions of the severity of environmental problems, coupled with the theoretical and conceptual baggage brought to bear on the empirical data. On the first point, it is obvious that from the perspective of the survivalist tradition, what has been achieved in the international arena is entirely inadequate. For those who do not accept the imminent catastrophe postulated in this tradition, on the other hand, the assessment of environmental regimes will be less critical.

These competing perceptions explain, for instance, why commentators have differed over the significance and achievements of the Rio Summit (for critical views see Chatterjee and Finger, 1994 and Richardson, 1997, p. 54; for general accounts see Brenton, 1994, pp. 223–35 and Elliot, 1998, pp. 17–26). On the one hand, UNCED failed to produce the stringent conventions many environmentalists were looking for. Only two binding conventions (on the preservation of biological diversity and climate change) were signed, and as we have seen, the former is bereft of timetables and targets, the latter excludes the participation of developing countries and the United States initially refused to sign either. Moreover, even for industrialized countries, the language of the climate convention avoids making the target agreed to obligatory. The text states that 'developed country Parties shall adopt national policies ... *with the aim* of returning individually or jointly to their 1990 levels' of greenhouse gases (Paterson, 1992, p. 269; see also Rowbotham, 1996).

On the other hand, it might be argued that the significance of the Rio Summit was not the failure to agree on cast-iron commitments, but the fact that it is thought to be the largest diplomatic event ever held and that world leaders thought the issues important enough to warrant their attendance. Moreover, the Summit further developed the international machinery – through the creation of the CSD and the utilization of the GEF – which made further progress in the future more likely. As Thomas (1992, p. 258) points out, 'No-one wanted to be seen not to be there, even if most were unprepared to make real concessions once there'. For Stephen Young (1993, p. 46) likewise, the Summit represented 'a useful first step, a pause for further thought akin to a driver on a snow-bound motorway thinking about slowing down to a safer speed'. Whether first steps are an appropriate response, of course, depends on perceptions of how far down the road towards irreversible environmental damage we have gone.

Perceptions of international environmental regimes will also be coloured by the general approach to international relations adopted. Traditionally, there have been two main theoretical traditions. From the perspective of the so-called 'realist' tradition the difficulties associated with concluding effective environmental agreements will come as no surprise (Morgenthau, 1962; see also Waltz, 1979 and Dryzek 1987, ch. 6). The natural condition of relations between sovereign states, according to this state-centric tradition, is one of anarchy. The world's political system is equivalent to Hobbes' state of nature with each sovereign state seeking to defend its own self-interest and being extremely suspicious of others. Given that a world government is unrealistic (Ophuls, 1977), the prospects for effective international co-operation are bleak, even if the parties concerned stand to benefit equally, because without a Leviathan – a body with power over the participants – there can be no guarantee, as in the critique of the Green emphasis on decentralization discussed in Chapter 4, that some 'free riders' will not try to get the benefits without paying the costs (Weale, 1992, p. 189).

The central problem of concluding international agreements is, then, that the participants are all sovereign states with no higher legal force standing above them. In environmental terms, the problem is particularly acute because of the dichotomy between the interdependence of the world's ecology (and markets) which recognizes no political boundaries, on the one hand, and the fragmented nature of the world's political system consisting of 170 sovereign states on the other (Hurrell and Kingsbury, 1992b, p. 4). The realist school of thought sees no answer to the problem raised by this dichotomy.

However, without wishing to question the fact that political sovereignty can provide obstacles for the development of international co-operation, or that nation states remain key actors in international environmental politics, the realist perspective does not sit well with the number of international agreements which have been made, and, more to the point, with the fact that at least some of them seem to work reasonably well. In the environmental field, UNEP lists 152 multilateral agreements up until 1990, the vast majority of which have been concluded in the last 20 years (Hurrell, 1992, p. 10). This growth of international co-operation gives credence to the utility of the alternative, pluralist or liberal-institutionalist, model of international relations (see Keohane, 1989). This model devalues the importance of nation states and emphasizes the determining role that can be played by other actors such as international organizations, NGOs and epistemic communities in the creation and effective implementation of international regimes. As Hurrell (1995, p. 137) describes, according to this view, 'power is shifting to institutions above the level of the state, driven by the need to solve common problems in an increasingly interdependent world' (see also Held and McGrew, 1993).

There is some empirical support for the liberal-institutionalist theory. Paterson (1996), for instance, argues in his case study of global warming that by emphasizing the important role played by international organizations and epistemic communities, the model provides a more satisfactory account than the realist approach. Moreover, as we saw above, the assumption made by advocates of the realist approach that states act as unitary actors and are not subject to the often competing demands of domestic actors is to ignore the pluralistic nature of Western liberal democracy and the opportunities available for interest groups to influence negotiating positions. Having said this, one only has to look at the weak character of the agreements made at Rio, as well as the difficulty of ensuring compliance with the agreements that were reached, to realise that state sovereignty remains a central feature of international politics.

It is important to point out here that, from an environmental perspective, the devalued role of the nation state is not necessarily beneficial. Indeed, the continuing degradation of the environment and the difficulty of concluding effective international treaties may best be explained, not by the unwillingness of nation states to act, but by the role of powerful, globally organized, economic interests. A political economy approach, therefore, may have greater explanatory utility than the two traditional models described above (Hurrell, 1995, pp. 141–4; Williams, 1996). An alternative approach is to focus on gender, and the subordinate role of women, as a key factor in explaining environmental decline. From a normative perspective, feminists would suggest that reversing this position requires women to be much more centrally involved in international negotiations (Bretherton, 1996; Elliot, 1998, pp. 148–57).

Factors determining the effectiveness of international environmental regimes

Whatever the theoretical approach adopted, it is clear that there are a range of factors which help us to predict the likelihood of efforts to conclude a particular environmental agreement being successful. First is the *identification and acceptance of a problem*. Here, it can be suggested that there is a significant relationship between the level of recognition of a problem and the effective action to tackle it. This explains why science plays such a crucial role in environmental politics. It was, for instance, the undisputed scientific evidence about ozone depletion that led to the stringent measures agreed in the Montreal Protocol and subsequent agreements. By contrast, the causes and consequences of global warming are nowhere near as clear-cut, although it was the identification of the problem by scientists and the work of the IPCC which did so much to get the parties to the negotiating table in the first place. Recognizing the power of scientific opinion, the fossil fuel industry has sought to employ maverick scientists who have attempted to challenge the consensus emerging over the causes and consequences of global warming.

Secondly, there is the related issue of *scope* – what and who should be included? Environmental problems tend to be multi-causal and the more factors there are to consider, the more difficult it is to reach agreement. This goes a long way towards explaining why the treaty on ozone depletion exists and has been regarded as successful, whereas a long-term agreement on cutting CO_2 emissions has been much more difficult to arrive at. In the former case, as a uni-causal phenomenon – CFCs are known to be overwhelmingly the main culprit – it was relatively easy to focus on what needed to be done. Compare this with global warming where there are great uncertainties about the role played by numerous complex factors – fossil fuel combustion, the thorny issue of car use, the contribution of forests and oceans as carbon sinks and so on – and therefore a diverse group of actors too to take into account (Richardson, 1992, pp. 166–8). It is not surprising, therefore, that one diplomat has described climate change, in perhaps only slightly exaggerated terms, as 'the most complex public policy issue ever to face governments' (quoted in Elliot, 1998, p. 60).

In the context of treaty content, a further distinction worth making is between treaties concerned with 'common pool' resources and those concerned with 'common sink' resources (Weale, 1992, pp. 192–5). Common pool resources are those, such as the conservation of fish stocks and forests, which 'provide a source of benefit to those who have access to them'. These can be compared with common sink resources, such as the quality of seas or the atmosphere, which are 'pure public goods, either for the world at large ... or for some portion of it'. The point of this distinction is that treaties concerned with the former are usually easier to conclude than those concerned with the latter. In particular, it is much easier to monitor the 'taking' of common pool resources and to allocate responsibility than it is to monitor, say, emissions into the sea or the atmosphere. Further, treaties based around common pool resources usually involve attempts to ensure the ability of the parties to continue gaining economically from exploitation. As such, there is a considerable incentive to conclude a treaty and comply with its provisions (see the example of whaling in Chapter 3). Considerable sacrifices, on the other hand, may be involved in treaties designed to limit the exploitation of common sink resources.

A third factor is the *sacrifices* required of the signatories to an environmental agreement. Again, a contrast between ozone depletion and climate change is instructive. In the case of CFCs, alternatives are now readily available and are relatively cheap. Phasing CFCs out, then, does not raise question marks against continued economic growth in the developed and developing worlds. In addition, financial assistance from developed countries for developing countries to adjust to CFC alternatives was made available (Connolly and Norris, 1991, p. 99). On the other hand, the sacrifices required of the signatories to an effective agreement on global warming are considerable and, as we saw, developing countries are unwilling to participate in such an agreement, at least unless the developed world offers financial assistance. For their part, the developed countries have not only been unwilling to provide the kind of sums that would be necessary to persuade the developing countries to alter their behaviour, but, some at least, have even been unprepared to reduce their own greenhouse gas emissions. Beckerman (1992, p. 281) sums up the disturbing reality: 'The prospects of China or India making sacrifices of current standards of living or immediate growth prospects in order to improve the standards of living of the world in 100 years time', he writes, 'are virtually non-existent'.

Given the difficulties identified above, it is hardly surprising that reaching binding agreements is problematic. For this reason, the level of *flexibility* built into an international regime can be important. In general, the more flexible an agreement is, the more countries will sign up to it. The goal of maximizing participation explains why framework conventions are couched in terms of vague commitments, general principles or guidelines rather than specific, meaningful obligations. Had the Vienna Convention, for example, insisted on specific reductions in CFCs, it is unlikely at the time that Britain, France and Italy would have signed (Ward, 1990, p. 241). Another, classic, case of a 'lowest common denominator' agreement designed to incorporate as many countries as possible is the 1989 Basel Convention concerned with controlling the movement and disposal of hazardous wastes. Hazardous waste, it says, should be disposed of in an 'environmentally sound manner', but not defining what is meant by the term is tantamount to maintaining the status quo since each country can decide for itself how to interpret it (Susskind and Ozawa, 1992, p. 147).

Not all treaties are so vague. For example, two of the major wildlife conservation treaties, the International Convention for the Regulation of Whaling (ICRW), and the Convention on the International Trade in Endangered Species (CITES) impose stringent obligations on the signatories. In order to maximize the number of countries involved, however, both treaties allow for some flexibility. The ICRW has the authority to set quotas for the number of whales that each member state is permitted to catch or, as it did in 1986, prohibit any catch for commercial purposes. In order to maximize participation, however, the treaty also includes a get-out clause which enables members who disapprove of a decision to register an objection within 90 days and thus not be bound by it. Furthermore, the treaty also allows nations to catch whales for 'scientific' purposes irrespective of the quotas set or the existence of a moratorium prohibiting commercial whaling. So far, this has had the effect of persuading most of the whaling nations, and particularly Japan, to abide by the treaty. In the context of scientific evidence revealing the recovery of whale numbers, even the present flexibility of the treaty may not be enough to prevent the whaling nations from breaking away. In this climate, the Irish delegation to the annual IWC meeting in 1997 proposed that limited whaling, under strict controls, be allowed within Japan's and Norway's territorial waters. This was rejected the following year after a report was prepared, but it is likely to return to the agenda in the future.

The CITES treaty is equally stringent. The main instrument of the treaty is the lists of species contained in the Appendices. The main categories are Appendix I, containing 'endangered' species in which a commercial trade is completely prohibited and Appendix II containing 'threatened' species in which a commercial trade is restricted. Around 1000 species are listed as endangered and 30 000 as threatened. Some trade for other purposes, including, for instance, scientific research, is allowed in endangered species, and for this and the commercial trade in threatened species, permits issued by member states are required (Cooper, 1987, p. 171). The CITES convention is administered by a secretariat, based in Switzerland, and the parties meet every two years to discuss the allocation of species to the various different categories offering different levels of protection. One of the key problems with the treaty is that not all countries are members and some of those which are not, in the Far and Middle East, trade heavily in the products derived from endangered species. In order to try to maximize participation, countries are allowed to declare a reservation against a particular species when they join, and against any species added to Appendix I or II while they are members, thus exempting them from the provision (Lyster, 1985, p. 9).

Another key factor to be considered is the effectiveness of *implementation and enforcement procedures*. One method increasingly used is to enforce treaties through domestic legal systems by obliging signatories to enact treaty provisions in national legislation, as EU directives and some treaties such as CITES do (Hurrell, 1992, pp. 28–9). A problem here is the one mentioned earlier, that the greater the stringency, of both the content of a treaty's provisions and the enforcement mechanism, the fewer the countries that are willing to commit themselves. There are at least three other dimensions to the implementation and enforcement issue. First, as we saw above, international political and diplomatic attention can be focused on those nations who have been unwilling to implement and enforce treaties. One possible sanction is the employment of international publicity and diplomatic pressure. In this respect, the role of environmental groups may be crucial in publicizing non-compliance and, in addition, their expertize can be invaluable for governments genuinely seeking to comply with their treaty obligations. Potentially more effective is the use of trade sanctions (see above) although increasingly these fall foul of the WTO's mandate to prevent the imposition of obstacles to free trade (Porter and Brown, 1996, pp. 132–6).

The second dimension relates to assessments of a treaty's provisions. Here, it should be observed that, even if a treaty's enforcement mechanism is reasonably effective, assessing the effectiveness of the provisions themselves is extremely problematic. Not only is it expensive and time-consuming to gather the relevant information, but interpreting it is fraught with difficulties. The complexity and interdependence of the world's ecology is such that one can never be totally sure of cause and effect. Environmental degradation may not be an indication of a failure to enforce a treaty since a new factor not covered by it may be responsible. Equally, mere evidence of environmental improvement does not mean that the treaty was responsible. A decline in SO_2 emissions, to give one example, may have been caused by the recession rather than any direct action by a particular government (List and Rittberger, 1992, p. 106).

The final dimension relates to weak states. Where factors such as civil unrest, ethnic strife, lack of financial resources and general economic problems exist, the likelihood of effective enforcement is reduced. In some countries, for example, minimal effort is made to enforce the provisions of the CITES treaty and smuggling and poaching is a serious problem. Customs officers may have little training and/or incentive to determine whether or not a species being imported is included in the CITES appendices and, in addition, the lenient penalties imposed on those who are convicted provides little disincentive (*BBC Wildlife Magazine*, April 1991, pp. 254–60). Finally, it is not always in weaker states where treaty agreements are not enforced. Evidence exists, for instance, that there is a significant illegal trade in CFCs within Europe which is threatening the success of the treaty designed to repair the ozone layer (*Guardian*, 4 September 1997).

* * *

This chapter has sketched out the major characteristics of international environmental politics – the nature of international regimes, the actors involved, and the factors likely to determine a treaty's chances of success. We have seen that, while international co-operation has increased, the provisions of many treaties are weak; some crucial environmental issues, such as deforestation, are not subject to any treaty, and the quality of implementation and enforcement remains questionable. These dimensions are inextricably linked with the dominant theme – the relationship between North and South, between the developed and developing worlds – running throughout the chapter. The environmental consequences of Third World development are, and will remain, acute. The concept of sustainable development is much easier to promote in general terms than to put into practice. Crucial questions still remain. How much and what forms of development can be justified on ecological grounds? What is the balance to be struck between environmental protection and the needs and demands of indigenous peoples? Such questions go to the heart of the modern politics of the environment and, indeed, the very future of the human race depends upon finding adequate answers to them.

Further reading

Relatively brief introductory accounts of international environmental politics are provided in Young (1993), McCormick (1991) and Weale (1992). There are two very thorough textbooks written by Elliot (1998) and Porter and Brown (1996), the latter of which is now in its second edition. An excellent chronological survey of developments between Stockholm and Rio is provided by Brenton (1994). There are a number of useful collections of articles, the two most significant edited by Hurrell (1992) and Vogler and Imber (1996).

On more specific issues, Thomas (1993) contains a valuable collection of articles on the Rio Summit; Paterson (1996) and the collection of articles edited by O'Riordan and Jager (1996) provide a comprehensive coverage of climate change; Benedick (1991) has produced the same for ozone depletion and on the environment and the Third World the book by Miller (1995) is an advisable first port of call. Finally, the best introductory account of international relations theory as it relates to the environment is the article by Hurrell (1995).

6

Europe and the Environment

This chapter focuses on the role of one particular international organization, the European Union (EU). The EU is a unique international organization because, as McCormick (1991, p. 128) points out, it is the only one 'with the power to agree environmental policies binding on its members'. Legislation emanating from the Council of Ministers does not have to be ratified by national legislatures although scrutiny does, or is expected to, take place before the decision is made. Moreover, the EU (a term used, for the sake of simplicity, to describe the present constitutional arrangement and its predecessors the European Community and the European Economic Community) now plays an important role in negotiating for member states in various international environmental arenas such as those concerned with climate change and ozone depletion (see Chapter 5).

The environment is often regarded as an EU success story. Not only are there compelling reasons for arguing that environmental policy should be dealt with at a European level, but, in a rare case of consensus, opinion polls suggest that the citizens of the EU seem to think so too (Lowe and Ward, 1998c, p. 286; Bomberg, 1998, p. 13). Between 1957 and the early 1990s, almost 300 items of environmental legislation were adopted and the scope of these has gradually increased (Haigh, 1992, p. 235). In the 1970s about 5 items of environmental legislation emanated from the EU each year; by the following decade this had increased four-fold and by the early 1990s there had been a further rise to over 30 (Lowe and Ward, 1998b, p. 13). EU legislation now covers issues as diverse as water quality, air pollution, chemicals, waste, and wildlife and habitat protection. This chapter seeks to record and explain the historical development of the EU's environmental role, before going on to provide a general assessment of its record. Finally, the chapter considers the impact of the EU on British environmental policy.

The history of EU environmental policy

It is possible to identify four main periods in the development of the EU's concern for the environment (Hildebrand, 1993; Baker, 1997, pp. 91–8; Lowe and Ward, 1998b, pp. 11–16). First, the period between 1957–72 was marked by minimal involvement. The Treaty of Rome made no reference to the environment and although a number of pieces of legislation were introduced (a total of nine directives and one regulation) they 'cannot be regarded as adding up to any sort of proper and coherent policy' (Hildebrand, 1993, p. 19). Indeed, the Treaty of Rome provided no legal competence for the EU to be involved in environmental issues – not surprising given that its remit was to promote the economic well-being of member states. Most of the measures that were carried were justified (under Article 2) on the grounds, first, that the commitment to raising the standard of living incorporated the idea of environmental quality and, secondly, that they promoted the harmonization of laws throughout the Union, thereby providing a level playing field for economic competition. Articles 36 (providing a justification for restricting imports and exports on the grounds of morality or the protection of humans, animals and plants) and 235 (a catch-all clause enabling action to achieve the objectives of the Treaty for which no powers are clearly granted) also provided some, albeit obscure, justifications for environmental policy (Hildebrand, 1993, p. 17; Wurzel, 1993, pp. 181–2).

Stockholm to Maastricht – the rise of the environment in Europe

The second period, between 1973–85, was marked by greater EU involvement in environmental issues. In 1973, the first Environmental Action Programme (since followed by four successors) was produced by the Commission, setting out the policy direction which it thinks the EU should follow. These programmes are accepted as guides to EU policy by the Council of Ministers who are thus not committed to every proposal in them (Haigh, 1990, p. 11). Despite the fact that no legal competence yet existed, the first Action Programme established the principle that the EU had the authority to act in environmental matters 'whenever real effectiveness is attainable by action at Community level' (Hildebrand, 1993, p. 20), a phrase vague enough to justify the considerable intervention which did occur.

Between 1973–85 there was a significant increase in EU environmental legislation – 120 directives, 27 decisions and 14 regulations, to be exact – covering a wide range of issues such as the quality of bathing and drinking water, air quality and the disposal of hazardous waste. Indeed, in the 1980s proposals on the environment constituted the fastest growing area of EU policy (Hildebrand, 1993, p. 27, p. 42; Lowe and Ward, 1998b, p. 13). As the environmental activity of the EU increased, there was a concomitant need for bureaucratic support. In the early 1970s, a new service department responsible for the environment was created in the Commission and in 1981, its status was enhanced as it became DGX1, a directorate general for the Environment, Nuclear Safety and Civil Protection (Liefferink, Lowe and Mol, 1993, p. 4).

The Action Programmes in particular, and greater EU involvement in general, came about for a number of reasons (Hildebrand, 1993, pp. 24–5; Wurzel, 1993, p. 180; Lowe and Ward, 1998b, pp. 13–15). The decision to introduce Action Programmes was taken at a Summit Conference of heads of member states held in Paris in October 1972. The Summit was held at a time when environmental concern was near the top of the political agenda of many countries, when the survivalist *Limits to Growth* report had just been published and after the UN Conference in Stockholm. Further, a series of environmental disasters, notably at Flixborough in England in 1974 and Seveso in Italy in 1976, helped to reinforce the need for the continuing development of EU environmental policy. In the 1980s, this growing interest in environmental issues was reflected in the increasing representation of European Green parties in the newly (since 1979) elected European Parliament.

The internationalist emphasis of much contemporary environmental discourse was bound to focus attention on the EU as an already existing international body with considerable powers. In addition, it was becoming increasingly apparent that, as countries such as Germany and the Netherlands were adopting more stringent environmental regulations, they were being disadvantaged in terms of trade with other member states, thereby challenging the success of the economic harmonization strategy. Crucially, it was as much business interests as environmentalists within these countries who were calling for action at an European level.

The third period, between 1986 and 1992, was marked by the establishment of the EU's legal competence to deal with environmental issues. The Single European Act (SEA) of 1986, a significant amendment to the Treaty of Rome, added an environmental dimension to the EU's responsibilities in Title VII which 'formalised and made explicit the strong Community involvement in the environmental field which had developed over the preceding fifteen years' (Lowe and Ward, 1998b, p. 13).

As a consequence of the introduction of a formal legal framework for environmental policy, the environment has a much higher status within the Commission, and DGXI can seek, with greater authority, to influence other, particularly economic, aspects of the EU's work. Article 130R of the new treaty explicitly promotes the aim of integrating environmental protection measures into other EU policy areas, an objective which has also been central to the fourth and fifth Action Programmes (Weale and Williams, 1993, p. 46). In addition, the SEA introduced new institutional structures which, coupled with further changes made at Maastricht (see below), have increased the EU's capacity to adopt environmental measures (Judge, 1993).

The SEA introduced qualified majority voting for nearly all legislation related to the internal market (under Article 100a of the new treaty). This included environmental protection since national legislation could distort trade if it was more stringent in one member state then in another. The introduction of qualified majority voting has made it more difficult for a small number of member states to block environmental proposals in the Council of Ministers. Further, decisions taken in this way are subject to the co-operation procedure which gives more influence to the European Parliament, a body which tends to be greener than the Commission and the Council of Ministers (Bomberg, 1998, pp. 40–2).

Prior to the SEA, the Parliament had a purely consultative role whereby the Council of Ministers had to seek the Parliament's view on Commission proposals but could then ignore it. Under the co-operation procedure, the Council of Ministers is obliged to adopt, by qualified majority voting, a 'common position' after the initial opinion is received from the European Parliament. This is then relayed back to the Parliament which has a 'second reading' after which it can decide to approve, amend or reject the proposal. If the latter option is taken, the Council of Ministers can override the will of Parliament but only by a unanimous vote. Not only does this new procedure provide greater opportunities for the Parliament to influence policy, it also allows time for the environmental lobby to mobilize support for or against a measure.

The Maastricht legacy

The fourth period, from 1992 to date, in the historical development of the environmental role of the EU, has been marked by considerable uncertainty. On the one hand, the role of the EU in tackling environmental problems has solidified. The latest (fifth) Action Programme (1992–2000) moves further down the integration road. Moreover, the Maastricht Treaty on European Union (1992) established the EU's legal right to represent member states in international environmental fora, in addition to extending the areas where qualified majority voting applies. Even more importantly, further changes to the EU's decision-making structure has given even more power to the European Parliament. Thus, under the so-called 'co-decision making' system, the Parliament, although it still cannot initiate legislation, has the power to veto some legislation and to negotiate with the Council of Ministers on amendments (Bomberg, 1998, p. 42).

The entry of Sweden, Finland and Austria to membership in January 1995 was also beneficial to the environmental dimension of the EU. In addition to Germany, the Netherlands and Denmark, there are now six member states who act as 'forerunners' in the advocacy of environmental policy (Liefferink and Skou Andersen, 1998). All three new members were keen to keep the environment on the agenda for the negotiations surrounding the revision of the Maastricht Treaty. The resulting Amsterdam Treaty of 1997, which came into effect on May 1 1999, furthers the EU's environmental role by making the integration of environmental considerations into the EU's activities a more explicit objective, in addition to extending the areas which are to be subject to the co-decision procedure (Duff, 1997, pp. 74–8).

There is another side to recent developments. Since 1992 there has been a rapid slow-down in EU environmental activity. The number of proposals emanating from the Commission has significantly declined and those that do emerge tend to take the form of framework directives and non-binding codes of practice as opposed to regulations and detailed directives (Golub, 1996a, pp. 699–702; Lowe and Ward, 1998b, p. 24). The major casualty has been the carbon or energy tax, seen as a vital plank of the strategy to meet the CO_2 targets set at Rio, and subsequently at Kyoto (Collier, 1997, pp. 14–17). After much discussion, the carbon tax proposal was defeated by the Council of Ministers and by the end of 1994 had been 'all but abandoned'. As a fiscal measure the tax required unanimity in the Council. The leading opponent was the UK who, significantly, invoked the subsidiarity principle (see below). Finally, some directives, most notably one which set down minimum standards for zoos, have even been downgraded to recommendations (Collier, 1997, p. 10).

There are a number of inter-related reasons for this slow-down. First, there have been general doubts about the wisdom of further European integration. In the Maastricht Treaty, an attempt was made to address these doubts by highlighting the concept of subsidiarity which had originally been mentioned in the SEA specifically in relation to environmental policy. Subsidiarity, as Golub (1996a, p. 687) explains, 'holds that decisions should be taken at the most appropriate level of government and establishes a presumption that this level will be the lowest available'. A Euro-sceptic, Golub argues that a considerable amount of EU environmental measures cannot be justified if subsidiarity is invoked, and shifting some environmental decision-making back to member states is a positive step, not least, because democracy is enhanced by taking decisions at the lowest possible level. Collier (1997), on the other hand, suggests that in many cases subsidiarity is not necessarily inimical to the continuation of a viable EU environmental strategy, in the sense that there are good reasons for thinking that, more often than not, effective environmental decision-making requires a supranational dimension. In practice, however, Collier reveals that subsidiarity has been used as an excuse for reducing the environmental role of the EU.

Subsidiarity, it should be pointed out, is not the cause of declining EU involvement in environmental decision-making, but rather an effect of other political and economic factors reducing the attractiveness of both EU interference in general and EU environmental measures in particular. This is confirmed by the fact that subsidiarity first appeared in the SEA but played little or no role in the development of EU environmental policy up to the Maastricht Treaty (Golub, 1996b, p. 714). By the early 1990s, however, more widespread doubts about the utility of greater European integration existed and these were accompanied by economic recession and rising unemployment, making more stringent environmental measures seem a luxury that could no longer be afforded, even for Germany a previously fervent supporter of environmental measures. Although the economic situation has improved since the early 1990s, the proposed enlargement of the EU to take in countries with both poor economic *and* environmental records will raise acute harmonization difficulties (Hewett, 1997, pp. 15–18). Attitudes to greater European integration are likely to wax and wane thereby making the future direction of EU environmental policy difficult to predict.

Integration, enforcement and EU environmental policy

Two particular issues dominate an assessment of the EU's environmental record. The first concerns integration. It is accepted wisdom that a genuinely effective environmental strategy (at the national and EU level) requires environmental quality measures to be built into decision-making on agricultural, industrial, energy and transport issues (see Chapter 8 for a consideration of integration in the British context). This need for integration was, as we saw, recognized by the SEA, the Amsterdam Treaty and by the most recent Environmental Action Programmes (Liberatore, 1997, pp. 108–13). Despite this, it is widely accepted that integration has not gone very far. Weale and Williams (1993, p. 49), for instance, point out that 'implementation of integration has been a faltering and haphazard affair, without serious resonance in the central policy activities of the EC'. Confirming this judgement, the Commission's interim review of the Fifth Environmental Action Programme stated that: 'There is insufficient awareness of the need and a lack of willingness to adequately integrate environmental and sustainable development considerations into the development of other policy actions' (quoted in Collier, 1997, p. 5).

An examination of EU policy reveals that environmental considerations have either been, at worst, completely ignored or, at best, regarded as a relatively unimportant afterthought. The circumstances surrounding the provision of an environmental dimension to the SEA is a classic example. As Hildebrand (1993, p. 29) points out, this addition was not, for most, a priority when the revisions to the Treaty of Rome were being made. Instead, the environmental commitment was eventually tacked on at the end of the process as a belated recognition that the creation of a single market and the hoped-for economic growth would have environmental consequences in terms of a general rise in economic activity, and the generation of more road traffic in particular. Similarly, although integration was cited as an important objective in the Amsterdam Treaty, there are no references to environmental considerations in the Titles relating to transport, agriculture and so on, despite the fact that environmentalists lobbied for this and that it had the backing of the Environment Ministers of all 15 member states (Liefferink and Skou Andersen, 1998, pp. 88–9).

Since the establishment of the EU's legal competence to take environmental action, and the recognition that integration was the chief means by which environmental quality could be assured, surprisingly little has changed. The 'single most environmentally damaging European policy', as Hewett (1977, p. 12) describes the Common Agricultural Policy (CAP), just happens also to be the single most expensive item in the EU's budget. The basis of the CAP has traditionally been to maximize production through encouraging intensification which, in turn, has had devastating environmental consequences (Lowe *et al.* 1986, ch. 2). Some green tinges have since been added to the CAP but the fundamental principles behind it have not changed.

Large amounts of EU funds are also spent on the Structural and Cohesion Funds, both of which are designed to increase the economic well-being of Europe's poorer regions. Again, environmental quality has often been the loser (Hewett, 1997, pp. 11–15). Much of the Cohesion Fund, for instance, goes on the building of transport infrastructure and, in particular, roads, and even though, since the early 1990s, the Commission has instituted environmental impact assessments as part of the application procedure for the Structural Fund, monitoring and enforcement problems still exist. In July 1999, at least partly as a result of a campaign by the World Wide Fund for Nature, five member states, Germany, France, Ireland, Portugal and the Netherlands, were given written warnings that their share of the annual structural funds would be withheld until they complied, to the Commission's satisfaction, with EU environmental legislation (*Guardian*, July 9 1999). Finally, in general, the EU's transport programme is disproportionately skewed towards road building whereas a 'minuscule' amount is spent on railways (Richardson, 1997, p. 55).

Energy is another policy area which has enormous environmental implications and yet these are rarely considered a high priority. We have already seen how a carbon tax, an exemplar for an integrated approach to environmental policy, was rejected. In the context of the CO_2 targets agreed to at Kyoto, the remaining elements of the EU's energy policy – focusing on energy efficiency and renewable energy measures – 'look decidedly inadequate' (Collier, 1997, p. 16). Moreover, energy conservation measures sit uneasily with the EU's strategy of liberalizing the energy market with the aim of reducing prices. As a result, the EU's stated pursuit of a more sustainable energy policy 'remains largely an illusion' (Collier, 1997, p. 17).

Describing the failure to integrate environmental policy into other aspects of the EU's work is easier than explaining it. Part of the problem is undoubtedly an unintended consequence of administrative practice. Policy-making has become increasingly sectorized and it is problematic to adopt the holistic approach demanded by environmentalists (Baker, 1997, p. 95). More convincing, perhaps, is the argument that the EU's environmental record is a product of the dominant role played by economic interests, who have a vested interest in minimizing the impact of environmental policy, in the development of EU policy. It is certainly the case that the transport and agricultural lobbies remain very powerful (Weale and Williams, 1992, pp. 53–7) and that, at an organizational level, DGXI remains small compared to the development-oriented parts of the Commission. Economic interests have a powerful position primarily, of course, because the EU's overriding objective has always been to encourage economic growth, thereby reducing unemployment and poverty. This, in turn, reflects the economic priorities of member states. In so far as there is a perception, within EU institutions as well as national governments, that there is a conflict between economic and environmental well-being – as the UK, for instance, did over a carbon tax – then more often than not the former will prevail.

Another obstacle to effective EU environmental policy is the difficulty of enforcement. The EU has no agents of its own to ensure its policies are implemented and enforced and therefore has to rely upon the member states to do it (Haigh, 1990, p. 1). This has led to considerable problems. Infringement of EU measures can occur either through partial compliance – whereby national measures do not fully incorporate EU law; through non-notification which essentially means that the measure has not been implemented at all; and through incorrect application where the measure has been introduced but wrongly (Collins and Earnshaw, 1993, p. 216). A Commission report revealed that up to the end of 1989, there had been no less than 362 infringements (90 for partial compliance, 60 for non-notification and 213 for incorrect application) and infringement proceedings brought by the Commission had increased from 16 in 1982 to 217 in 1990 (*ibid.*, pp. 216, 219).

Solutions to this problem have been varied (Collins and Earnshaw, 1992, pp. 235–46). The creation of an EU inspectorate has been mooted but is widely thought to be financially prohibitive and

politically unrealistic. Further suggestions have included a rationali-
zation of national reporting requirements, greater access to national
courts and a greater use of fines that could be applied by the
European Court of Justice. One positive step was the creation of
the European Environment Agency (EEA) in 1990 (Connelly and
Smith, 1999, pp. 242–7). The remit of the EEA, which is based in
Copenhagen and began its work at the end of 1993, is to gather and
analyze environmental information. Not only can this information be
used to aid improved enforcement but it can also provide the
justification, through identifying environmental problems, for additional legislation. The EEA remains independent of the Commission
but the major weakness is that it relies unduly on national governments to provide information (Wynne and Waterton, 1998). In
addition, despite the best efforts of former Environment Commissioner Ripa Di Meana, the EEA is only concerned with the gathering
of data and has no inspectorate arm to monitor implementation and
compliance (Bomberg, 1998, pp. 52–3).

The major problem with these suggestions for reform is that they
tend to assume the reason for failure to implement and enforce EU
measures is primarily a product of political expediency. While this
does play some part, the evidence suggests that this is not the only, or
even the main, factor. For example, Germany and the Netherlands
are justly regarded as having a high awareness of, and concern for,
environmental protection. Yet, in the figures mentioned above,
neither country has a particularly good record, both, for instance,
near the bottom of the table of member states for partial compliance
with only France and Spain below them. This would suggest we need
to look at a variety of factors – the problem of reconciling EU
legislation with existing laws and regulations, the complexity of the
administrative machinery (a problem particularly apparent in federal
systems such as Germany), and the level of consultation with
interested parties allowed for – to explain the enforcement failures
(Collins and Earnshaw, 1992, pp. 217–18; see also Ward, Lowe and
Buller, 1997).

Britain, the EU and the environment

A thorough assessment of the impact of EU environmental policies,
of course, requires an examination of their effects in individual
member states. This final section focuses on the relationship between

Britain and the EU. A detailed consideration of British environmental policy and politics is provided in Chapter 8, but this section seeks to provide a broad overview of the impact the EU has had on British environmental policy.

A laggard state?

Britain's relationship with the EU has traditionally been regarded as 'reluctant, sceptical and awkward' (Lowe and Ward, 1998b, p. 5), the popular perception being that Britain lags behind her European partners in the environmental sphere (McCormick, 1991, p. 133). The reality is undoubtedly more complex than this. Lowe and Ward (1998b, pp. 16–25) identify three distinct phases in the environmental relationship between the UK and the EU. The first, between 1973–83, was marked by Britain's insularity. The few environmental directives emanating from the EU were treated on their merits but there was a general assumption within Britain that the country had little to learn from EU intervention. Not only was the British system perceived to be the best but it was also regarded as particularly appropriate for her national characteristics.

The second period, between 1983–92, was marked by 'defensiveness and isolation'. For much of the 1980s, Britain's apparent disinterest, and sometimes outright hostility, to environmental measures proposed by the EU earnt for her the title 'dirty man of Europe' (Rose, 1990). Such a perception sits rather uneasily, however, with Britain's environmental heritage, as the country with the oldest pollution inspectorate and the most comprehensive land-use planning system in the world (see Chapter 8). Nevertheless, there were some high-profile conflicts between Britain and the EU, particularly over acid rain, radioactive contamination of the Irish Sea and falling standards of water and air quality. This conflict came to a head in the run-up to the signing of the Maastricht Treaty in 1991. The catalyst was the appointment of the Italian socialist Carlo Ripa di Meana as the environment commissioner in 1989. Unlike most previous incumbents, he was determined to be inflexible in the interpretation of directives and to pursue miscreants in the European Court (Haigh and Lanigan, 1995, p. 25).

Britain had been threatened with court action on a number of occasions, including the failure to comply with directives dealing with the quality of bathing water. The key decision, however, occurred in 1991 when Ripa di Meana called a halt to seven British construction projects on the grounds that they had failed to comply with a 1985 EU directive which insisted on an environmental assessment preceding any major development. These included, most importantly, the M3 extension at Twyford Down and the Channel Tunnel rail link. Major allegedly responded by threatening to obstruct the signing of the Maastricht Treaty and, according to Haigh and Lanigan (1995, p. 27), since the Commission was well aware that the actions of DGXI could increase the influence of the Euro-sceptics in the Conservative Party, 'DGXI was ordered to tone down its actions'. Whether or not this is correct, it is true that, in July 1992, legal action was dropped against most of the construction projects and delayed in the case of the alleged infringement of the bathing water directive (McCormick, 1993, p. 275).

Despite the publicity given to the conflicts described above, it is possible to exaggerate the differences between Britain and the EU over environmental policy. The British Government's 'aggressive rhetoric' was arguably designed to appease the Euro-sceptics within the Conservative party and belied the generally constructive nature of the Government's approach to EU environmental policy (Haigh and Lanigan, 1995, p. 27). It is true that the Commission has received more complaints about Britain's failure to comply with EU directives than any other member state but this has more to do with the strength of the British environmental movement and its willingness to use the Commission as an outlet for their complaints, than an objective measure of non-compliance (Ward, Lowe and Buller, 1997, pp. 201–2). Indeed, Commission records reveal that in this period Britain usually came about half-way up the league table of member state infringements, not so good as countries such as Denmark and Germany but much better than Spain, Greece and a number of others (Collins and Earnshaw, 1992, pp. 219, 232–3). Finally, in the third phase since 1992, headline conflict between the UK and the EU over environmental policy has subsided. This is partly because of the post-Maastricht slowing-down of EU environmental activity (see above), but it also reflects a growing convergence between a much-revamped British environmental strategy and an emerging European consensus.

Assessing the impact of the EU

A common viewpoint is that membership of the EU has had a profound impact on the character of environmental policy and politics in Britain, and, in particular, that membership has resulted in higher environmental standards in the UK than otherwise would have been the case. When assessing the impact of the EU in the environmental sphere, it is helpful, following Lowe and Ward (1998b, pp. 25–8), to distinguish between impacts on 'policy style' and 'policy substance'. The first relates to the way in which policy is made while the second refers to policy outcomes.

In terms of the first of these potential impacts, it is often claimed that the biggest impact the EU has had on British environmental policy concerns the challenges to the traditional British style of policy-making. Here, it has been suggested that the conflict between the voluntarist, consensual, pragmatic and secretive approach to environmental regulation (traditionally favoured in Britain) and the more open imposition of rigid and impersonal uniform standards (favoured in much of Europe) has led to previously unknown levels of debate in Britain and some legislative movement from the former to the latter (see Chapter 8). One of the effects of this has been a trend towards greater centralization of policy-making in Britain. In the area of air pollution, for instance, the EU has placed an obligation on the British Government to ensure that specified standards are enforced for concentrations of smoke, sulphur dioxide, lead and nitrogen oxide and this, in turn, has led to increased direction of local authorities (Haigh, 1986).

On the other hand, there has been a debate within Britain, facilitated, but by no means caused, by the association with the EU, about the viability of traditional administrative practices to which academics, environmental groups, statutory bodies such as the Royal Commission on Environmental Pollution, and regulators themselves have contributed. Moreover, as Jordan (1998, pp. 175–6) has pointed out, one can exaggerate the extent to which Britain has abandoned its traditional approach to pollution control, and the extent to which uniform standards and an adversarial regulatory structure are preferable to the traditional British approach (see Chapter 8).

In terms of policy substance, it has already been indicated above that a common perspective is that British Governments have had to be brought into line kicking and screaming, most notably over action to combat sulphur dioxide emissions implicated in acid rain, and over water quality. EU directives also provided much of the impetus for major pieces of legislation such as the Wildlife and Countryside Act in 1981 and the Environmental Protection Act in 1990 (Young, 1993,

p. 49). According to this negative view, the British Government only accepted the environmental provisions in the SEA because it thought (mistakenly as it turned out) that most environmental measures would still be subject to the British veto and could be headed off by appeals to the subsidiarity principle, the latter strategy still being pursued in the Maastricht Treaty negotiations (Golub, 1996b).

As with the impact on policy style, however, there is an alternative view challenging both the EU's influence and force for environmental improvement. First, many of the reforms that have occurred would have happened anyway as a result of Britain's wider international obligations. The commitments entered into at Rio and Kyoto on climate change, for instance, have been the guiding force behind much of the present Labour Government's environmental strategy (see Chapters 5 and 8). Secondly, as in the case of the Integrated Pollution Prevention and Control Directive, British experience has played a significant role in the content of some EU environmental proposals, and not least in the field of environmental integration (see Chapter 8). Thirdly, it is possible to identify areas of environmental policy, most notably, land-use planning, which have barely been touched by EU directives. Last, but not least, membership of the EU has proven to be counter-productive in terms of agricultural policy where, as we saw, the CAP's emphasis on intensification has been environmentally damaging. Successive British Governments have taken the lead in the development of environmentally sensitive agriculture within the EU.

In animal welfare terms too, a much neglected but increasingly important policy area, membership of the EU has had the effect of holding back more enlightened member states (Goddard Svendsen, 1996). It was the single market, for instance, which prevented the British Government from prohibiting the export of live calves to the continent, despite the protests and overwhelming public opposition to the trade, and despite the fact that many of the exported animals ended up in husbandry systems already banned in Britain (see Chapter 9). Moreover, the British Government was the dominant force behind the inclusion of a Declaration on the protection of animals in the Maastricht Treaty, and has sought to achieve reforms, in particular, to various aspects of factory farming.

Determining accurately the level of impact the EU has had on the character of British environmental policy is ultimately impossible because, as Lowe and Ward (1998b, p. 28) point out, 'one is making comparisons with the hypothetical scenario of what might have happened had the UK remained outside the EC'. It should have become apparent that there is sufficient doubt about the influence of the EU to give some credence to the following three responses to the claim that the EU's impact on British environmental policy and politics has been considerable. First, it might be suggested that the degree of change in UK environmental policy since the 1970s can be exaggerated; second, that the changes determined by EU membership have not necessarily produced more beneficial outcomes and third, that the changes that have occurred are not necessarily the responsibility of the EU anyway.

The powers exercised by the EU are not equivalent to those of a nation state. Member states have the legal right to secede and, even while remaining members, they are relied upon to implement and enforce directives. As a result, 'European Union politics and policy are still heavily shaped by the culture, agendas and actions of the individual member states' (Lowe and Ward, 1998b, p. 3). The emphasis on subsidarity since 1992 has reinforced this national dimension so that while the EU has undoubtedly influenced the environmental policies of member states, and not least Britain, it remains difficult to drag them to places they do not wish to go. That Britain has edged closer to the adoption of a Europeanized environmental theory and practice is partly a product of intellectual conviction, and partly because Britain regards the environment as an issue it can 'sacrifice' (Lowe and Ward, 1998c, p. 297) in return for greater obstruction in other areas.

Further reading

The literature on the EU and the environment has expanded significantly in the past decade. A useful introductory chapter is provided in Connelly and Smith (1999) and there are also overviews in Haigh (1992) and Wurzel (1993). A special edition of the journal *Environmental Politics* (April 1993) contains the articles by Hildebrand, Weale and Williams and Collins and Earnshaw. Bomberg's book (1998) focuses on the role of the Green movement in Europe but it also contains a useful general chapter on the development of environmental policy and politics in Europe. The book edited by Liefferink *et al.* (1993) is mostly hard going and sometimes impenetrable but it does contain some useful material. On Britain's relationship with the EU, Haigh (1990) is the standard text, updated in his co-written 1995 article. There is also an extremely useful and accessible set of articles in Lowe and Ward (1998a).

7

The Environmental Movement in Britain

This chapter is concerned with examining the environmental movement. The term *movement*, here, is perhaps something of a misnomer in that it is expected to encompass individuals, groups and parties with very different organizations and outlooks (Jordan and Maloney, 1997, p. 1). Can we really, for example, include the respectable, establishment-oriented, National Trust in the same 'movement' as the radical direct-action group Earth First!? Nevertheless, it is hoped that in the course of this chapter, the varying characteristics of the environmental movement will become clearer. Following Bomberg (1998), the account in this chapter is based around the distinction between environmental interest or pressure groups, Green political parties and Green movements. As with this book in general, the focus is on Britain but comparative references are made from time to time when deemed appropriate.

The environmental lobby

As John McCormick (1991, p. 34) points out: 'Britain has the oldest, strongest, best-organized and most widely supported environmental lobby in the world'. This section seeks to explore the origins and development of this now established lobby, before going on to examine how it might best be categorized to make sense of its defining characteristics and significant divisions. Finally, we embark on a preliminary investigation (to be built on in Chapter 9) into the environmental lobby's capacity to influence public policy outcomes.

Origins and evolution

Concern for the countryside was the major impetus for the formation of the first environmental groups in the nineteenth century. From the sixteenth century, the activities of amateur field naturalists made more people aware of the beauty of the countryside and by the latter part of the nineteenth century, with the help of much improved transport provision aiding access, hundreds of natural history societies existed with a combined membership of around 100 000 (Lowe and Goyder, 1983, p. 18; Evans, 1991, pp. 18–20; McCormick, 1991, p. 29). Even though they were concerned primarily with studying and enjoying the countryside rather than conserving it, these societies drew attention to, and felt strongly about, the damage being caused. (McCormick, 1991, p. 30).

From its early days, the emerging environmental movement had three distinct strands. In the first place, there were those groups concerned with preserving the countryside as an amenity to which people could escape from the squalor and grime of urban and industrial Britain. This was the rationale behind the creation of the Commons, Open Spaces and Footpaths Preservation Society (1865), the National Trust (1895), the Council for the Preservation of Rural England – later the Council for the Protection of Rural England (CPRE) (1926) – and the Ramblers Association (1935). The second strand consisted of those groups concerned with nature conservation. Thus, the Royal Society for the Protection of Birds (RSPB) was created in 1889 and the Society for the Promotion of Nature Reserves (since 1981 the Royal Society for Nature Conservation – RSNC) was set up in 1912 initially to persuade the National Trust to use some of its resources to create nature reserves. The distinction between nature conservation and amenity has been an important divide in the history of countryside politics in Britain, not least determining the division of responsibilities of the state environmental agencies (see Chapter 8). There can obviously be conflicts between the two strands since the most ecologically important areas may not be those that are sought on recreational or aesthetic grounds. With the emergence of ecology as an important scientific discipline, the conservation strand has become increasingly dominant.

The third strand in the emerging environmental movement was the growing concern for animals which precipitated the emergence of the animal protection movement in the nineteenth century, a movement which has different organizational and ideological roots from the broader environmental movement (Garner, 1993a, ch.2). In the early part of the nineteenth century, the major causes of concern were the cruelties inflicted on animals by the urban working class such as the treatment of carriage horses and the use of animals for baiting, whereas the cruelty inflicted on animals by the aristocracy (through hunting and shooting) and the scientific élite (in animal experiments) was, by contrast, largely ignored. As Harriet Ritvo (1987) suggests, this class bias was at least partly the product of a desire for social control, since animal cruelty, and baiting in particular, was associated with drunkenness and absenteeism from work.

Whatever the motive, the first law in this country (and probably the world) designed to protect animals was passed in 1822 and two years later the Society for the Prevention of Cruelty to Animals (the royal prefix was added later) was formed to police the legislation. As the century progressed, the concern for animals expanded to include experimentation and the protection of wild animals and birds. Of the 30 or so major animal protection groups now in existence in Britain, no less than eight were formed in the nineteenth century and 13 existed by the outbreak of the Second World War (Garner, 1993a, p. 43).

The late 1950s and early 1960s witnessed the beginning of a period of renewed interest in environmental issues which resulted in dramatic increases (see Table 7.1) in the membership and income of existing groups, and the creation of new ones (McCormick, 1992, pp. 47–68). In 1980, Lowe and Goyder (1983, p. 1) identified nearly a hundred national environmental groups and several thousand local ones, with a combined membership of 2.5–3 million (or about 5 per cent of the total population). This membership figure was roughly double that of 1970, which in turn was double that of 1960. A more recent estimate puts the figure a decade later at about 4.5 million, some 8 per cent of the total population (McCormick, 1991, p. 34). Overshadowing the others is the National Trust with more members than all of the political parties combined, closely followed by the RSPB whose membership now also tops one million. Extra income means, of course, that groups can employ more and better quality staff, and this in turn leads to better organized and more extensive campaigns. Between 1984 and 1989 staff numbers at Friends of the Earth increased by 900 per cent, and at Greenpeace by 570 per cent (McCormick, 1991, p. 155).

In the early 1990s, there was evidence of some decline with Friends of the Earth suffering a 10 per cent reduction in income, and similar problems besetting Greenpeace (*Guardian*, October 19 1994; Jordan and Maloney, 1997, p. 16), but there is nothing to suggest that this is anything more than a transitory phenomenon caused, perhaps, by the recession. Even if this decline occurs across the board, the long-term growth rates remain impressive (Young, 1993, p. 19). The member-

Table 7.1 Increases in the membership of the major environmental groups, 1971–89.

	1971	1980	1985	1989	1995
Greenpeace		10000	50000	320000	380000
FOE	1000	12000	27000	120000	110000
WWF	12000	51000	91000	202000	220000
Ramblers Assn.	22000	36000	50000	73000	109000
National Trust		950000	1.32m.	1.75m.	2.29m.
CPRE	21000	27000	26500	44500	45000
RSNC	64000	140000	165000	205000	250000
RSPB	98000	321000	390000	433000	890000

Sources: McCormick (1991, p. 152); Grant (1989, p. 14); Connelly and Smith (1999, p. 69).

ship of the RSPB, for instance, stood at around 4000 in the 1930s compared to over a million today.

Another indicator of the rise of the environment as a political issue is the existence of a much larger 'attentive public', consisting of those who are not members of any specific group but who express an interest in the issues raised by environmental groups (Lowe and Goyder, 1983, p. 9). MORI polls in 1989 revealed that 18 million people regarded themselves as environmentally-conscious shoppers, while between May and June 1989 the proportion of people rating the environment as the most important issue rose from 17 per cent to 35 per cent (Ward, 1990, p. 223; McCormick, 1991, p. 108).

The new wave of environmental concern that emerged in the 1970s was different in at least two important respects from the first wave in the nineteenth century. In the first place, not only did group member-ships increase but the members of some newer groups in particular were encouraged to be more active in terms of participating in demonstrations and even in direct action. In this sense, there is an overlap between characteristics of 1970s' environmentalism and the contemporary Green movement discussed later in the chapter. Many of the older, pre-1970s, environmental groups, on the other hand, tend to be much more cautious, relying on their technical expertize and ability to engage in quiet negotiations with decision-makers, the wider membership only being called upon in specific and limited cases to back up the leadership's position.

Obviously, the symbol of this new 1970s activism was the formation of Greenpeace and Friends of the Earth which, as Table 7.1
reveals, secured the greatest increases in membership during the
1980s. Greenpeace dates back to the late 1960s and earned its spurs
in a Canadian-based sea-bound protest against US and French
nuclear testing before turning its attention to whaling (McTaggart,
1978). The organization flourished during the 1970s with a British
branch created in 1977. By 1989, the worldwide membership of
Greenpeace was estimated to be 3.5 million, the British section
contributing over 300 000 of these (Yearley, 1992, p. 72). Friends of
the Earth was founded in 1969 in the United States by David Brower
who had fallen out with the Sierra Club, a major conservation group,
because of his desire to adopt a sharper campaigning edge (McCormick, 1991, p. 33). The British branch was set up a year later, and by
the early 1980s more or less independent branches existed in 29
countries (Lowe and Goyder, 1983, p. 124; Jordan and Maloney,
1997, pp. 37–42).

Both Greenpeace and Friends of the Earth have moderated their
image somewhat since the late 1960s. Greenpeace tends now to spend
much of its time seeking to work with the business sector rather than
confront it. Similarly, Friends of the Earth spends much of its time
producing well-documented technical evidence of the causes and
consequences of environmental degradation and possible resolutions,
as opposed to encouraging confrontation with industry and mass
action to highlight environmental problems (McCormick, 1991,
pp. 117–8; see also Hajer, 1997, pp. 89–94; Jordan and Maloney,
1997, pp. 18–25; Connelly and Smith, 1999, pp. 79–82).

The second characteristic of the new wave of environmental
concern is a far greater recognition of the interdependence of
environmental problems. A characteristic of Greenpeace and Friends
of the Earth has been their generalism: prepared to campaign on
many different fronts. Further, ostensibly single-issue organizations
now concern themselves with a whole range of environmental issues.
The RSPB, for instance, recognizes that birds can be harmed by
a wide variety of human activities threatening them and their
habitats.

Classifying the environmental lobby

There are a number of classificatory schemes that can be utilized to
help us understand the nature of the environmental movement.

Interests and causes

The most heavily utilized distinction in the pressure group literature is that between groups that exist to serve the, often economic, interests of their members – trade unions and business organizations being the obvious examples – and those concerned with promoting a cause which is not, exclusively at least, in the interests of their members. Most environmental groups can be classified as cause groups although, particularly in the United States, they are known as public interest groups (to be contrasted with sectional or special interests) as a consequence of their aim to achieve objectives which are beneficial to the wider public.

Lowe and Goyder (1983, p. 35) make a further refinement to this by distinguishing between 'emphasis' groups and 'promotional' groups. Emphasis groups are those that have achieved some success and at least part of their role is concerned with defending these gains. This applies mainly to the older environmental groups such as the RSNC and the CPRE. Promotional groups such as Friends of the Earth, on the other hand, are concerned almost exclusively with promoting change. The implication here is that a group that fails over time to make some gains will struggle to survive, particularly if it relies on its membership for its income.

Not all environmental groups are concerned primarily with promoting a cause. Some, such as the British Waste Paper Association, Environmental Resources Ltd and the Body Shop, are trade associations or companies which have a vested economic interest in promoting an environmental message. In addition, many groups concerned with their particular local environments can be described as non-economic *interest* groups since their major purpose is to protect their own areas from development (such as the building of more houses or a road) even if it would benefit others. Sometimes this can have an economic dimension too when, for instance, property prices could be affected.

The classic case of a successful local campaign involved the Wing Airport Resistance Association whose opposition to the building of the third London airport near the small Buckinghamshire town of Wing is often used as a model of how to resist major developments effectively (Kimber and Richardson, 1974). Crucially, in the present context, the strategy of WARA was based, not upon opposing the idea of an airport *per se*, but on why it was inappropriate to build it in *their* back yard. The fact that they were happy to suggest alternative sites demonstrates that their concern was their own interests and not the environment in general. This applies equally to the dumping of nuclear waste. Even those who recognize the value of nuclear power would be none too happy if it was proposed that the waste be dumped in their areas.

Most environmental groups are cause groups, having a voluntary and sometimes also a charitable status. Such organizations, it has been argued, face problems which do not affect interest groups. These problems derive from the rational choice theory of group behaviour most associated with the work of Mancur Olson (1965). For Olson, it is against the interests of individuals to participate in the achievement of collective goals, even if they value these goals. This is because rational individuals will take a 'free ride' by calculating that it is not worth paying the costs of participation since he or she will enjoy the benefits gained by the group anyway. This makes the organization of a group problematic since, if Olson is right, it is not clear why anyone ever bothers to become a member. Olson's answer is that groups are able to recruit members in so far as they offer 'selective incentives' which are only available to members. The problem for cause groups is that they do not have the same capacity to provide such incentives as interest groups do. If Olson is right, cause groups would appear to be at a serious disadvantage. At the same time, membership of cause groups, including, as we have seen, environmental groups, has greatly increased. How, then, do we explain this? (See the attempt to answer this in Jordan and Maloney, 1997, chs 3–6.)

One response is to point to the fact that some environmental groups do provide selective incentives. The National Trust, for example, provides access to heritage sites and, likewise, RSPB membership provides free access to nature reserves. In addition, most groups provide literature to members, some of which is very well produced and by itself has some value. Another response is to say that Olson is wrong and that other motivations underlie group membership. People may, for instance, join groups because of the intrinsic satisfaction they receive from participating in group activity in terms of, say, the social life that membership provides. It may be possible to rescue Olson here if rational choice analysis is stretched to 'subsume non-material incentives' such as this (Jordan and Maloney, 1997, p. 2). Alternatively, it might be suggested that the achievement of public policy goals is the key motivation. Whether Olson is right or wrong, he did direct attention at the issue of group mobilization (see McCarthy and Zald, 1977), a topic that had previously been taken for granted, and, in the case of environmental groups at least, one that still requires a good deal of research.

Primary and secondary activity

Another useful distinction to make is between primary and secondary group activity. The former consists of those activities designed to secure legislative change through influencing decision-makers. The latter consists of those activities designed to provide a service to group members or those on whose behalf a group seeks to work (Grant, 1989, ch.1). In reality, many environmental groups engage in both types of activities but it is important to note that much secondary activity does take place.

In particular, environmental groups carry out a great deal of their own conservation work. The National Trust acquires and maintains historic buildings and scenic areas; and since the 1920s, the RSPB has owned and maintained nature reserves of particular value to birds. Since the 1960s, the RSNC has been the co-ordinating body for a country-wide network of voluntary county trusts (or wildlife trusts as they are now known) who own and manage some 1500 nature reserves (Warren and Goldsmith, 1983, p. 346; Simpson, 1990, p. 165; Yearley, 1992, pp. 57–9). Likewise, the British Trust for Conservation Volunteers (BTCV) was set up in 1970 to train volunteers in nature conservation who then may go on to work, in a paid or voluntary capacity, for a particular nature reserve (*Green Magazine*, March 1991, pp. 54–6).

In the 1980s too, local clean-up campaigns and waste recycling schemes were set up, often with the help of government funding through job creation schemes (Young, 1993, p. 28). Thus, in the mid-1980s, the BTCV, the RSNC and Friends of the Earth linked up with the Department of the Environment, the Manpower Services Commission and the private sector to create UK 2000, an organization involved in various environmental projects at the local level (Porritt and Winner, 1988, p. 163; Lowe and Flynn, 1989, p. 272). Some environmental groups also have a policing role. The RSPCA was created in 1824 with the primary function of policing the first animal welfare legislation carried through Parliament two years earlier, and its uniformed inspectorate is a familiar sight in Britain (Garner, 1993a, pp. 183–5). Similarly, RSPB inspectors try to ensure that protected bird species are not killed or their eggs stolen. Finally, and more recently, a number of local badger groups have been created to keep an eye out for badger baiters.

Geographical sphere of influence

The third way of classifying environmental groups is in terms of their geographical sphere of influence. Here, we can make a distinction between those groups which have a national, international or local focus. This distinction is not clear-cut, of course, because many groups work in all three spheres. As environmental decisions are increasingly taken at a supranational level, it is not surprising that environmental groups have adopted an international role (see Chapter 5). But, even though the European Union is obviously crucial and the growing number and importance of international environmental treaties makes pressure group involvement essential, groups do not ignore the lobbying of their own governments.

There are a variety of reasons for the continued national focus of environmental pressure groups. First, national governments still exercise a great deal of influence and it remains necessary for groups to persuade their government to reflect their views in the international arena (Grant, 1989, ch.5). Moreover, since, as with European Union directives, the implementation of supranational decisions is usually left to national governments, there is still a need to apply pressure at the national level in order to ensure compliance. In addition, participating in EU decision-making can be difficult. The financial costs, the weakness of umbrella organizations, and the complexity of the EU policy process all militate against effective lobbying. Lowe and Ward's research (1998c, pp. 100–1) reveals that almost half of the British environmental groups they questioned had no contact with EU institutions, and only 16 per cent had regular contact with more than two directorates (see also Long, 1998).

A further point is that there is still plenty of scope for environmental groups to exercise influence at the local level. As Chapter 8 explains, local planning authorities in Britain are responsible both for drawing up development plans for their areas and for granting consent for individual development proposals. Both provide opportunities for local environmental groups to participate in decision-making and they have grasped this opportunity. To give one indication of their involvement: the number of local amenity societies increased rapidly from about 150 in the mid-1950s to over 1000 20 years later (Lowe and Goyder, 1983, ch.5; see also, Blowers, 1984 for an extended case study of one particular planning decision). Local authorities have also often taken the initiative by drawing up general environmental plans, and this process was encouraged by the Rio

Summit which emphasized the need for local authorities to produce so-called Agenda 21 documents detailing how they are putting the principle of sustainable development into operation (see Chapter 5; and Ward, 1993).

Issue concern

There is a large number of environmental groups campaigning on a wide variety of issues. Lowe and Goyder (1983, p. 80) divide issue concerns into four distinct areas: conservation, recreation, amenity and resources. In addition, they identify a 'central core' of groups (the CPRE, the Civic Trust, the National Trust, the RSPB, Friends of the Earth and the Council for Environmental Conservation) who have the most extensive movement-wide contacts. The issue focus in Britain has been predominantly on wildlife and countryside issues, as opposed to wider issues of pollution. The biggest and most well-established groups are those, such as the RSPB, the RSNC, the National Trust and the CPRE, which focus exclusively on conservation and amenity issues. Conversely, the National Society for Clean Air (NSCA) is the only national group which has, over the past three decades, worked exclusively on pollution issues. The NSCA, in its previous manifestation as the National Smoke Abatement Society, was regarded as a key influence leading to the 1956 Clean Air Act (Kimber and Richardson, 1974).

The focus on conservation politics is not at all surprising. Damage to the countryside is much more visible than all but the worst cases of air or water pollution. In addition, improved transport infrastructure and the much wider ownership of cars has made the countryside more accessible for many people. Finally, the greater opportunities for environmental groups to participate in decisions affecting the countryside (compared with the secrecy with which pollution control has traditionally been associated in Britain) have also made it an issue which lends itself towards group activity.

Another distinction worth making is the breadth of concern different groups have. Some groups, such as the RSPB and the Soil Association, have a fairly narrow remit, while groups, such as the WWF and the RSNC have a much wider one. What distinguishes the modern environmental movement is the extent to which they are now much more ecologically informed. Thus, even groups which ostensibly have fairly narrow interests recognize the extent to which their particular concern, whether it be insects or birds, can be affected by a

wide variety of activities from intensive agriculture to urban encroachment.

In the animal protection field, there has always been a mixture of
single issue groups (such as the National Anti-vivisection Society and
the League Against Cruel Sports) and more broadly based groups,
most notably the RSPCA. In recent years, though, there has been a
tendency for individual groups to emphasize a range of issues –
factory farming, vivisection, blood sports and so on. This has an
ideological cause deriving from the emergence of animal rights, a
philosophical position which can be consistently applied to all forms
of animal exploitation. If one accepts that animals have rights, it is
inconsistent to campaign against hunting while ignoring the use of
animals for food, clothes and as laboratory subjects (see Chapter 3).

The pressure group perspective

Most environmental groups do, at least some of the time, seek to
influence public authorities, and one of the key elements of an
analysis of group politics is to assess how successful they are in
achieving their objectives. Political scientists have long recognized
that groups do play an important role in determining public policy
outcomes, with the pluralist perspective, in particular, emphasizing
their central role in democratic politics (see Chapter 9)

It is extremely difficult, however, to determine the extent of this
influence. We could, for instance, simply look at decisions made, see
how far they coincide with a particular group's objectives and impute
influence accordingly. This is, of course, to disguise some major
problems. It is, for instance, to overlook the possibility that some
issues are consciously or unconsciously excluded from the decision-
making arena so that the decisions made do not involve the most
important issues (Bachrach and Baratz, 1962). Further, it cannot be
proved that a particular decision would not have been made anyway
without a group campaigning for it because, for instance, of the
strength of public opinion or through the personal commitment of
decision-makers (Grant, 1989, pp. 114–16). We will return to consider
the political processes involved in environmental decision-making in
Chapter 9. Here, the basic framework for an analysis of the influence
of the environmental lobby is sketched out.

Environmental groups, like all other pressure groups, have a
number of targets which they seek to influence. We have seen that

the nature of environmental decision-making has put a premium on the supranational level but that lobbying government departments and agencies and local authorities is still important. Distinctive features of the British political system, of course, are the unitary nature of the British state and the dominance of the legislature by the executive. This means that gaining access to the executive, or so-called 'insider status', is crucial for pressure groups and the environmental lobby is no exception (the role of Parliament is discussed further below). Not only can the government of the day be virtually assured of getting its legislation through Parliament without being significantly amended, it is also the case that an increasing number of Acts are skeletal in nature, and authority is delegated so that the executive is able to make regulations in the form of statutory instruments. This is the case, for instance, with the Wildlife and Countryside Act which gives the Secretary of State for the Environment responsibility for deciding which species are to be granted protection (Grant, 1989, pp. 63–4). Parliamentary scrutiny of such secondary legislation is so limited that it is important for pressure groups to gain access to the executive in order to influence the content of regulations.

The nature of insider status needs to be further refined. In the first place, there are a variety of different levels of access ranging from written consultation and an occasional meeting with officials and even ministers to regular, high-level consultation (Grant, 1989, p. 60). Further, it should be recognized that access is not the same as influence. Thus, Lowe and Goyder's research (1983, pp. 63–5) revealed, in the early 1980s, that while environmental groups regarded most government departments and agencies as either 'entirely accessible' or 'very accessible', many departments were regarded as generally unreceptive to their point of view.

It has also been pointed out that environmental groups risk being 'imprisoned' by the executive, forced to moderate their demands in order to gain access to decision-makers without gaining the influence that this strategy requires (Sandbach, 1980, ch.1). It might be argued, for instance, that one of the main functions, or at least one of the consequences, of the state conservation agencies has been to provide a pseudo-governmental arena within which environmental groups can participate, thereby giving the impression of influence, while officials and ministers are left alone to make the major decisions (Lowe and Goyder, 1983, p. 67). Nevertheless, despite these reservations about access, it is fair to say that influence without access is unlikely, not least because if the demands made by a particular group generate a significant degree of support, access of one kind or another is likely to follow.

A cursory glance at the ability of the environmental lobby to influence decision-makers reveals, from their perspective, a somewhat depressing picture. A crucial problem faced is the need to influence a number of government departments. Environmental groups have always had reasonably good access to the Department of the Environment, Transport and the Regions (DETR), and prior to that the Department of the Environment (Lowe *et al.,* 1986, p. 121). Targeting the DoE by itself, however, is not sufficient because, despite its name, environmental issues are only part of its remit and, in addition, it is not responsible for many of the major decisions that impact on the environment (see Chapter 8). It is the development-oriented departments – in particular, Trade and Industry, Transport (before its merger with the DETR) and the Ministry of Agriculture, Fisheries and Food (MAFF) – which hold the key to effective environmental policy, and these are the very departments which the environmental lobby has found difficulty in penetrating (Lowe and Goyder, 1983, p. 63).

Access to the development-oriented departments, then, tends to be restricted to a small number of powerful interest groups which have a vested economic interest in preventing environmental protection issues from being considered. The road lobby, for example, was traditionally influential within the Department of Transport and the industrial lobby within the Department of Trade and Industry. The classic case of this type of decision-making structure, which political scientists have characterized as a policy community, is the close relationship between MAFF and the National Farmers Union. This relationship is examined in depth in Chapter 9. Here, it is worth mentioning an important illustration of the policy community at work. This concerns the Wildlife and Countryside Act 1981. Despite being one of, if not *the*, most important conservation measures passed since 1945, only one conservation group, the RSPB, was consulted thoroughly by MAFF during the formulation stage. Not even the state conservation agencies were involved until after the proposals were announced and by then it was too late to make radical changes (Lowe *et al.*, 1986; Cox and Lowe, 1983).

There is some evidence that the relationship between environmental groups and key government departments has 'improved markedly' in recent years (McCormick, 1991, p. 40). Young (1993, pp. 62–3) suggests that MAFF has become more responsive to environmental concerns and our case study in Chapter 9 does confirm this. As Young himself admits, however, there has not been a fundamental change in patterns of decision-making and, as Chapter 8 demonstrates, environmental policy in Britain has been cautious and, particularly if one accepts that environmental problems are severe, inadequate. Unable to gain regular and intense access to decision-makers, then, most of the environmental movement's attention is directed to outsider activity which involves campaigning to raise media and public awareness of environmental issues in order to influence public authorities directly. As a result, demonstrations, petitions, public meetings and the distribution of literature remain important activities.

It might be argued too that Parliament's impotence in the British system puts the lobbying of MPs in the outsider category, although the influence of the House of Commons will vary, depending particularly upon the size of the governing party's majority. In normal circumstances, since the Second World War, only when no party lines are attached to a bill will significant numbers of MPs be open to persuasion. The importance of much environmental legislation, and the fact that much of it is dictated by decisions made by the European Union, means that it is extremely rare for Parliament to become a genuine decision-making arena. Environmental groups can take advantage of its scrutiny role, though, and many groups do give evidence to relevant select committees in the House of Commons and Lords.

One factor, albeit not the only or even the most important one, which may explain the relative lack of access that the environmental lobby has (and, in turn, the nature of environmental policy outputs), is the resources that groups can utilize in an attempt to achieve their objectives. A number of resources can be identified. First is a group's *expertize*. Decision-makers, all things being equal, are not interested in sloganizing or in moral arguments. What they appreciate is accurate information and practical solutions to technical problems. The RSPB's great expertize in bird conservation, for instance, gives it considerable advantages when approaching government (Lowe and Goyder, 1983, p. 58). Similarly, Friends of the Earth has focused increasingly on providing technical information and one would expect it to reap the benefits of this change in strategy.

Another factor is the *resources* a group can muster. Money does not just buy competent lobbyists and the means to publicize a group's objectives, but also enables the appointment of highly qualified researchers to provide the expertize a wealthy group, like the RSPB, can muster. Resources apply not just to finance but to the advantages a group's membership can provide. This can be in terms of mobilizing the membership to put pressure on public authorities. It can also refer to the quality of the membership. In particular, articulate professionals can be a great asset. As Lowe and Goyder (1983, pp. 91–6) point out, local conservation groups have predominantly middle-class professional memberships. More importantly, many can boast architects, planners and even appointed and/or elected members of local authorities among their number. Such groups are usually given consultative status because they can help a local authority meet its statutory obligations to both consult interested parties and fulfil conservation objectives (Young, 1993, p. 20).

The most important resource a group can muster is its ability to exercise *sanctions*. Here the economic functions performed by interest groups, such as farmers and industry, in terms of providing employment and generating wealth, can be a crucial factor in determining how a government, ever aware of the electoral consequences of an economic downturn, will respond (Lindblom, 1977). Clearly, this is extremely relevant to environmental measures which many perceive, rightly or wrongly, to have economic costs.

Environmental groups, however, have some sanctions of their own. One is their ability to cause delays through the planning system. This is a form of influence which may be anticipated by developers who, to avoid a costly and time-consuming enquiry, may change their plans to incorporate the objections of environmentalists. A related sanction is the use of direct action which may have the effect of delaying development projects and increasing the costs involved because of the greater security provision necessary (see below).

A further sanction relates to the ability of environmental groups to generate public support for their objectives which governments may have to take into account (Lowe and Goyder, 1983, pp. 59–60; Marsh, 1983, p. 15). One example was the highly publicized campaign against the veal trade which forced a response from the government, however inadequate. The evidence does suggest that once an issue creates problems for governments, in terms of public disorder or electoral opposition, for instance, they are forced to act (Gamson, 1975). A crucial point here, though, is that mere public support is not enough since it is the saliency of an issue, or the strength of feeling relative to other issues, that matters. In this context, it might be argued that the high level of public support for environmentalism is somewhat deceptive since, when it came to the crunch, elections in the 1980s and 1990s were still won or lost on the so-called 'feel-good' factor which relates to narrow material standards of living.

The environmental lobby's ability to take advantage of the resources noted above can be enhanced by the building of alliances or coalitions. Groups will often join forces for particular campaigns, but more permanent umbrella organizations have been created over the years. The Council for Environmental Conservation, for instance, was founded in 1969 to co-ordinate the environmental lobby. After a rather troubled existence, at least in part because groups were not prepared to give up enough of their autonomy to make it viable, it was renamed the Environment Council in the mid-1980s. One of its committees, the Wildlife Link, has been reasonably successful in providing a means whereby various groups can exchange information and present a united front to government departments (McCormick, 1991, p. 37). Also worth mentioning is the Green Alliance, which helps provide groups with information on the workings of the political process and how the environmental movement can use it to their best advantage (*ibid.*, p. 38).

The environmental lobby's chances of success are enhanced even further in so far as a set of shared objectives can be agreed with a wide range of organizations. This was the logic, for instance, behind the creation of Transport 2000 in 1973. Designed to lobby for a more sustainable transport policy, Transport 2000 has a membership consisting, not just of environmental groups such as Friends of the Earth and CPRE, but also other interested bodies such as the rail unions and public transport user groups. The same logic was, more recently, behind the creation of the Real World Coalition. Formed in 1996, this coalition of 32 NGOs sought to bring together all of those organizations concerned with sustainable development issues – including Friends of the Earth, Christian Aid, Charter 88, Oxfam and the Save the Children Fund – by identifying shared objectives in a manifesto which was then used to lobby political parties in the run-up to the 1997 election (Jacobs, 1996).

Green political parties

Green Parties now exist in many countries. The Values Party, formed in New Zealand in 1972, was the first Green party in the world and the forerunner of the British Green Party – the People Party – was established a year later to become the first of its kind in Europe (Rainbow, 1992). In some countries Greens have succeeded in achieving representation in national and state legislatures (two Swiss Greens elected in 1979 being the first to be elected at the national level) as well as the European Parliament. In some countries too Greens have also occupied governmental posts. Most notable has been the German Green Party which secured increasing levels of support in the 1980s. Between 1983 and 1987, the Party held the balance of power in the Hesse Parliament when it formed a coalition with the SPD, and in 1998 the Greens entered into national government as the coalition partners of the SPD. Greens have also held ministerial office in Italy, Finland and France, and have held the balance of power in Liege in Belgium in 1982–8 and Tasmania in 1989–91 (Young 1993, p. 40).

Early historical development

The People Party was founded in a Coventry estate agent's office in February 1973 by a group of professional people who had been influenced by the growing environmental threat as represented in the survivalist literature of the time. Edward Goldsmith's *Blueprint for Survival* was, and still remains, a key text for British Greens and Paul Ehrlich's work on population was equally influential (Rudig and Lowe, 1986, p. 266; Parkin, 1989, pp. 217–18; McCulloch, 1992, pp. 425–7). The first few years of the party's existence were hardly auspicious. After fighting a small number of seats in the two 1974 general elections (see Table 7.2), most of the founding members left and the party came close to folding (Rudig and Lowe, 1986, p. 272).

That the party did survive was due to the emergence of a new set of national leaders including, most notably, Jonathon Tyler, Jonathon Porritt and David Fleming. In 1975, the People Party was renamed the Ecology Party and in the 1979 general election the brave decision was taken to fight 50 seats, the minimum necessary for a party to be entitled to a five-minute election broadcast. Although the party's electoral support remained stubbornly low, the extra publicity did attract new members and the Ecology Party entered the 1980s an established party in reasonably good health. In 1985, another name change took place and the present name was introduced in place of the rather neutral and sterile 'Ecology' label.

Organization

There have been organizational disputes within most Green parties and in Britain they have been particularly acute. These disputes have not occurred by accident. They reflect the perennial strategic problem facing radical organizations seeking to make fundamental changes to society. The choice facing the Green Party has been to adopt one of two strategies. In Germany, the labels 'realos' and 'fundis' have been used to describe the advocates of these two positions, while in Britain the terms 'electoralists' and 'radicals' have been in more common usage, but the distinction remains essentially the same (see McCulloch, 1992, pp. 419–20; Doherty, 1992b, pp. 94–8).

The realos or electoralists advocate the adoption of a traditional hierarchical organization with a relatively autonomous leadership working within the existing political framework, fighting elections and being prepared to make electoral compromises and, if necessary, striking deals with other parties. The fundis or radicals, on the other hand, argue that Green parties should seek to maintain ideological purity by refusing to compromise their principles for electoral expediency. Organizationally, the creation of a decentralized, democratic organization with tight controls placed on those occupying leading positions is necessary. This is partly to protect against a leadership becoming deradicalized and compromising the party's principles in search of electoral success and partly because a hierarchical organization is anathema to the Green emphasis on decentralization and egalitarianism. In addition, this alternative strategy would mean being prepared to engage in extra-parliamentary action in support of environmental objectives and other social movements – anti-nuclear and road protesters, the feminist movement and so on – when their interests coincide (see Bomberg, 1998, who discusses the conflict between purity or participation in the context of Green parties in the European Union).

The split identified above has been particularly evident in the British Green Party and the radicals have usually had the edge over the electoralists. This is partly because British Greens, unlike their German counterparts, have never had to tackle the difficult decisions faced by parties making significant electoral and representational progress (see Doherty, 1992b, pp. 107–8). Such divisions are also apparent, however, in other European Green parties (see Bomberg, 1998, pp. 27–31, for details of the internal disputes within the German Green party). In Germany, for instance, the Green's prospects of remaining as the SPD's coalition partner have been threatened by the radical's bitter hostility to the Schroder government's failure to quickly phase out nuclear power and its support for the NATO bombing of Serbia (*Guardian*, 14 May 1999; 5 July 1999; see also *Guardian*, 17 May 1999 for details of the environmental damage caused by the NATO campaign). British Greens, though, have been much more strongly influenced by radical ecocentric views than Greens in the rest of Europe (see, for instance, Dodds, 1989). Such views, of course, put the Greens at odds both with the prevailing ideology of the main parties, making compromises unthinkable, and with the political system itself.

The divisions within the Green Party (then the Ecology Party) began in the early 1980s when a growing membership brought an increasing number of radicals, committed to the 'fundi' position, into the party (Rudig and Lowe, 1986, p. 275). At the same time, the electoralists within the leadership wanted reforms to transform the party into a conventional electoral organization. The affair came to a head in the mid-1980s. At the 1986 conference, amendments to achieve the electoralist's objective were put forward and rejected. As a result, leading electoralists, such as Tyler and Ekins, discussed setting up a parallel organization (a party within a party) called Maingreen to campaign for the electoralists' point of view, putting forward, for instance, a slate of candidates for the party council (Parkin, 1989, pp. 226–7). A passage from Tyler's paper for the Maingreen meeting illustrates the electoralist viewpoint nicely. 'Organisation, image, leadership: these are the substance and backbone of real-world politics', he wrote. 'We may wish they were not', he continued, but 'our reward for continuing to pretend they are not will be eternal marginality' (quoted in Robinson, 1992, p. 213). When news of the attempt to set up this organization filtered through to the party council, however, the move was roundly condemned and, feeling disillusioned about the prospects of ever changing the party, a number of leading electoralists, including Ekins and Tyler, resigned (Doherty, 1992a, p. 294).

The departure of leading electoralists left the radicals in a very strong position, but this was not the end of the matter. In the late 1980s the dispute re-emerged (the following account is based on Doherty, 1992a). This time, a new set of electoralists containing some of the best-known figures in the party, including Caroline Lucas, David Bachelor, Jean Lambert and Alec Pontin, formed a party faction called Green 2000. The aim was to capitalize on the Green vote in the 1989 European election by creating the conditions, through reform of the party's decentralized structure, for major electoral success and Green participation in government early in the twenty-first century.

At the Autumn 1991 conference, Green 2000 got the changes they wanted passed by the necessary two-thirds majority. This was achieved by using the proxy votes of the more passive party members who did not attend the conference. Thus, just as Neil Kinnock and Tony Blair have reduced the influence of left-wing activists in the Labour party by appealing over their heads to ordinary, more moderate, party members, Green 2000 were able to dilute the influence of the more active fundis by utilizing the less committed members (Rudig, 1993).

The reforms achieved were as follows. Although the conference remained the supreme authority in the party, the original Party Council, which had overall political and organizational authority, was replaced by two new bodies, a Political Executive and a Regional Council. The former, consisting of 11 members elected by an annual, secret ballot of the membership, became the dominant institution with the Regional Council, consisting of 28 members elected from Area Parties, performing only an advisory role. Moreover, the principle of rotating offices – a central Green device to prevent a party hierarchy developing, whereby no one person was permitted to serve in office for more than three consecutive years – was abolished.

The success of the Green 2000 campaign was revealed in the first elections to the new party bodies in January 1992. Supporters of Green 2000 took the vast majority of the positions on the Political Executive and Sara Parkin was elected to the Chair. As a result, a recognizable leadership was beginning to emerge with authority to direct the party in an electoralist direction. This did not, however, end the infighting. Poor election results, financial problems and a declining membership provided a stick with which the fundis, who dominated the Regional Council and had been alienated by the success of the Green 2000 strategy, could beat the electoralists. Only £50 000 was spent on the 1992 campaign (30 times less than the Natural Law Party), and by the Autumn of 1992 the party's membership had fallen to 8000 (from a high-point of 20 000 in 1990) (*Guardian*, 10 September 1992). As a consequence, in 1992, after a disappointing general election performance, Sara Parkin and a number of other members

Table 7.2   Green Party electoral record

General elections

	seats fought	% of vote	% in seats fought	total vote
Feb. 1974	5	–	1.8	–
Oct. 1974	4	–	0.7	–
1979	53	0.1	1.5	–
1983	108	0.2	1	54,077
1987	133	0.3	1.4	89,354
1992	253	0.5	1.3	173,008
1997	95	–	1.4	64,021

European elections

	seats fought	% in seats fought	% of Vote
1979	3	3.7	–
1984	16	2.6	0.6
1989	79	14.9	14.9
1994	84	3.2	3.2
1997	84	6.2	6.2

Sources: Young (1993, p. 37); *Guardian*, 25 June 1994; 15 June 1999.

of the Political Executive resigned, thus further weakening the party (Young, 1993, p. 39). Such was the party's woes that, by the time of the 1997 election, the party considered, on financial grounds, not putting up any candidates. In the event, a motion to that effect was defeated at the party's conference in September 1996, but the party eventually only fought 95 seats, compared to 253 in the previous election (see Table 7.2).

Electoral support

As Table 7.2 reveals, the Greens have found it difficult to make an electoral breakthrough. In general elections, the gradual, albeit very slow, increased share of the vote, from 0.1 per cent in 1979 to 0.5 per cent in 1992, is almost entirely explained by the additional seats contested by the party (53 in 1979 and 253 in 1992), although the ability to contest more seats does itself indicate some growth. In 1997, as we saw, the party only contested 95 seats, and secured the lowest number of votes since 1983. The highest share of the vote won in a particular constituency in each general election has hovered around the 3 per cent mark, with 3.9 per cent in Coventry North West in 1979 remaining the highest. Finally, the Greens have had some success in local elections where the party's lack of resources does not, perhaps, matter quite so much and where personalities and local issues have more of an impact. In 1989, for instance, the Greens won one county council, 11 district council and 90 parish council seats with an overall 4.1 per cent share of the vote. The share of the vote obtained by the party in the seats it contested was about 8 per cent and in parts of Avon and Kent the Green share was over 20 per cent (Rootes, 1991, p. 41).

Only the 1989 European Parliament election result does not fit the pattern identified above and it is instructive to discuss this outcome in some detail. The 14.9 per cent share of the vote was the highest ever won by a Green party in any national election in any European state. In addition, the party won over 20 per cent in 17 constituencies, came second ahead of Labour in 6 and failed to come at least third in only 2 (Rootes, 1991, p. 39). Despite this impressive showing, the general consensus, with which the present author agrees, has been that this result was an aberration, reflecting not so much an emerging environmental consciousness as a series of special circumstances unlikely to be repeated (the following account is based upon Rootes, 1991; and Rudig and Franklin, 1991; see also Curtice, 1989).

The obvious evidence for this interpretation is that the Green vote was much lower before and has declined since the 1989 election. This is not, however, sufficient evidence for our claim. It may be that the 1989 result reflected the heightened concern for environmental issues quite clearly emerging in the late 1980s, in which case the subsequent decline in the Green vote may simply reflect the fact that since 1989 the environment has been relegated, due, perhaps, to the recession and the re-emergence of economic issues at the forefront of voter concerns.

Certainly, the period immediately preceding the 1989 election was one in which the environment had played an unprecedented role in British politics. It does not automatically follow, however, that the Green Party would be the major beneficiary of this heightened concern, particularly as the major parties had sought to adapt to it (see Chapter 9). A more persuasive argument for the Green Party surge in 1989 is that, as Rootes points out, it was made possible by a change in the balance of political competition among British parties.

The election was held during the mid-term of a Conservative government which is often the occasion for a protest vote, particularly in an election which is not concerned with choosing a government. Moreover, the Conservative government in 1989 was particularly unpopular due largely to the introduction of the poll tax and the general economic malaise. Added to this was the extremely negative campaign run by the Conservatives in the European election itself.

The unpopularity of the Tories, however, does not explain why it was the Greens who were the beneficiaries of the protest vote. Here, two factors were at work. First, the natural repository of a protest vote by disillusioned Conservatives is the party or parties of the centre. At the time, however, the Liberal Democrats had just been established as a result of the rather acrimonious merger of the Liberal Party and the Social Democratic Party. The new merged party was therefore not in a position to fight an effective campaign. Secondly, the whole trend of this argument depends on the accuracy of the added assertion that Green votes tended to come from disillusioned Tory or Alliance voters and this indeed was the case. An NOP poll in July 1989 revealed that 29 per cent of those who voted Green in 1989 said they had voted Conservative in the preceding general election compared to 27 per cent Alliance and only 18 per cent Labour. Furthermore, the Green vote was heavily skewed towards the South, where the vast majority of seats was held by the Conservative party. Finally, where another minor party had campaigned strongly, such as in Scotland, Wales and the South West, the Greens polled less effectively.

If the preceding analysis is right, one would expect the Green vote to be very fragile. The subsequent decline in support for the Greens provides some evidence for this but as we pointed out above, this is not sufficient. Evidence from a sample of the electorate who voted in 1989, undertaken by Rudig and Franklin, reveals the true state of long-term Green prospects. They found that under a third of 1989 Green voters identified strongly with the party, that just under a third of Green voters said it was highly improbable they would ever vote Green again at a future European election and, finally, that virtually no one in their sample who voted for a party other than Green in 1989 was prepared to switch to the Greens at any future election. Thus, not only was Green support extremely fragile, but there was no sign of future support coming from elsewhere.

Explaining the weakness of the Green Party

There are a number of possible explanations for the Green Party's failure to make a significant impact on British politics. The most obvious of these, although not necessarily the most important, is the *electoral system* (Rudig and Lowe, 1986, pp. 277–8). As is well known, Britain's first past the post system has the effect of penalizing smaller parties with evenly spread support (unlike the nationalist parties in Scotland and Wales). Under a 'pure' system of proportional representation (PR), the Greens would have won 19 per cent of the British allocation of European Parliament seats in 1989, and, as a result of PR being introduced for the 1999 European parliament elections, the British Greens did win 2 seats (held by Jean Lambert and Caroline Lucas) on a vote share of only 6.2 per cent. In Germany, a hybrid system combining elements of first past the post and the party list system operates, whereby each member of the electorate has two votes, one in a constituency contest and one additional vote for a party. It is significant that all Greens elected at the national level in Germany have been elected by this second vote rather than in constituency contests (Yearley, 1992, p. 89). In 1983, for example, 27 green delegates were elected to the Bundestag on an overall 5.6 per cent share of the vote and 44 were elected on a 8.3 per cent share in 1987. Under varying proportional systems, Greens have also been elected to national parliaments in Sweden, Italy, Belgium, Switzerland and Austria with relatively small shares of the vote (Callaghan, 1990, p. 2).

There are a number of additional factors relating to the British electoral system which are also worth mentioning. In the first place, the requirement that each electoral candidate has to put down a substantial deposit, which is not returned if the candidate fails to win at least 5 per cent of the vote, puts a significant financial strain on small parties. In a similar vein, there is, unlike in Germany, no state funding for political parties in Britain which benefits Labour and Conservative financial links with trade unions and business respectively. Secondly, it may be that the first past the post system discourages voters from choosing the Green Party because many feel it is a wasted vote. Reluctantly, in such circumstances, voters may decide it is preferable to vote tactically for one of the major parties to prevent the other one from winning.

Finally, there is the broader constitutional distinction between unitary and federal structures. In the latter type of system, Greens can gain media publicity and political experience by participating in state elections and governments with considerable executive power. This can be enormously useful in building a national party. Thus, when the German Greens held the balance of power in Hesse after 1982, the experience of government and the media coverage that followed it was indispensable (Parkin, 1989, pp. 116–17). In Britain, by contrast, local politics, particularly after the reforms in the 1980s reduced the power of local authorities still further, is a much more peripheral activity. Thus, it is not widely known that the Green Party has polled reasonably well in some areas of the country in local elections and has sitting councillors in a number of them.

The Green Party's performance cannot be explained merely by the particular electoral system it has to work within. Even if we were to assess the Green Party in narrow electoral terms, it should be remembered that the existence of an alternative electoral system is unlikely to have made much difference to the Party's position. In Germany, the share of the vote won by the Green party in the 1980s and 1990s (5.6 per cent in the 1983 general election, 8.3 per cent in 1987, 7.3 per cent in 1994 and 6.7 per cent in 1998) was far higher than the British Greens have ever managed in equivalent elections. Indeed, under the 5 per cent barrier operating in Germany, the British Greens would still have won no seats. The Greens were seriously handicapped by the electoral system in 1989, of course, but one wonders what impact the election of Green MEPs from Britain would have had, given the European Parliament's limited powers and the lack of interest accorded in Britain to the institution.

It should be noted too that other Green parties in Europe have not done dramatically well in electoral terms despite more favourable electoral systems. Where many of them have outshone their British counterpart is in the degree to which they have become the focal point of mass environmental movements, influencing the direction of environmental campaigns and lobbying, as well as seeking electoral success. To some degree, the British Green Party's electoral weakness has caused its failure to play a more central role in the environmental movement, since political representation provides an important platform for promoting environmental objectives. Nevertheless, there are additional factors we have to take into account.

It was implied in the preceding paragraph that an important dimension of Green Party politics in Britain has been the *indifference of the environmental lobby* towards the Green Party. This has, indeed, been the case. Despite repeated efforts by the latter to encourage co-operation with the former, these have largely been unsuccessful. One highly significant statistic here is that, according to Jordan and Maloney's research (1997, p. 117), only 2 per cent of Friends of the Earth members claimed also to be members of the Green Party. There are a number of explanations for this failure of the Green Party to attract the interest of the environmental lobby (Rudig and Lowe, 1986, pp. 269–70, 278–9). In Britain, environmental groups have felt it worthwhile, with some justification, to focus on conventional pressure group lobbying. Many of the older, more moderate, groups have a long history of respectable advocacy and, as a result, have the kind of access to decision-makers denied to similar groups in other European countries, such as France. For these groups in Britain, it is regarded as simply unnecessary to support a separate Green Party. For those who do not have effective access, there is still a great deal of outsider activity to focus on and sufficient hope of gaining access to decision-makers at some point in the future. For both, being associated too closely with a radical Green Party may risk alienating them from centres of influence and may also alienate supporters or potential supporters who vote for other parties.

The Green Party has also failed, unlike other European Green parties, to forge links with major new social movements, such as those concerned with gender and race politics, peace campaigners, and those opposed to nuclear power, in addition to the older and more established labour movement. Of particular importance has been the weakness of the anti-nuclear movement in Britain. Again unlike other European countries and particularly France, Britain has not been exclusively reliant on the nuclear option and, when the government has gone down that route, as in the case of Sizewell, it has allowed for an extensive consultation procedure – however biased towards the nuclear industry – thus enabling protest to be channelled in a safe direction. Local opposition to the siting of power stations has also not materialized, primarily because the locations were carefully chosen, more often than not, to ensure that the provision of employment opportunities took precedence over the safety fears (Ward, 1983, p. 184). As a consequence, the Greens have not been able to capitalize on the potential for concentrated support (Rudig, 1985, pp. 67–8; Rudig and Lowe, 1986, p. 279). In addition, the opposition to nuclear power that did exist in the 1980s was absorbed by the Labour party (Ward, 1983, pp. 186–7). By the time Labour had softened its anti-nuclear approach, nuclear power, for reasons explored in Chapter 9, was no longer a major part of the government's energy strategy.

A further weakness of the British Greens has been their *inability to attract the support of the broad Left*. The 'watermelon' label – green on the outside and red on the inside – attached to the German Greens indicates the Left's substantial contribution to the development of that particular party. The majority of Green supporters in Germany are recruited from the Left (Hulsberg, 1987) whereas, as we have seen, British Green support in electoral terms tends to come from the disillusioned right of centre voters. There are a number of possible explanations for this. In particular, the British Left has not been tinged with Green to the same degree that the Left in many other European countries has (Weston, 1986). It is notable, for example, that the majority of the participants in the recent spate of protests against road building and the export of live animals have been drawn from either the 'respectable' Tory-leaning middle classes or from those on the periphery of society. One the other hand, the traditional preoccupation of the organized Left in Britain has been with conflicts relating to industrial relations or general economic issues (such as the poll tax demonstrations in the 1980s), reflecting the continuing importance of class-based politics in Britain. Moreover, as was illustrated in the case of nuclear power, successive governments have been careful enough to avoid provoking conflicts over environmental issues which might have drawn in a variety of groups on the Left (Rudig and Lowe, 1986, pp. 280–1). Finally, in so far as the Left has been concerned with environmental issues, the Labour party has been a broad enough church to accommodate them (see Chapter 9).

It should be said, in addition, that the Green Party has not sought to encourage alliances with the Left. The ideology of British Greens, influenced by Goldsmith's particular variety of deep ecology, has emphasized the view that the Green approach goes beyond the 'old' divisions between Left and Right (Porritt, 1984, pp. 43–4; Doherty, 1992b, p. 105). This in turn has been reinforced by the Green leadership which has tended to be middle class and moderately Left of Centre. Jonathon Porritt, for instance, threatened to leave the Green Party if the views of Green 2000 did not prevail but the party he threatened to defect to was not Labour but the Liberal Democrats. One related, and perhaps crucial, point in this section is that ultimately the failure of the Green Party may be mainly a product of the fact that environmental issues have been taken on board by the major parties. If so, we are left with the conclusion that the threat posed by the Greens, particularly evident in 1989, was the architect of their downfall.

The Green movement and direct action

In recent years, the environmental lobby and the Green Party has been joined by a third element which can be described as the new social movement strand of the environmental movement. New social movements differ from traditional pressure groups and political parties in that they are not interested in seeking to directly influence decision-makers or in participating in conventional electoral politics. Rather, new social movements stress the importance of wider cultural changes as opposed to piecemeal legislation, and are usually prepared to engage in direct action in pursuit of these objectives. Moreover, new social movements reject hierarchical organizational structures as well as the old political divisions based on capital and labour. They are, to quote Bomberg (1998, p. 22), 'amorphous, spontaneous, non-professional groups that emerge to campaign on or protest about a given issue'.

The characteristics of new social movements are not, perhaps, as new as the advocates of the concept suggest, and there is some overlap between the activities of some pressure groups and so-called new social movements which leads some scholars to advocate discarding the concept (Jordan and Maloney, 1997, pp. 46–73). In the environmental field, it is certainly the case that political protest and direct action has been a feature of campaigning since the emergence of Greenpeace and Friends of the Earth (Bomberg, 1998, p. 24), and, likewise, direct action in defence of animals dates at least as far back as the formation of the Hunt Saboteurs Association in 1964. Nevertheless, as we pointed out earlier in this chapter, there is much evidence to suggest that the initial radical edge of Greenpeace and Friends of the Earth has been blunted, and a new breed of activists has emerged to fill the gap.

In order to locate the new breed of protesters within a typology of the environmental movement, it is important to distinguish between those activities that reflect a reluctant outsider status and those that reflect a suspicion of normal decision-making channels. In the latter category we can make a further distinction. On the one hand are those groups and individuals that remain outsiders because they are aware of the dangers of being 'captured' by government, but who, nevertheless, have legislative objectives. On the other hand are those who seek to bypass the public policy route entirely, in favour either of directly influencing those (non-state figures) against whom action is directed or with the intention of a wider cultural change in civil society. The new breed of environmental protester fits most comfortably into this latter category.

Direct action is an increasingly important aspect of the environmental movement's armoury. It covers a huge variety of activities. Strictly speaking, for instance, direct action can include attempts to influence consumer behaviour and, as a consequence, the behaviour of producers and retailers. Indeed, the emphasis on the 'Green consumer' has been an important strategy of environmentalists and in the late 1980s it began to reap dividends (see Chapter 10). Direct action is more usually associated, however, with those individuals who engage in a continuum of activities, stretching from the mildest of non-violent civil disobedience at one end to criminal and even life-threatening actions at the other.

The more extreme end of environmental activism is associated in particular with organizations such as the Sea Shepherd Conservation Society, Earth First! and the Animal Liberation Front. The Sea Shepherd Conservation Society was formed in 1977 by Paul Watson, who was expelled from Greenpeace for his willingness to pursue a more rigorous and aggressive form of direct action. Sea Shepherd has been responsible for attacking pirate whaling ships and, in one particularly notable action, for causing extensive damage to a whale-processing station in Iceland. It now claims 30 000 members worldwide, over half of whom are in the United States (Allaby, 1986, p. 213; *Guardian*, 21 September 1994).

Earth First! was founded in the United States in 1979 by David Foreman, unhappy with the 'institutionalisation of more mainstream environmental groups such as Greenpeace and Friends of the Earth' (Seel, 1997b, p. 172). Since then, it has spread to a number of other countries including Britain where a group was initiated in 1991. Under its name, activists have carried out attacks (known as ecotage or monkey wrenching) on equipment used on construction sites, and, even more controversially, have driven long nails into trees with the intention of, at best, deterring loggers and, at worst, seriously injuring them. The deep ecology focus of Earth First! has sometimes led it to anti-human conclusions, some followers advocating illiberal policies such as mass sterilization and others contemplating with equanimity the possible effects of the Aids virus (Vincent, 1993, p. 267).

There is no reason to believe, however, that such misanthropic views are widely held amongst Earth First! activists and, in as far as they are, it tends to apply more to the movement in the United States than in Britain. In Britain, where it is estimated there are now between 60 to 70 local Earth First! groups, non-violent civil disobedience is the norm. Moreover, whereas Earth First! in the United States has focused on protecting wilderness from human intervention, the British version has been involved with issues such as roads, genetically modified food and the Criminal Justice Act, which could be regarded as human-centred (Seel, 1997b). Even in the United States, a considerable proportion of Earth First! activists has wanted the organization to widen its issue concern to take on social justice issues as well as wilderness preservation, and, in 1990, a split involving these two factions (labelled the 'socials' and the 'naturals') occurred (Nyhagen Predelli, 1995).

The Animal Liberation Front (ALF) was founded in Britain in 1976, and there are now ALF organizations in many other countries. ALF activists have adopted a wide range of direct action strategies (Garner, 1993a, ch. 8). This has, most notably, included breaking into factory farms and laboratories where the animals may be released, equipment destroyed and evidence of ill-treatment compiled. Some animal rights activists have also been associated with planting incendiary devices in the premises of fur retailers and even seeking to target the homes of scientists engaged in vivisection. The ALF denies responsibility for much of this, seeking to draw a distinction between harming people and harming property. Such a distinction is, theoretically at least, possible to make and it is important to note that not one person associated with the ALF's targets has been killed as a result of the activities of radical animal liberationists. The ALF, however, consists of autonomous cells of activists and, for obvious reasons, has no hierarchical organizational structure. The important fact, therefore, is that some activists are prepared, rightly or wrongly, to intimidate those involved in the use of animals, and risk physically harming people.

In the 1990s, non-violent direct action in pursuit of environmental objectives has markedly increased. Much of it is associated with opposition to the building of new roads (Doherty, 1999). Campaigning against the building of roads dates back at least to the 1970s, but whereas traditional campaigns focused on the public enquiry process, the new brand of protest begins after permission to build has been granted. Local protest groups, formed to fight the proposal through the planning procedure, are usually prepared to support the direct action of the so-called eco-warriors, creating alliances between 'Vegans and Volvos' as one *Times* leader put it (quoted in Griggs *et al.*, 1998). Not surprisingly, perhaps, tension between these two groups can arise over the justifiability of direct action as well as over different reasons for wanting to prevent the building of the road (North, 1998, pp. 5–10).

Activism against road building mushroomed following the, ultimately unsuccessful, attempt to prevent the building of the M3 through Twyford Down near Winchester (Doherty, 1998). The violent eviction of eco-activists from the site in December 1992 provoked considerable media interest and encouraged protesters to embark on similar occupations at a number of other sites, such as Wanstead, in East London; Pollock, in Glasgow; Newbury in Berkshire; and Fairmile in Devon (where a number of the protesters and most notably 'Swampy' became minor celebrities). A national anti-roads movement quickly emerged and an umbrella organization, Alarm UK, was created to co-ordinate the activities of protesters (see *Guardian*, December 28 1996).

As well as anti-roads activism, protest has also been evident against genetically modified foods (*Guardian*, 13 June 1998; 1 June 1999), in pursuit of animal rights objectives in general, and most significantly, against the export of live animals (Mcleod, 1998). Ironically, too, the Conservative government's draconian Criminal Justice and Public Order Act (1994) has had the effect of mobilizing a previously disparate group of protesters against a common enemy (*Guardian*, 6 August 1994). It is also tempting to see environmental protest as only a part of a new DIY sub-culture encompassing squatting, the dance culture, the creation of alternative communities and a general opposition to capitalism, the latter particularly evident during the so-called 'Carnival Against Capitalism' held in London in June 1999 (Jordan and Lent, 1999; *Guardian*, 24 June 1999). Groups with an environmental focus who have also been associated with wider campaigns include Reclaim the Streets, formed in 1991, who, among other things, seek to disrupt motor vehicle traffic in urban areas by holding impromptu street parties (*Guardian*, 22 July 1995; *Sunday Times*, 30 July 1995; *Guardian*, 15 June 1998); Critical Mass, consisting of large groups of cyclists who assert their rights to use roads; and The Land is Ours Movement, associated with the academic and journalist George Monbiot, which has been responsible for occupying sites in both urban and rural areas to illustrate the misuse of privately-owned land, and the community purposes to which it could be put (Doherty, 1998, pp. 72–3). Finally, mention might also be made of the opposition to the building of the M77 through part of Glasgow which centred around a group of protesters who set up a 'temporary autonomous zone' known as the Pollok Free State. As Seel (1997a, p. 124) points out: 'Although the core group's primary focus was the M77 being built through Pollok Park, they were well aware of issue linkages, seeing this as just one instance within a wider resistance movement against unfettered market forces, centralised (un-) "representative" government and the erosion of rights.'

Assessing the extent to which direct action is justified is a difficult task (see Singer, 1974; Garner, 1993a, ch. 8; and Goodwin, 1997, ch. 15). One initial consideration is the extent to which the objectives of the direct action is met. This is difficult to judge, not least because the objectives may be varied and imperceptible at least in the short term. The wider purpose of eco-protesters, for instance, 'is to pose a cultural challenge to mainstream society which makes people question the existing way of life' (Doherty, 1998, p. 73). Even if we limit the objectives to, say, the altering of road building programmes, assigning influence is not easy. All of the camps have, so far, been removed and the vast majority of the planned roads ultimately built. However, it is equally the case that the road building programme has been significantly cut by successive British governments. There are a range of possible reasons for this though. At the very least, it can be argued that the protests have been a contributory factor in the transformation of transport policy, publicizing the issue, and adding to the costs of road building projects (Doherty, 1998, p. 66).

In addition to the utility of the direct action being pursued, there are at least three other factors that need to be taken into account. First, the nature of the activity is obviously a crucial criteria. Most would regard non-violent civil disobedience, defined by Goodwin (1997, p. 363) as 'a principled, purposeful, and public disobedience of the law', as an acceptable pursuit in a democracy, provided that the adherents are prepared to accept the legal consequences of their actions. Far fewer, however, would be prepared to accept direct action which led to criminal damage, and even fewer if the welfare of humans was put at risk.

Secondly, the justifiability of direct action is also related to the nature of the decision-making system being challenged. Environmental and animal rights activists regularly complain that direct action is justified because their voices are ignored in the political process. Anti-roads activists, for instance, point to the biased nature of the public enquiry process whereas animal rights activists argue that the interests of agribusiness and pharmaceutical companies always take precedence over the interests of the animals they exploit (see Chapter 9).

Finally, and particularly relevant to environmental protest, direct action may be deemed justifiable by a moral imperative. In this context, those who hold that nature has intrinsic value or that animals have rights could, and do, argue that they are morally obliged to obstruct those seeking to carry out their lawful activities, if the interests of non-human nature are damaged in the process. Such a position could be taken independently of the way in which a particular law is made.

We have seen in this chapter that the environmental movement has grown extensively in the past 20 years or so and that it has become even more complex in terms of ends and means. Despite the rise of eco-protest and the willingness of activists to take direct action in pursuit of environmental objectives, the vast majority of groups still seek, at least part of the time, to influence public policy outcomes by using traditional campaigning and lobbying methods. To assess how successful they have been in Britain we need to examine how the political system has responded. This is the subject matter of the next chapter.

Further reading

There is a shortage of general texts on the environmental movement. Lowe and Goyder (1983) is thorough but is now somewhat dated as is Kimber and Richardson (1974) although the latter does provide some case studies of important issues. There are chapters in Young (1993), McCormick (1991) and Connelly and Smith (1999) worth reading; Porritt and Winner (1988) is also useful as is Grant's (1989) study of pressure groups in general. Jordan and Maloney (1997) is the result of a research project with particular emphasis on Friends of the Earth. Environmental protest is covered admirably well in the collection edited by Jordan (1998).

The international environmental movement is tackled by McCormick (1992), Mazey and Richardson (1993) and Boardman (1981). There are studies on particular parts of the movement. Much useful information on the conservation movement is provided in Evans (1991), Warren and Goldsmith (1983) and Lowe *et al.* (1986). The animal protection movement is examined in Garner (1993a, 1993b, 1996 and 1998) and Thomas (1983) and the anti-nuclear lobby is discussed in Ward (1983). McTaggart (1978) is a very personal account of the development of Greenpeace.

The Green Party's development has not been the subject of a book-length study, although see Parkin (1989) for an insider's account of Green parties throughout the world. For the British Greens, it is necessary to plough through a number of articles. The main ones are Rudig and Lowe (1986), McCulloch (1992), Doherty (1992a, 1992b) and Rudig (1993). The electoral development of the Greens is covered convincingly in Rootes (1991). See also Rudig (1985), Rudig and Franklin (1991), Curtice (1989) and Carter (1992b).

8

Political Institutions and Environmental Policy in Britain

This chapter examines environmental policy and the structure of environmental decision-making in Britain. It will describe the institutions responsible for environmental decision-making and the major pieces of legislation giving rise to this institutional structure and the way in which its constituent parts operate. In addition, some of the major issues arising from this decision-making structure are considered. In the first place, it will be asked how effective Britain's system of land-use planning is. Secondly, it will be asked how far Britain's pollution control system has changed from the traditional emphasis on pragmatism, flexibility and fragmentation to a more rigorous, standardized and integrated one. Thirdly, the case for at least partly replacing the traditional regulatory approach with a system of economic instruments is assessed. Partly as a summary of the chapter as a whole, the final section examines the attempt by successive British governments to develop an environmental strategy in the light of the agenda set by the Rio Summit. In the process, this section will also attempt to provide an interim evaluation of the new Labour administration's record in the environmental field.

British environmental policy and policy-making

When considering Britain's environmental legislation, the haphazard and piecemeal way in which it has been introduced quickly becomes apparent. Indeed, at least until recently, and perhaps not even now, Britain did not have a policy for the environment, in the sense of a clearly laid-out and consistent plan integrated across the whole range of governmental activities (Young, 1993, pp. 65–6). Consequently, Britain's environmental protection system machinery is very difficult to describe.

Figure 8.1 Major environmental measures in Britain

1853	Smoke Nuisance Abatement (Metropolis) Act
1863	Alkali Act
1876	Rivers Pollution Prevention Act
1906	Alkali and Works Regulation Act
1947	Town and Country Planning Act
1949	National Parks and Access to the Countryside Act
1953	Navigable Waters Act
1954	Protection of Birds Act
1955	Rural Water Supplies and Sewage Act
1956	Clean Air Act
1958	Litter Act
1960	Radioactive Substances Act
1960	Estuaries and Tidal Waters Act
1961	Rivers (Prevention of Pollution) Act
1963	Deer Act
1963	Water Resources Act
1968	Countryside Act
1968	Agriculture (Miscellaneous Provisions) Act
1969	Creation of the Royal Commission on Environmental Pollution
1970	Creation of the Department of the Environment
1972	Deposit of Poisonous Wastes Act
1973	Water Act
1974	Control of Pollution Act
1974	Dumping at Sea Act
1975	Conservation of Wild Creatures and Wild Plants Act
1976	Endangered Species (Import and Export) Act
1980	Local Government, Planning and Land Act
1981	Wildlife and Countryside Act
1986	Housing and Planning Act
1986	Agriculture Act
1986	Food and Environment Protection Act
1986	Animals (Scientific Procedures) Act
1987	Creation of Her Majesty's Inspectorate of Pollution
1988	Agriculture Act
1989	Water Act (created the National Rivers Authority)
1990	Environmental Protection Act
1990	(September) White Paper *This Common Inheritance* published
1995	Environment Act (among other things, created the Environment Agency and the Scottish Environmental Protection Agency)
1998	Scotland Act (devolving environmental responsibilities to a new Scottish Parliament and Executive
1998	Government of Wales Act (devolution of some secondary environmental responsibilities to the Welsh Assembly and its committees)

For many centuries, attempts have been made to deal with the environmental problems that emerge from time to time. A decree issued by Edward I in 1273 to prohibit the burning of sea coal is said to be the first environmental regulation in Britain (Vogel, 1986, p. 31). Modern practice, however, dates back to the nineteenth century. Since then, numerous measures have moulded the system which exists today (see Figure 8.1)

The most effective way of making sense of this list of measures is to distinguish between the two main systems through which environmental policy is implemented (Blowers, 1987, p. 279). In order to avoid complications here, I have excluded the policy machinery involved in regulating the welfare of animals (for a more detailed treatment see Garner, 1993a and 1998). However, some reference to animal welfare policy-making is made in Chapter 9, particularly in the case study on agricultural policy-making. In this chapter, we shall focus on development and conservation issues which are resolved through the land-use planning system and the pollution control system concerned with regulating emissions into the air, water and soil.

A number of points can be made about these two systems before we go on to describe them in detail. First, in both cases, Britain is unique in having the world's first national pollution agency and a more comprehensive system of land-use planning than anywhere else (Vogel, 1986, p. 144). Secondly, as pointed out in Chapter 7, much of the controversy surrounding the environment in the post-war years have centred on development and conservation issues. This is a direct consequence of the greater visibility of the issues, both in terms of the effects of decisions (or inaction) and in terms of the ability of interested actors to participate in the making of these decisions. It is also a product of the fact that agriculture, protected by extensive state support, had grown throughout the 1970s and early 1980s, whereas, in the same period, industrial pollution and major capital projects (such as the Channel Tunnel) were constrained by the recession.

Thirdly, it should be noted that the two systems are not entirely separate administratively, since the Department of the Environment, Transport and the Regions (DETR) figures heavily in both systems. The DETR was created in 1970 as the Department of the Environment (DoE), as a result of the amalgamation of the Ministries of Housing and Local Government, Public Buildings and Works, and

Transport. Transport issues were initially devolved to a separate department before being amalgamated with the DoE when Labour took power in 1997, and the Department of Energy was abolished in 1992, most of its environmental functions going to the DoE. Despite its name, environmental protection has proved to be a relatively small part of the DETR's responsibilities. Particularly in the 1980s, it spent a disproportionate amount of time and effort on more general local government affairs and, as McCormick (1991, p. 17) points out, until the appointment of Chris Patten in 1989, no Environment Secretary had shown any particular interest in the natural environment.

Despite the return of transport to the environmental fold, many key environmental responsibilities remain with other departments such as Trade and Industry (responsible for elements of energy policy), and MAFF (responsible for environmentally sensitive areas, pesticide control, farm waste management and farm animal welfare). Further, the Treasury has a profound influence as the holder of the purse strings. Moreover, there is a whole network of so-called quasi-governmental agencies with responsibilities that impact on the environment. As well as those specifically concerned with promoting environmental objectives (on which see below), mention can also be made of urban development corporations, the Agricultural Development Advisory Service, British Rail, as was, and the British Tourist Authority (Young, 1993, p. 57).

British environmental policy has become even more fragmented as a result of Scottish and Welsh devolution. The new Scottish Parliament has legislative authority in a range of policy areas, including the environment, transport, agriculture, fisheries and forestry, in addition to having limited tax-varying powers. In the future, this could lead to significant differences between environmental policy in Scotland and the rest of the United Kingdom. On the other hand, one should recognize, first, that some differences already exist as a result of the autonomy exercised by the Scottish Office, which the Scottish Parliament and Executive replaces. Secondly, Scottish environmental policy has to conform with EU directives in the area (as well as any other international commitments entered into by the UK government), and the UK's relations with the EU will still be largely the responsibility of the UK government. In Wales, the new National Assembly takes over the powers exercised by the Welsh Office, which includes policy relating to the environment, agriculture, transport, and planning. However, the Assembly's impact on environmental policy in general will be limited since, unlike the Scottish Parliament, it does not have the power to make primary legislation. Rather, it can only fill in the details of primary legislation passed by the Westminster parliament.

The distinguishing characteristic of environmental problems is their interdependence, and it is entirely artificial to draw a hard and fast distinction between pollution policy and countryside and land-use planning policy. A planning decision to allow a road to be built, for example, will not only effect the ecological and amenity value of the countryside but will cause pollution and, because flora provides a sink for CO_2 (the primary greenhouse gas), also contributes to climate change. Indeed, such is the complexity (and potential seriousness) of climate change that most of the environmental issues facing governments in the world relate to it in one way or another. For example, transport policy does have implications for public health, resource depletion and the protection of the countryside as a resource for humans and wild animals but, since road vehicles are one of the largest sources of CO_2 emissions, it also has a central role to play in the politics of global warming. Although British decision-makers may not fully recognize the interdependence of environmental issues (and numerous constraints operate against the successful implementation of a holistic policy), there have been attempts, particularly since the Rio Summit in 1992, to develop an overarching sustainable development strategy.

Development and conservation

As Figure 8.2 demonstrates, the centrepiece of the system designed to resolve development and conservation conflicts in Britain is the land-use planning system. In the nineteenth century, local authorities were given powers to clear slum areas for redevelopment, but the modern land-use planning system dates back to a series of Town and Country Planning Acts introduced since the 1920s (Vogel, 1986, p. 108). There were attempts by the Thatcher governments, which were ideologically opposed to restrictions on the free market and hostile to Labour-controlled local authorities, to remove some planning powers, particularly in urban areas (Blowers, 1987), but the system remains largely intact and, as we shall see, from an environmental perspective at least, it has been positively added to (Pennington, 1997).

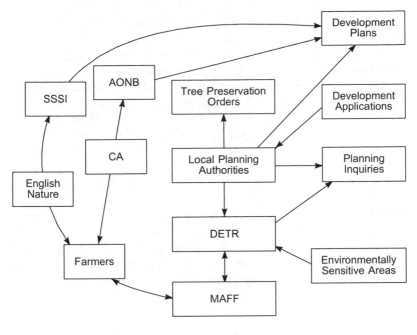

AONB   Areas of Outstanding Natural Beauty
CA   Countryside Agency
DETR   Department of the Environment, Transport and the Regions
MAFF   Ministry of Agriculture, Fisheries and Food
SSSI   Sites of Special Scientific Interest

Figure 8.2 Development and conservation: institutional structure

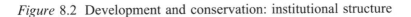

The major piece of legislation remains the Town and Country Planning Act 1947. This effectively took the development of private property under public control. The legislation requires that all proposed development be subject to planning permission by the relevant local authority. Thus, local authorities draw up extensive development plans and will consider individual development applications in the light of the overall plan, either rejecting the proposal outright or attaching conditions to their permission. Since 1968, the public have had a statutory right to be consulted over individual applications. Although a meeting of the full council is usually required to approve decisions, the real power lies with local planning authorities, which consist of those councillors who are members and the planning officials who serve them.

Ultimate authority rests with the Secretary of State for the Environment since, if the planning authority rejects an application or insists upon conditions unacceptable to the applicant, there is a right of appeal (to the DETR in England or the devolved Welsh or Scottish authorities). Only the applicant has the right of appeal so that an environmental group, for instance, cannot appeal against the granting of an application. The Secretary of State (or Scottish or Welsh equivalents) can then decide to reject or uphold the appeal or, which is most likely in controversial cases, order the setting up of a public inquiry. The Inspector appointed by the Secretary of State will then hold an inquiry and submit a report usually containing a recommendation which the Secretary of State can accept or reject (Vogel, 1986, pp. 108–9). One other option the Secretary has is to 'call in' an application before it has been discussed by the local planning authority, thereby bypassing the usual procedure.

The state conservation agencies

In addition to the planning system, development and conservation issues are also the direct concern of the state conservation agencies, namely English Nature and the Countryside Agency, responsible to the DETR, and the Forestry Commission, responsible to the MAFF in England and the Welsh and Scottish devolved authorities. English Nature was created by the National Parks and Access to the Countryside Act 1949 as the National Parks Commission, was later renamed as the Nature Conservancy and then, in 1973, the Nature Conservancy Council (NCC). Its present name derives from changes made in the late 1980s and enshrined in the Environmental Protection Act 1990. In Scotland and Wales, the NCC and the Countryside Commission, now part of the Countryside Agency, were combined to form a Scottish National Heritage and a Countryside Council for Wales while in England, the traditional division between conservation and amenity remains (Young, 1993, p. 58). The motives for these changes was in part cost-cutting and in part the government's irritation at the Nature Conservancy Council's opposition to Scottish Office conservation policy. Thus, the new Scottish National Heritage could be controlled more effectively by the Scottish Office (now the Scottish Executive) than the DoE-sponsored NCC (Ward, 1990,

p. 226). The criticism of the conservation community was placated somewhat by the creation (also in the 1990 Act) of a Joint Nature Conservation Committee.

English Nature is based in Peterborough, employs about 700 people and has an annual budget of over £40m. Its major task is to identify areas of the country which have a particularly important flora, fauna or geology. Once identified, it then recommends to the Secretary of State that these areas be designated as sites of special scientific interest (SSSI). At present, there are about 6500 SSSI in Great Britain, covering 7 per cent of the land. It also has responsibility for creating national nature reserves, of which there are 242 in Great Britain, and, in consultation with local authorities, it may also designate areas as 'local nature reserves' (Rydin, 1993, p. 127). The Countryside Agency (CA) was formed on April 1 1999 as a result of a merger between the Countryside Commission, originally created in 1949, and the Rural Development Commission. The CA was created in an attempt to integrate rural concerns into one body. In keeping with the historical distinction between conservation and amenity in Britain, the Countryside Commission had traditionally been concerned with identifying areas which can be designated as Areas of Outstanding Natural Beauty (AONB) or as national parks. There are now 39 AONB in England and Wales, covering some 13 per cent of the land area (*ibid.* p. 122). There are seven national parks in England and three in Wales, which, once designated, are run by separate authorities. Similarly, in conjunction with local authorities, the Countryside Commission also identified coastlines with a particularly scenic quality (designated as 'heritage coasts') and established 'countryside parks'.

The final agency with a specific conservation function is the Forestry Commission. This was set up in 1919 as a result of a post-war timber shortage and performs both a productive and a regulatory function, existing as a nationalized forestry concern selling timber from forests it has grown on its own land, as well as regulating the private forestry sector. The Forestry Commission is responsible to MAFF as well as to the Welsh Assembly and Scottish Executive. The environmental effects of both deforestation and inappropriate afforestation (the planting of uniform coniferous forests and the destruction of ancient woodlands) can have severe environmental consequences (Lowe *et al.*, 1986, pp. 46–50) and, although the Forestry Commission has had responsibility for recreation and conservation since 1967, critics contend that it is far too close to private timber interests and therefore pays insufficient attention to the damage caused by their activities (Grant, 1989, pp. 141–5).

The planning system – pros and cons

There are two main positive aspects of the planning system. First, by allowing for a great deal of public participation, environmental groups can have a significant input into important conservation issues. As we saw in Chapter 7, local authorities will often seek the help of conservationists when making decisions, not least during the process of drawing up their development plans. Secondly, local authorities must increasingly take into account environmental factors when drawing up a development plan, and, indeed, many local authorities, particularly since they have been encouraged to develop local Agenda 21 plans, have taken their sustainable development role seriously (see Rydin, 1997; Young, 1997; Connelly and Smith, 1999, ch. 10). Since 1991, the DETR has specifically instructed planning authorities to pay particular attention to the way in which local authorities can help to promote sustainable development and the effects development is likely to have on global warming and the quality of air and water. Likewise, a 1985 European directive (implemented in 1991) makes it mandatory for developers seeking permission for major projects such as oil refineries and power stations to produce an environmental statement, documenting the environmental effects of the development. This is potentially very useful for environmentalists who, as Young (1993, pp. 61–2) points out, have often been at a disadvantage because they lacked the resources to gather such information (see also Rydin, 1993, p. 101). Now, they hope their opponents will provide it for them.

From an environmental perspective, however, there are still weaknesses in the land-use planning system. Indeed, such are the flaws in the system that there has been enormous pressure on the Labour government to introduce comprehensive countryside legislation strengthening the protection granted to flora and forna. A White Paper is expected early in 2000. At the time of writing, however, the weaknesses remain. The first of these is that environmentalists cannot appeal against a decision to grant planning permission, nor can they insist on a public inquiry. Furthermore, not only are the terms of major public inquiries (known as public local inquiries) usually narrow – environmentalists cannot challenge the need for a motorway but only challenge the chosen route (Vogel, 1986, pp. 135–7; Connelly and Smith, 1999, pp. 94–7) – but also the financial resources available to developers are usually far greater than those of any environmental groups (see Chapter 9). Thirdly, in some circumstances, the element of public participation in planning-decisions can work against environmentalists, since developers can draw support from the local community by pointing to the economic benefits a particular project can bring. As Vogel (1986, p. 127) points out:

> In the case of pollution control, the lack of opportunities for public participation may mean that less weight is given to environmental considerations; in the case of the planning system, however, it is often precisely the relative accountability of local planning authorities to public pressures that undermines the political influence of amenity interests.

A classic instance of this was documented by Andrew Blowers (1984), who demonstrated how opposition to further development at a Bedfordshire brickworks in the late 1970s was defeated by the recession of the early 1980s which changed the priorities of the local trade unions.

An additional, and crucial, weakness of the planning system is the relative positions of the state conservation agencies and farmers. We have seen that neither the Countryside Commission (now the Countryside Agency) nor English Nature (or, prior to 1991, the NCC) have played any significant part in the formulation of conservation legislation. Likewise, the planning system takes precedence over the designation of SSSI and AONB. In other words, while there may be a presumption against development in designated areas (and such areas are marked on local authority development plans) English Nature and the Countryside Agency have no statutory authority to determine land use, only the right to persuade and cajole.

By far the biggest problem faced by the state conservation agencies is their inability to control agricultural development. For reasons that are explored in Chapter 9, the Town and Country Planning Act 1947 excluded agriculture from any planning constraints and, despite attempts to close this gap since then, the position is largely unaltered today (Rydin, 1993, p. 117). English Nature and the CA have been given the authority to conclude management agreements with farmers, and some funds to offer as compensation, but their resources are generally considered to be inadequate for the task (Vogel, 1986, pp. 140–2; Pearce, 1993, pp. 111–13). A WWF report published in 1997 severely criticized English Nature for its failure to prevent the physical deterioration of about two thirds of the 6500 designated

SSSI, focusing on the agency's unwillingness to prosecute offenders. In response, English Nature, which now has Barbara Young (the noted conservationist and former head of the RSPB) as chair, has argued that the laws are weak and any effective action requires the co-operation of landowners (*Guardian*, 24 November 1997; see similar reports published by the RSPB and Friends of the Earth, *Guardian*, 14 May 1998; 26 October 1998; *Sunday Times*, 9 May 1999).

One final point is worth making here. Even if the state conservation agencies did have statutory power to insist upon the protection of land as an SSSI or AONB, which they do not, this would still leave the vast majority of the countryside unprotected. As Evans (1991, p. xxiv) points out, the designated National Parks, nature reserves and country parks amount to no more than 10 per cent of the total British land area of 22.7 million ha.

Pollution control

Pollution control mechanisms have been subject to a great deal of change in the past two decades or so, and it is important to document these changes before going on to examine their character and significance.

The traditional approach to pollution control

The traditional British approach to pollution control was based on a regulatory system focusing either on particular substances (for example, radioactive or toxic waste) or particular media (air, water, soil). As a result, a whole range of inspectorates grew up in a haphazard way to check emissions from industrial processes. The first of these was the Alkali Inspectorate set up in 1863 to enforce the Alkali Act of the same year, which sought to remove most of the hydrochloric acid emitted by alkali manufacturers (Vogel, 1986, p. 32). Over time, the Alkali Inspectorate became a more general air pollution inspectorate as more and more industrial processes came under its control. To reflect this wider remit, in 1982 it was renamed the Industrial Air Pollution Inspectorate (IAPI). By the early 1980s, the IAPI was just one of a network of inspectorates including the Wastes Inspectorate, the Radioactive Substances Inspectorate and the Water Quality Inspectorate (Weale, 1992, p. 105). In addition, local authorities were responsible for domestic sources of pollution and those industrial processes not covered by the inspectorates. For instance, local authorities were given powers to control smoke emissions from coal fires under the Clean Air Act 1956 passed in response to the London smogs of the 1950s (Scarrow, 1961).

Despite the number of agencies concerned with pollution control, the operating procedures of the inspectorates were remarkably uniform (Hawkins, 1984; Smith, 1997, ch. 3). Typically, inspectors would visit factories and enter into negotiations until agreement was reached on the amount and nature of the pollution that would be permitted. The stringency of the conditions applied to authorizations would therefore vary from plant to plant depending upon the inspectorate's definition of the 'best practicable option' (BPO) operating principle established in the Alkali and Works Regulation Act 1906.

This procedure enabled inspectors to take into account the ability of the plant to meets the costs of improvement, the economic importance of the process, the environmental threat posed by the pollutant and the ability of a particular medium to absorb a particular substance (Vogel, 1986, pp. 70–80; O'Riordan and Weale, 1989, pp. 278–9). This negotiated consent was concluded in secret with little public access to information, on the grounds that

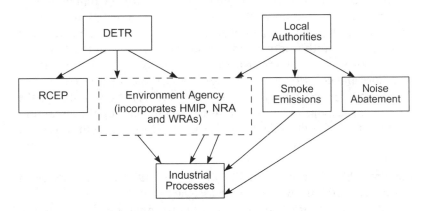

DETR	Department of the Environment, Transport and the Regions
HMIP	Her Majesty's Inspectorate of Pollution
NRA	National Rivers Authority
RCEP	Royal Commission on Environmental Pollution
WRAs	Waste Regulation Authorities
– – –	Institutions to be combined in new Environmental Protection Agency

Figure 8.3 Pollution control: institutional structure

co-operation could only be sustained if confidentiality was maintained (Jordan, 1993, p. 408). Moreover, formal legal action was very rarely taken, the inspectors preferring to persuade and cajole. As a result, between 1920 and 1966 only two firms were prosecuted for breaches of the inspectorate's authorization (Vogel, 1986, p. 88). Finally, because the emphasis was on single medium control (air, water or soil), if an industrial process was polluting in more than one medium it would have to seek multiple authorization or multiple permissions (Weale, 1992, p. 95).

The changing nature of pollution control

Considerable changes have occurred in the institutional structure of British pollution control in recent years, and it is worthwhile sketching out the present state of affairs (see Figure 8.3) before we move on to consider some of the key debates behind these changes. These changes have been typically haphazard and incremental but the traditional structure of pollution control has been at least modified if not transformed.

We noted earlier that the DETR is itself a relatively new institution dating back to 1970. Relatively new too is the Royal Commission on Environmental Pollution (RCEP), which was created in 1969 in response to environmental concern. It has no executive powers but its reports are authoritative and can sometimes, as with the 1994 and 1997 reports advocating measures to cut car use significantly, hit the headlines and contribute to a change in government policy (*Guardian*, 27 October 1994; *Guardian*, 19 September 1997). Most notably, the RCEP was responsible in the 1970s for recommending the streamlining of pollution control agencies (Weale, 1992, p. 102), but it was not until 1987 that this became a reality with the creation of Her Majesty's Inspectorate of Pollution (HMIP) within the DETR, and not until the Environmental Protection Act 1990 that it was given powers concomitant with the role assigned to it.

HMIP was an amalgam of the separate pollution inspectorates, with IAPI at the centre. The aim was to integrate pollution control in order to rationalize the existing system, preventing the inefficiency and the cross-media transfer of pollutants inherent in multiple-permitting (see below). Thus, the aim is to introduce a system of overall site licences based upon the 'best practical environmental options' (BPEO), a principle reflecting the multi-medium approach of integrated pollution control (IPC) (Ward, 1990, p. 227). This will operate in tandem with the principle of 'best available techniques not entailing excessive costs' (BATNEEC), the term replacing, but meaning much the same as, BPO in the Environmental Protection Act. BATNEEC will apply where pollutants can only be released to one medium (Young, 1993, p. 60).

A further change of note was the creation of the National Rivers Authority (NRA) in 1989, which came about as a consequence of water privatization (see Chapter 9). The NRA had regulatory power over water pollution as well as responsibility for land drainage, fisheries, conservation and recreation. Prior to this, all aspects of water management, including sewage treatment and disposal and industrial emissions, was in the hands of ten Regional Water Authorities created by the Water Act 1973. By splitting water use from environmental responsibilities, however it came about, there is an assumption that water quality will improve, although there is only some evidence (see below) that this has actually occurred.

A final, crucial, move toward greater integration occurred with the creation of the Environment Agency (EA). This new body, which combines the work of the NRA, HMIP and the waste regulation functions previously performed by local authorities, began its work in April 1996. The initiative had been suggested in *This Common Inheritance* in 1990 (Department of the Environment, 1990, p. 43), was announced by Major in 1991 during his first environment speech as prime minister (Carter and Lowe, 1995, pp. 38–9) and was the only domestic environmental commitment in the 1992 Conservative manifesto. The initial proposals were later modified to meet some of the concerns expressed by environmentalists, but weaknesses in the proposals were still evident (see below).

Pollution control debates

The preceding sketch of Britain's pollution control system raises a number of issues which we shall now consider. In the first place, there is a consensus among environmentalists, and increasingly, governments too, that a move towards *integrated pollution control* is a key part of the ecological modernization strategy (Weale, 1992, p. 96). We need here, then, to explain what is meant by the concept, what advantages are claimed for it and how far Britain has moved towards it.

Integration, of course, can be contrasted with fragmentation. Fragmentation in the environmental sphere occurs in two dimensions. First, there is the fragmentation which occurs because a number of government departments are responsible for policy action or inaction impacting on the environment. One form of integration (often called 'external integration'), therefore, refers to the attempt to incorporate an environmental dimension into all relevant policy areas – transport, energy, agriculture and so on. External integration occurs, therefore, as Weale and Williams (1993, p. 46) point out: 'when decision-makers in other policy sectors take into account environmental consequences in the making of their decisions and make suitable adjustments to their plans and the execution of those plans when environmental implications are recognised'. Following Jordan (1993, p. 407), this form of integration is 'comprehensive, precautionary and preventative' in nature, in that it seeks to deal with environmental problems at source (through, for instance, promoting public transport or prohibiting the use of certain substances) rather than dealing with pollution once it has occurred.

Another form of fragmentation occurs when a number of separate agencies are responsible for regulating emissions into the air, water or soil. Another form of integration (often called 'internal integration'), therefore, refers to the attempt to combine under one authority the responsibility for regulating all emissions into all mediums, whether it be air, water or soil. Again following Jordan (1993, p. 407), this form of integration is 'reactive' in nature in that it seeks to deal with waste once it is produced.

The advantage of IPC is that it is more in accord with the nature of the problem. As Jordan (1993, p. 406) points out: 'One of the inherent failings of environmental management systems in many countries has been the fundamental mismatch between the complex and holistic nature of environmental problems and the fragmented and sectorized institutions that have been created to deal with them.' In the case of internal integration, then, a fragmented regulatory system is not only inefficient, requiring a number of visits and separate authorizations, but also tends not to produce an optimal distribution of emissions (or pollution in the round) since an overall perspective is difficult to arrive at and pollution tends merely to be displaced from one medium to another (Dryzek, 1987, pp. 10–13; Weale, 1992, pp. 93–5). Likewise, in the case of external integration, the ability of the DETR to deal with environmental problems is limited if those departments and agencies responsible for policy areas having an impact on the environment do little or nothing to incorporate an environmental perspective.

When discussing the extent to which Britain has moved down the integration road, it is important to recognize that integration is an ideal system which does not exist anywhere in the world. Some countries though, for example, Sweden and the Netherlands, have come closer than most (Weale, 1992, p. 94, p. 98, 125–52; Connelly and Smith, 1999, pp. 271–6). In Britain, the creation of HMIP was guided by the principle of internal integration, and the Environmental Protection Act 1990 formally recognized the principle through the adoption of the BPEO operational criteria (Bradbeer, 1994, p. 124) which was designed, as the RCEP pointed out, to provide 'the most benefit or the least damage to the environment as a whole' (O'Riordan and Weale, 1989, p. 289). Similarly, the amalgamation of HMIP and the NRA in a new Environment Agency marked a further step down the integration road.

There remains some doubts, however, about successive government's commitment to internal integration. The resources of HMIP, for instance, were limited, the agency having a deficit of £3m in 1991–2 (Jordan, 1993, p. 415), hampering its ability to attract qualified staff able to undertake the complicated task of fulfilling IPC. Furthermore, IPC was not introduced very quickly. It took four years from its creation for HMIP's powers to be made available (in April 1991) and even then, not all processes were to be subject to the BPEO procedure (*ibid.*, p. 414).

The EA, 'employing 9000 staff with a budget of just over £500m a year', is 'one of the largest organisations of its kind in the world' (Connelly and Smith, 1999, p. 259). Moreover, the fact that the bulk of the EA's positions, (including 11 of the top 15 posts) went to former NRA employees, offered the prospect of the EA adopting the NRA's more legalistic and confrontational 'regulatory culture' (Smith, 1997, p. 217). Its ability to function as an effective regulator, however, is hindered by its varied and onerous responsibilities (*ibid.*, pp. 259–60). Moreover, the original draft proposals for the EA were criticized by environmentalists and opposition MPs and were only partly improved to take account of the objections.

In the first place, the powers given to the EA in the proposals were less formidable than the existing powers of its constituent elements. In the original proposals, the EA was merely to 'have regard to the desirability of conserving and enhancing the environment' whereas the NRA was required to '*further* the conservation and enhancement' of the environment. As a result of this criticism, John Gummer, the then Environment Secretary, announced in November 1994 that the wording of the legislation would be amended so that the EA had to 'further' conservation and the enhancement of the environment as opposed to just considering it. Additional clauses were also inserted. These give the EA powers to deal with contaminated land and overspill from abandoned mine workings (*Guardian*, 19 November 1994).

However, other weaknesses identified by environmentalists remain. First, the clause which requires the EA 'to take into account costs which are likely to be incurred, and the benefits which are likely to accrue', from environmental measures potentially allows industry to avoid pollution control measures on the grounds of costs alone, taking court action, if necessary, to establish their case. Further, the EA has little independence from government, its ten board members being chosen by the government, and largely under its control. There is also no representation for environmentalists, local authorities, trade unions or the business sector (*Guardian*, 10, 11, 14 October 1994). Finally, the ties to government are further tightened by the provision that EA capital expenditure requires the full support of the Treasury.

These weaknesses were confirmed in the EA's first year, with some commentators (including the former chairman of the NRA) describing the Agency as a 'toothless tiger' (Tickell, 1997), unwilling to prosecute offenders and generally failing to keep a healthy arm's-length distance from those it was regulating. Since then, however, the evidence suggests that the EA has become tougher with polluters. In 1999, for instance, the Agency produced a list naming and shaming the worst polluters. Moreover, EA prosecutions have increased by about 30 per cent since 1997, culminating in 744 in the year up to March 1999. The fact that courts have imposed relatively small fines is not the Agency's fault (*Guardian*, 22 March 1999).

Turning our attention to external integration, we note that some progress has been made, particularly since Labour came to office in 1997. The White Paper, *This Common Inheritance* (Department of the Environment, 1990) did address the issue of external integration by advocating policy co-ordination across the whole range of government activities and, to reflect this concern for integration, the document was presented not just by the DoE but also by the DTI, the Departments of Health, Energy, Employment, Transport and Education as well as MAFF. The language of *This Common Inheri-*

tance was impeccably integrationist, seeking to ensure that 'policies fit together in every sector; that we are not undoing in one area what we are trying to do in another; and that policies are based on a harmonious set of principles rather than on a clutter of expedients' (p. 8). To this end, the White Paper proposed that the cabinet committee (chaired by the Prime Minister) responsible for drawing up the White Paper should continue for the purpose of co-ordinating the government's environmental approach. In addition, it advocated the creation of a committee of ministers to draw up an energy efficiency programme and it recommended that each department should nominate ministers responsible for environmental issues in their departments (Weale, 1992, p. 124).

Little progress towards external integration was made under the last Conservative government where, it seems, John Gummer (the Environment Secretary) was fighting a lonely battle. It appears that the cabinet committee on the environment met rarely (Weale, 1992, p. 124), and Gummer has subsequently admitted that the 'green ministers' met only seven times between 1992 and 1996 (Connelly and Smith, 1999, p. 263). Moreover, the White Paper in general disappointed environmentalists severely, some commentators suggesting that the then Environment Secretary Chris Patten's original intentions (involving, in particular, a commitment to the introduction of a carbon tax) were considerably watered down, if not blocked completely, through the intervention of the Treasury, the DTI and the Department of Transport (Bradbeer, 1994, p. 126). In some ways, the White Paper was a 'milestone' since it did represent the first comprehensive statement of Britain's environmental policy (Flynn and Lowe, 1992, p. 33). The reaction of the press, however, was probably closer to the mark – the *Independent*, for instance, called it 'as feeble as it is lengthy' (it ran to 296 pages). Most of the 350 measures listed had already been implemented or announced and there were very few new commitments.

Since Labour came to power in 1997, there has been some further progress towards integrating environmental concerns into a range of policy areas. Three main initiatives can be noted. First, as we have seen, the departments of transport and environment were merged to create a new Department of Environment, Transport and the Regions with one minister (John Prescott) in overall control. This is a minimum requirement for the effective delivery of an integrated transport policy, a central part of Labour's environmental strategy (see below). Secondly, in November 1997, the government established a new House of Commons Environmental Audit select committee (as promised in the manifesto) designed to scrutinize the government's environmental progress. This committee has a Labour majority (nine Labour MPs, four Conservatives, one Liberal Democrat and one Plaid Cymru), but has a Conservative chair.

Finally, it seems that the Labour government has taken the idea of 'green ministers' more seriously than its predecessors. A formal programme of meetings between these ministers has been instituted by Michael Meacher (Minister for the Environment) and the co-ordination of environmental policy has undoubtedly been enhanced as a result. This initiative, it might be argued, is a symbol of growing environmental concern throughout government. MAFF, for instance, now emphasizes the conservationist role of agriculture far more than it used to and even the Department of Transport has scaled down its road building programme. The Foreign Office, under the control of Robin Cook, one of the greenest ministers in the government, has made the greatest strides. The department now has an environment department, which grew 50 per cent to 23 staff in a year between 1998 and 1999, and a new fund has been established to help developing countries use pollution control technology and be able to exploit renewable sources of energy more effectively (*Guardian*, 16 February 1999).

Despite the above, we should not exaggerate the significance of the moves towards integration in general, nor Labour's commitment to the idea in particular. In terms of agricultural policy, for instance, farmers are still not subject to many compulsory environmental controls (see above and Chapter 9) and the cuts in the road building programme over recent years arguably owe more to the pressure on public spending than to environmental considerations (see Chapter 9) (*Guardian*, 30 November, 20 December 1994). In addition, Labour's lack of commitment to environmental issues is, perhaps, revealed by the fact that the environment portfolio (at present held by Michael Meacher) is not deemed significant enough for a seat at the Cabinet table. Moreover, there is a conspicuous absence of environmental integration in the 1998 comprehensive spending review (HMSO, 1998). Despite the fact that the DETR's environmental review states that its 'central objective' is to promote sustainable development and that the government has an 'intention to use the tax system where appropriate to reduce environmental damage', the idea of green taxes in particular, and (with the exception of the countryside review) the environment in general, is not discussed elsewhere in the government's review. The Department of Trade and Industry review mentions 'sustainable growth' without explaining what it means and, indeed, whether it is being used in an environmental sense at all. Even more crucially, the objectives of the Treasury review are to 'expand economic and employment opportunity for all through productive investment, competition, better regulation and increased employability'. The potential environmental impact of such an objective is not mentioned.

Environmental standards

Another debate that has emerged in recent years concerns the choice between the traditional pragmatic British regulatory system involving negotiation, compromise and a case by case approach, on the one hand, and the imposition of rigorous uniform standards on the other. The advantages of the latter is that it avoids the dangers of what has been described as an implementation deficit whereby the regulators 'go native' by becoming too close to the regulated (Weale, 1992, pp. 17, 87; see also Sandbach, 1980, p. 56). On the other hand, the enforcement of uniform standards may well lead to greater corporate resistance and much time-consuming and expensive litigation. David Vogel's (1986, p. 23) comparative study of regulatory practices in Britain and the United States, for instance, revealed that:

> Britain's emphasis on voluntary compliance has not proved any more or less effective in achieving its objectives than the more adversPS9A11 and legislative approach adopted by policy makers in the United States. American regulatory policy has been more ambitious, but as a result it has produced greater resistance from business. British regulatory authorities demand less, but because their demands are perceived as reasonable, industry is more likely to comply with them.

It is true that setting specific strict emission standards for particular substances is likely to satisfy public opinion far more than a system based on consensus, informality and confidentiality. It may be the case, however, that the latter offers greater advantages on environmental grounds since it allows for the kind of cost-benefit, cross-media analysis not available to a more rigid system (Weale, 1992, p. 115; Jordan, 1998, pp. 183–4). It is important to remember here that the emission of a potential pollutant is not a problem (that is, it does not become a pollutant) until it damages targets (humans, animals and plants) in the environment (Haigh, 1990, p. 13). It is not necessary, therefore, to restrict emissions of potential pollutants completely and, furthermore, one particular medium may be able to absorb far more of a potential pollutant, without damage being caused, than another. Finding the right balance would be far more difficult with a rigid system of environmental standards. Moreover, a more open system of pollution control, which is likely to accompany a system of rigid standards, would probably result in public pressure (and environmental campaigns) for zero emissions into certain media although this would not necessarily be the best environmental option.

On the other hand, administering a system of fixed uniform standards may be easier than assessing the quality of, say, water. It is a relatively simple task to determine whether a particular emission has exceeded the standard set than to try to find out which discharges are responsible if water quality objectives have been breached (Haigh, 1990, p. 21). Quality standards and varying authorizations, though, do allow the flexibility required to protect particularly vulnerable parts of the environment and do prevent unnecessarily restrictive standards being set where the environment needs less protection.

There has been increasing pressure on Britain to replicate the uniform standards applied in other European countries, such as Germany, the Netherlands and Denmark, particularly since the European Union has adopted this idea. In recent EU Environmental Action Programmes, environmental objectives have been advocated whereby uniform emission standards are set as stringently as available technology allows, irrespective of the cost – the so-called BAT approach (O'Riordan and Weale, 1989, pp. 290–1). Subsequently, this was amended to 'best available techniques not exceeding excessive costs' (BATNEEC) which was incorporated into the Environmental Protection Act 1990 (Jordan, 1993, p. 417). This amendment, of course, is crucial since what constitutes excessive cost is contentious and can only be resolved by negotiation on a case by case basis. British governments have consistently resisted the idea of uniform emission standards, insisting, instead, on meeting environmental quality objectives which allow for the varying of authorizations depending on the capacity of particular media to absorb pollutants (Haigh, 1990, pp. 17–21). While the arguments in favour of this approach stand, it should also be noted that there is an element of economic self-interest in Britain's reluctance to accept uniform emission standards decided in the Council of Ministers. Britain has short, fast-flowing rivers which would require less stringent emission standards than other rivers in Europe (Haigh, 1990, p. 22).

Of all the agencies responsible for pollution control, the NRA came closest to adopting a more rigid system. Its approach was still based on statutory water quality objectives set by government rather than uniform emission standards, but the NRA aggressively sought to enforce water quality objectives through the courts if necessary (Jordan, 1993, p. 412; Pickering and Owen, 1994, pp. 137–8). In addition, between 1991–93, HMIP flirted with a more 'arm's length' approach, whereby the process of applying for an authorization became much more formal, and there was much more distance between regulators and the regulated than existed previously, with industry having to demonstrate compliance with fixed standards set centrally by HMIP rather than negotiate with on-site inspectors (Jordan, 1993, pp. 414–5; Skea and Smith, 1998, pp. 271–3). HMIP officially abandoned this approach in 1993, however, in favour of a return to the traditional British emphasis on pragmatism, flexibility and consensus (see Chapter 9) (Smith, 1997, ch. 6). This about-turn seems to have been accepted by the EA and, as Skea and Smith (1998, p. 275) point out: 'The result has been a return to the site-specific flexibility and close operator participation which characterised the former air pollution regime'.

Economic instruments

The final debate we shall consider in this section concerns the use of economic instruments as a means of replacing or supplementing regulatory standards (see Connelly and Smith, 1999, pp. 159–71). Those who advocate the use of economic instruments recognize that solving environmental problems requires that those who pollute should be made responsible for it, but they argue that regulatory standards are not the best way to internalize the externalities. Rather, they suggest that a system of incentives should be put into place to encourage good environmental practice.

The clearest example is a system of Green taxes whereby companies or individuals are made to pay if they want to continue using a production method which causes pollution, or to continue buying leaded petrol. In this way, what had previously been an external cost to the whole community is internalized, in so far as producers and consumers have to take the environment into account as an extra cost for themselves. A more elaborate system involves tradeable pollution permits. This is where pollution permits amounting in total to an acceptable level of emissions are allocated to waste generators in a particular area. Each individual firm can then decide whether to invest in cleaner technology and, if they do, they can sell the unwanted permits to other firms (Bradbeer, 1994, p. 127). The aim of the system, of course, is to encourage cleaner technology because the costs of not doing so will be passed on to the consumer in the form of more expensive goods, which will reduce the competitiveness of the company.

Economic instruments are, at least superficially, an attractive proposition. In particular, they minimize the problems of implementation deficit and non-detection prevalent in regulatory approaches; they encourage firms to go beyond what a regulatory regime might require, and they are potentially much cheaper to enforce. However, there are disadvantages. In the first place, environmentalists tend to be suspicious of economic instruments because, although the aim is to discourage pollution, it appears at the same time to legitimize polluting activities (Bradbeer, 1994, p. 127). Moreover, green taxes are notoriously difficult to set at an optimal level and complex adjustments would be needed on a regular basis. Finally, there is little to suggest that an extensive system of policing would not still be required to ensure that the economic instruments are enforced. At best, they would seem to constitute only a supplement to traditional regulatory practices, and not an alternative.

Green taxes, in particular, raise problems for governments at both a political and an ideological level (Weale, 1992, pp. 161–3). The (only partially successful) increase in VAT on domestic supplies of gas and electricity by the Conservative government in 1994 is a case in point here. The policy had a budgetary rather than an environmental objective but it was little different from a carbon tax aimed at encouraging energy conservation, so the problems associated with it are applicable to the environmental field. The major problem is that such a tax would hit the poorest hardest, a point emphasized strongly by the Labour opposition, raising questions not just of fairness but also of votes. The political problem may be alleviated by compensating the poorest but this is barely adequate in environmental terms since the incentive for conserving energy disappears for those receiving it (Weale, 1992, p. 163).

Economic instruments are becoming increasingly popular as a policy instrument in Britain and elsewhere. The idea was intrinsically attractive to Thatcherites who were hostile to regulatory bureaucracy. In addition, when Chris Patten became Environment Secretary in the late 1980s, he appointed David Pearce, a noted advocate of environmental taxes, as his advisor (Pearce *et al.*, 1989). Despite this, economic instruments did not play a large role in the Conservative government's environmental policy. Lead-free petrol is one notable exception as was the landfill tax, introduced in 1996. By taxing local authorities for the amount of waste they deposited in landfill sites, the aim was to encourage them to set up recycling schemes. Moreover, following the edict that taxation should be transferred from the 'good' things such as employment, income and savings on to 'bad' things such as pollution, resource-use and waste, the proceeds of the scheme were to be used to reduce employer's National Insurance contributions (*Independent*, 30 September 1996). Despite attacking their Conservative predecessor for introducing additional taxes which had the potential to be environmentally beneficial, the Labour government has offered some prospect of economic instruments playing a larger role in environmental policy. The landfill tax has been expanded, road pricing is on the agenda and a series of Green taxes were announced in the 1998 budget (see below for a more detailed examination of these proposals).

British governments and sustainable development

The post-Rio environmental agenda has been dominated by sustainable development and the new global problems exemplified by climate change and biodiversity. Since then, governments have been required to develop an overall environmental strategy, within which particular policies can be justified. This process began with the Conservative government in Britain in the early 1990s. We have already noted the pre-Rio attempt to draw together an environmental strategy in the White Paper *This Common Inheritance*. Further initiatives followed after Rio. Two new administrative bodies (an advisory panel of experts on sustainable development and a 'round table' of 30 members drawn from all sections of the community) were announced in January 1994 (Dodds and Bigg, 1995, pp. 13–15). In addition, the government published four documents (on sustainable development, climate change, biodiversity and sustainable forestry) outlining their post-Rio strategy.

As with *This Common Inheritance*, these post-Rio documents were heavily criticized by environmentalists for, as Andrew Lees of Friends of the Earth pointed out, being 'old commitments repackaged' and for lacking 'any meaningful targets and timetables' (*Guardian*, 26 January 1994). In practice, very little was achieved. For example, the land-use planning system, the chief instrument for ensuring biodiversity in Britain, remained largely unchanged between 1992 and 1997. The Environment Secretary John Gummer did introduce tougher planning guidelines in 1994, mainly to deter the building of out-of-town shopping centres, and these were strengthened even further early in 1997, but, while this led to a steep decline in planning applications, the failure to produce a concurrent strategy to deter the use of cars resulted in existing shopping centres reporting a huge increase in trade (*Guardian*, 15 February 1997).

The main planks of the government's strategy to achieve the goals of the Rio climate convention consisted of a plan to introduce Value Added Tax (VAT) on domestic fuel in two stages, to 8 per cent in 1994 and 17.5 per cent a year later, to increase road fuel duty and to introduce various schemes to encourage energy efficiency (Maddison and Pearce, 1995, pp. 131–5). Despite not being able to achieve the full increase in VAT due to political opposition, the government easily achieved the target set by the Rio Summit. Indeed, with a reduction in (1990) CO_2 levels of between 4–8 per cent, Britain's record was better than almost every other industrialized country (*Guardian*, 19 February 1997). The target, however, was not particularly exacting and was made to seem more impressive because of some 'wildly inaccurate' predictions which had suggested that CO_2 emissions in Britain were likely to rise substantially by the end of the century. The rise failed to happen, not as the result of the government's direct concern for the environment, but largely as the unintended by-product of a big reduction in the coal industry and the greater use of gas for energy generation.

The Labour government

The election of the Labour government in 1997 had the potential to be a significant event in the development of British environmental policy. Not only was this the first Labour government since the environment had become an important issue, but the transformation of the party seemed to remove the ideological and organizational obstacles which had previously prevented the party from being wholehearted environmentalists (see Chapter 9). Some of the Labour government's environmental decision-making has already been mentioned. What follows now is an overall analysis of the government's record so far.

At Labour's 1994 conference a far-reaching environmental policy document *In Trust for Tomorrow* was adopted, and some of the proposals in this document were included in the party's 1997 election manifesto. Of particular significance was the, previously unacknowledged, recognition that environmental policy requires an integrative approach. The protection of the environment, it stated, 'is not an add-on extra, but informs the whole of government, from housing and energy policy through to global warming and international agreements' (Labour Party, 1997, p. 4). The central promise in the manifesto was a commitment to reduce carbon dioxide (CO_2) emissions, the principal cause of global warming, by 20 per cent of their 1990 level by 2010 (*ibid.*, p. 28). This reduction, Labour argued, could be achieved by a shift to renewable energy resources and energy efficiency measures involving the creation of an environmental task force from the unemployed. Most importantly, it would also require the introduction of an integrated transport system which would discourage unnecessary car use. This latter promise was included as one of the party's ten major commitments to be achieved in the lifetime of a Labour government.

Since taking office, there have been some promising signs that Labour are taking environmental issues seriously. As we have seen, there have been important, albeit limited, steps towards a more integrative approach to environmental decision-making. Particularly noteworthy in policy terms has been the government's decision to give up Britain's prior opt-out from an EU ban on dumping radioactive waste at sea, and, after a damning report on its safety record, the announcement of the closure of the Dounreay nuclear reprocessing facility (*Guardian*, 6 June 1998). In addition, Labour has maintained the previous government's National Air Quality Strategy and intends to make the achievement of air quality objectives a statutory responsibility for local authorities (*ibid.*, 19 November 1997). The government has also taken much tougher action than its predecessor on the environmental damage caused by the water companies (*ibid.*, 24 September 1998). Of even greater importance was the leading role played by the British government at the Kyoto conference on climate change in December 1997 (see Chapter 5). Not only did Blair and other ministers chide the United States for their reticence, but the government also honoured its manifesto commitment by agreeing to a 20 per cent cut in CO_2 emissions (a 12.5 per cent cut in total greenhouse emissions) as part of an overall EU target of 8 per cent.

Agreeing to cuts in CO_2 is one thing, achieving them is quite another. On the positive side, the government has committed itself to a significant increase in the use of renewable energy sources (10 per cent of electricity needs must be produced from renewable sources by 2010); a major cut in the previous administration's road building programme was announced in August 1998 – of the 140 projects inherited from the Tories, only 37 survived (*Guardian*, 1 August 1998) – and the use of green taxes has been increased. From June 1999, car excise duty has been graduated according to engine size, the so-called 'fuel duty escalator' is designed to ensure that fuel duty is annually increased above the rate of inflation, and by 1999, the landfill tax had been increased from £7 a tonne under the last Conservative government to £10 (*Guardian*, 10 June 1998). The most significant development of all was the announcement, in the 1999 budget, of the government's intention to introduce an industrial energy tax whereby organizations will pay a surcharge on purchases of electricity, gas and coal, the proceeds of which will be used to reduce employers' National Insurance contributions by 0.5 per cent (*Guardian*, 10 March 1999).

Last but not least, the promised White Paper on an integrated transport policy was published in July 1998 (Department of the Environment, Transport and the Regions, 1998). Reducing car use is a vital plank of an effective environmental policy. Not only will it play a significant role in meeting the targets set at Kyoto (the transport sector accounts for about 23 per cent of Britain's CO_2 emissions of which 85 per cent comes from road traffic) but it also tackles problems of pollution, congestion and the destruction of the countryside. The most innovative proposal in the White Paper is the granting to local authorities of the power to raise revenue through the levying of charges for driving into city centres and for workplace parking. Prescott, it appears, fought hard to persuade the Treasury that local authorities should be allowed to spend the revenues on improving public transport in their areas. Known as 'hypothecation', this is a major shift in policy since it represents a 'retreat from the Treasury's long-sustained opposition to earmarking tax revenue' (*Economist*, 18–24 July 1998).

Despite these encouraging developments, however, there are still doubts about the Labour government's environmental commitment in general, and its ability to meet the ambitious Kyoto targets in particular. As we saw earlier, the spending review gave little indication that environmental protection was at the centre of government thinking, and yet it is going to have to be in order to meet the 20 per cent CO_2 reduction target. The green tax proposals are to be welcomed and yet can be criticized. The vehicle duty scheme, for instance, is very moderate and is unlikely to change behaviour significantly. Only those people driving cars with engine sizes of 1100cc or below will pay less (currently a £55 saving) while everyone else, however big the car, will pay the same.

Similarly, doubts remain about the effectiveness of the industrial energy tax scheme (see *Guardian*, 11 March 1999). The scheme will not be introduced until 2001 after consultation with industry. High energy users in the manufacturing sector have already raised objections to the surcharge and, disconcertingly from an environmental perspective, there are already signs that they may be treated more favourably. Moreover, even on Treasury figures, the estimate is that the scheme will only produce a 2 per cent saving in CO_2 emissions. It is not clear where the other savings are going to be made, particularly in the light of the government's reversal of the previous administration's decision to increase VAT on domestic fuel bills.

Finally, the government's proposed transport reforms have also been stuck at first base. Some of the road-building commitments of the previous administration have been retained, most controversially a further widening of the M25 and the Birmingham Northern Relief Road (a project that Labour opposed in opposition) which will go through two SSSIs. Moreover, the integrated transport White Paper was delayed, apparently because Prescott's initial proposals were regarded as too 'anti-car' by Downing Street, and the necessary legislation has also been delayed, allegedly for the same reason (*Guardian*, 4 May 1998; 30 April 1999). Even if implemented too, the proposals are arguably inadequate. First, no targets are set in the White Paper for the reduction of road traffic, which continues to spiral, one recent official report from the Office for National Statistics revealing a near 10 per cent increase on major roads since Labour came to power (*Guardian*, 6 August 1999). There is, therefore, no objective benchmark by which to assess the effectiveness of the policy. Secondly, while the road pricing and parking tax elements are welcomed by environmentalists, it might be argued that the government is passing the buck by making them the responsibility of local authorities rather than of central government. Moreover, the proposals are permissive, enabling rather than forcing local authorities to act. As a result, it is unlikely that local authorities will act if they perceive their neighbouring areas are gaining an economic advantage by not doing so.

The Labour government's perceived failure to implement fully its environmental programme, and to act quickly or decisively enough on the emerging issue of genetically modified food, seemingly provoked something of a backlash (see Gray, 1999). It seems likely, for instance, that the government's poor performance in the 1999 European elections was, at least partly, caused by disillusionment with its environmental record, a perception heightened by the election of two Green MEPs. It is transport policy, in particular, which has emerged as Labour's Achilles heel. Not only has the implementation of the White Paper been stalled, but also increasing road congestion and evident safety problems on the railways, revealed graphically by the Ladbrook Grove disaster, have pushed the government's transport policy close to, if not beyond, crisis point. Not suprisingly, perhaps, an Independent Communication and Marketing (ICM) opinion poll in July 1999 revealed that transport was the only major issue where less than 50 per cent of the public thought the government was doing a good job; only 35 per cent, compared to 50 per cent who thought the government was doing a good job on the environment in general, 70 per cent on the economy, 66 per cent on Northern Ireland and 55 per cent on education (*Guardian*, 13 July 1999).

The Hague-led Conservatives have recognized Labour's weakness on transport policy and have unveiled their own strategy. Designed more to appeal to motorists than to protect the environment, this strategy, based on the view that the motor car is 'a force for good that brings freedom and choice to millions across our society', includes proposals to reduce car taxes, increase road building and the speed limit, and improve parking at railways and bus stations (*Guardian*, 13 July 1999). Such proposals seem a throwback to an environmentally-insensitive individualist era and offer little that will ease the congestion that increased road use brings. Not for the first time, the Conservatives may have misjudged the public mood, which is arguably not against curbs on car use as such but is against continuing congestion coupled with inadequate public transport. In general, by demonstrating that action on the environment may be a vote winner rather than a vote loser, the events described in the last paragraph could prove to be a watershed in Labour's approach. One of Blair's first public responses to the European election results, for instance, was to announce the government's intention to introduce a bill banning fox hunting (see Chapter 9). This was followed by an announcement that bills relating to transport and countryside protection will appear in the next session of Parliament.

*   *   *

In conclusion, our survey of the development of environmental policy in Britain reveals an incremental and cautious pattern with occasional periods of heightened activity. In the early 1980s, the government showed little interest in environmental issues and the general consensus was that Britain was lagging behind many of her European partners. By the late 1980s, this situation changed with the government's greater interest reflected in the creation of HMIP, the passage of the Environmental Protection Act and the publication of *This Common Inheritance*. This progress has since been built on by the Labour government elected in 1997. However, the ability of this new government to initiate a genuinely sustainable economic policy and, in particular, to meet its own CO_2 targets must be questioned. Progress towards integration remains slow and patchy. There are significant gaps in the planning system and enforceable standards are too often overlooked in favour of exhortation and encouragement.

Further reading

Introductory accounts of environmental legislation and decision-making in Britain can be found in McCormick (1991), Young (1993), Flynn and Lowe (1992), Blowers (1987), Ward (1990), Bradbeer (1994), Gray, (1995) and Connelly and Smith (1999). An indispensable study of the development of environmental controls in Britain and the United States is Vogel (1986). Hawkins (1984) is also useful. Coverage of the planning law is provided by Rydin (1993) and a fascinating case study of the planning system in action can be found in Blowers (1984).

The integration of pollution control policy is the main theme of O'Riordan and Weale (1989), Jordan (1993), Smith (1997) and Skea and Smith (1998). Pearce (1989 and 1993), Weale (1992) and Hajer (1997) provide accounts of ecological modernization. The key government documents on the environment in recent years are *This Common Inheritance* (Department of the Environment, 1990), *Sustainable Development: The UK Strategy* (Department of the Environment, 1994) and *A New Deal for Transport: Better for Everyone* (Department of the Environment, Transport and the Regions, 1998).

9

The Political Process and the Environment

So far in this book we have focused mainly on two broad themes: questions concerning what ought and needs to be done to protect the environment on the one hand, and questions concerning what has been done at the national and supranational level on the other. It should have become apparent that even from the perspective of the shallow or reformist environmentalist, and despite greater environmental awareness by decision-makers, there remains a gap between the 'is' and the 'ought'. The main purpose of this chapter is to examine the political processes involved in producing policy outputs, with the aim of understanding why this gap between 'is' and 'ought' exists. The chapter is divided into four main sections. First, various approaches to public policy which may help us to order the empirical evidence are considered. Secondly, because they play a pivotal role in British government and politics, we examine the influence that political parties have had on environmental policy-making. This is followed, in the final two sections, by case studies of agricultural and pollution control policy-making.

Approaches to policy-making

The process of policy-making is extremely complex, and disentangling the relative importance of the various influences on public policy is notoriously difficult. Clearly, in Western liberal democracies, policy decisions come about as a result of the interaction between elected politicians, bureaucrats working within public authorities, interest groups and public opinion. In addition, this interaction is mediated through the particular historical, social, economic and political contexts within which policy decisions are made. The situation is complicated, as we saw in Chapters 5 and 6, by the fact that environmental policy no longer takes place primarily within any one country, and the supranational nature of policy-making vastly increases the number of participants involved and in turn the variables one has to take into account.

Students of policy-making are faced with a mass of empirical evidence, and theory-building is a useful, albeit rather constraining, way of managing the information gathered. Numerous approaches from within the disciplines of political science and public administration have been suggested, and agreement over typologies or the validity of competing approaches is very rarely arrived at (compare, for instance, Greenaway et al., 1992, chs 1 and 2; Ham and Hill, 1984; see also Marsh and Rhodes, 1992). One recurring problem is that the development of theory tends to run far ahead of empirical application, a not surprising fact given the operational difficulties, such as time and cost, involved with the latter.

It is hardly surprising, therefore, that there has not been a surfeit of environmental studies which seek to relate empirical evidence to theoretical perspectives, although, as the rest of this chapter will demonstrate, there have been some. One such example is Albert Weale's (1992) account of pollution politics. In this work, Weale distinguishes between four idioms: rational choice theory, systems, institutions and policy discourse. While this is an innovative study, the choice of approaches is somewhat eclectic and Weale himself finds it difficult, because of the paucity of research, to relate them to actual cases of pollution politics.

A mention should be made of rational choice theory here (see Weale, 1992, pp. 38–46; Connelly and Smith, 1999, pp. 106–12) since it would seem to help explain certain aspects of environmental policy. Rational choice theory focuses on individual behaviour. It assumes individuals will make rational choices designed to maximize their own utility. This individualistic approach seems to offer a convincing explanation for the existence of a 'politics' of the environment. As we have seen, governments have to intervene to clean up the environment because, as an externality, individual polluters, not otherwise economically affected by the damage they cause, will have no incentive to do so unless penalized by a public authority. Moreover, in a classic case of the 'prisoner's dilemma', those affected by the pollution will not, if left to their own devices, contribute towards cleaning it up since their individual contribution will make no difference to the outcome. They will benefit anyway if enough of the others in the community contribute, since cleaning up the pollution is a public good which cannot be restricted. Further, if an individual does contribute and not enough of the others do, then he or she will have done so for no benefit and at a possible cost if the contribution cannot be repaid.

Rational choice theory also offers an account of the character of environmental politics. Collective action problems, as Chapter 5 revealed, are rife in the concluding of international environmental agreements. We saw in Chapter 7, in addition, that Olson's theory of group mobilization, which derives from the rational choice school, seeks to explain why environmental groups are weak *vis-à-vis* those sectional interest groups with a vested interest in preventing or diluting environmental measures (Olson, 1965). Moreover, as we shall see below, electoral expediency is at least one, albeit not the only or even the most important, factor in persuading the main parties to take environmentalism more seriously. This fits in nicely with the Downsian model of parties as mere vote maximizers, a theory which again can be accommodated within the rational choice tradition (Downs, 1959).

Pluralism and its critics

While not wishing to reject the rational choice approach entirely, it should be said that a great deal more importance has been attached to theories which seek to explain policy outcomes in terms of the power exercised by competing interests and, for better or worse, this chapter will focus on explaining environmental policy in terms of such theories. Again, stating the different perspectives is relatively straightforward while operationalizing them provides numerous methodological difficulties. The most appropriate way of beginning an examination of the enormous range of relevant material is to consider the pluralist approach.

The pluralist approach has been the dominant theory of the state in post-war Western political science (Dunleavy and O'Leary, 1987). It is particularly associated with the work of the American political scientist Robert Dahl (1961, 1971). For pluralists, in all complex societies where no state repression exists, the formation of groups to represent interests which people have in common is a natural phenomenon. In turn, public-policy making is a product of the interaction between groups. For some pluralist thinkers, government is itself the neutral arbiter between groups, its decisions reflecting the balance of power between them. For others, the government has its own agenda and exists as one competing set of interests among the others. For all pluralists, the key feature of modern Western liberal democracies is that power is diffuse. This does not mean that all groups have an equal ability to achieve their objectives, but that no one interest or small set of interests dominates the decision-making process. Thus, the assumption is that if a group has an interest to promote, it will be able to gain entry to the political system and, further, that at some point it will achieve at least some of its objectives. The competition between groups thereby ensures that governments remain accountable to societal demands, and these demands are an on-going feature of the political process not merely occurring during election campaigns.

Now, the pluralist approach has been subject to a great deal of criticism from those (often operating from within a Marxist, elitist or corporatist perspective) who claim that pluralists seriously exaggerate the extent to which the political system is open to a variety of competing groups (Ham and Hill, 1984, chs 2 and 4). Central here is a critique of pluralist methodology. Pluralists, it is suggested, operate with what Lukes (1974) has called a 'one-dimensional' theory of power. Thus, a typical pluralist analysis of decision-making involves looking at what decisions have been made and comparing these with the preferences of the groups involved. If a group's aims are met, they are attributed with influence. This approach, of course, might lead to non-pluralist conclusions but, the argument goes, if the pluralist hypothesis is confirmed, it may be unreliable and misleading because the methodology adopted cannot account for more subtle exercises of power.

The claim made by critics of pluralists, then, is that decision-making studies of the type described above do not tell the full story because they exclude the possibility that some decisions may not reach the decision-making arena or that, if they do, their resolution may not be dependent on the visible activities of particular groups. By appreciating the existence of what has been described as 'non-decision-making' (Bachrach and Barazt, 1962) or the 'second dimension' of power (Lukes, 1974), therefore, it might be possible to identify instances of covert grievances or concerns which are excluded from the political arena. This exclusion may occur for a variety of reasons (Dearlove and Saunders, 1984, pp. 209–12). It could be the product of the use of force. Alternatively, it can come about through the use of rules or procedures so that, for instance, issues are referred to Royal Commissions where they can languish, or challenging groups can be co-opted and tamed. Finally, exclusion can occur through the law of anticipated reactions whereby the reputation for power of a particular interest may be such that a challenging group or groups may anticipate that it is not worth their while entering the political arena.

A variation on this non-decision-making theme was provided by Charles Lindblom (1977). In this work, Lindblom, who had previously accepted the pluralist case, argues that business interests occupy a privileged position within the political system. This derives not just from the resources they can muster for conventional lobbying – which pluralist methodology would identify and take into account – but also, and most importantly, from their structural position in the economy. Thus, governments, he argues, will always take business interests into account, whether or not business organizations actually campaign openly for them, because the economic benefits that business provides, in terms of employment and investment, and so on, is crucial for the re-election prospects of any government.

Pluralism and the environment

There have been some attempts to utilize the theories discussed above in environmental case studies. Most notably, Matthew Crenson's study (1971) of air pollution politics in two US cities in Indiana specifically adopts the non-decision-making approach. He notes that air pollution regulations were introduced much later in one city (Gary) than in the other (East Chicago). His explanation was that in Gary, the economy was dominated by a single corporation (US Steel) whereas East Chicago had many steel companies. US Steel's reputation for power, Crenson argues, was so great that no environmental group thought it worthwhile to challenge its resistance to pollution controls. As well as the anticipated reactions involved in the reputation for power, there are elements of Lindblom's thesis here too. A major reason why US Steel could exercise such power was not because of its lobbying resources but because of the contribution it made to the local economy. There was an unstated assumption then that any attempt to introduce more stringent pollution controls could result in US Steel relocating elsewhere. This would have been far more catastrophic for Gary, reliant on one major employer, than in other cities with a broader employment base.

One British study along similar lines was Andrew Blowers' account (1984) of the relationship between a Bedfordshire brickworks and the local county council in the 1970s and early 1980s. Blowers, who was himself actively involved in the events he describes as leader of the Labour group on the council and a member of the planning committee, argues that while a pluralist model makes sense of the initial period in the 1970s when air pollution became a political issue and environmental groups were successful in obstructing London Brick's application for further planning permission, it cannot explain the company's eventual victory. In the early 1980s, the initial objection by the planning authority was overturned and this came about, Blowers suggests, because of the changed economic climate which led to the employment opportunities offered by the company (if planning permission was granted) taking precedence over the alleviation of air pollution. Again, Lindblom's assertion, that business has a privileged position because of the economic clout it can exercise, would seem to have some relevance here. In this case, unlike the Crenson study, it did not prevent the issue of air pollution reaching the political agenda but it did determine how the decision was resolved. On the other hand, the privileged position of London Brick only seemed to come into play at a particular (downward) point in the economic cycle. This suggests that the position of business is weaker, as one would perhaps expect, during a period of relative economic prosperity, particularly if we add to the equation the assumption that at such times post-material values become more pronounced (see Chapter 2).

There is also a case for saying that a class bias is central to the British planning system. Superficially at least, the land-use planning system would seem to be consistent with a pluralist analysis. It allows for extensive participation and consultation, and, in the event of a public inquiry, the final decision rests with a neutral inspector and, ultimately, with a democratically elected minister. We have already observed, however, that the more affluent and professional classes are more able to take advantage of the system (see Sandbach, 1980, pp. 132–3). Furthermore, developers have far more resources at their disposal compared to local or national environmental groups. The classic examples here were the nuclear inquiries (Windscale, 1977; Sizewell B, 1983–5; and Dounreay, 1986) where, despite marshalling their evidence effectively, the environmental lobby simply could not compete with the resources brought to bear by British Nuclear Fuels. BNF spent £750 000 in the Windscale Inquiry and £20 million in Sizewell B (Rydin, 1993, p. 236). It is not just hard cash that hinders the environmental case. The quasi-legal character of inquiries also militates against local groups making their voices heard (*ibid.* pp. 236–7).

Such arguments would seem to suggest that the system works in favour of particular groups within society, allowing Pepper (1986, pp. 180–1) to claim: 'At best the agencies and processes which are supposed to be neutral arbiters are heavily weighted towards and manipulated by the owners of capital. Through them, environmental protesters are put at immediate disadvantage when they try to make their cases in "democratic" forums.' Here, environmental reformers could benefit from taking on board the radical ecocentric insistence on the relationship between environmental protection and political organization. The argument, put most articulately by Dryzek (1990, chs 6 and 7), that effective resolutions to environmental problems must be accompanied by the democratization of policy-making is extremely relevant and is a point we shall come back to in the concluding chapter.

On the other hand, it should be said that while accepting that planning procedures are far from perfect, it is not clear that environmental conflicts can be reduced to class-based politics. For one thing, the building of nuclear power stations is a source of employment and, as we saw in Chapter 7, one of the reasons for the relative weakness of the anti-nuclear movement in Britain is the local support that has emerged for such developments. Furthermore, the opponents of development are themselves often (although by no means always) relatively affluent people adopting NIMBY attitudes. In this context, it might be said that at least some development is more beneficial to the working class and is prevented by those seeking to protect their relatively high standard of living (Blowers, 1984, pp. 264–5).

Policy networks

One of the central claims of pluralism is that no one interest dominates decision-making in all areas of policy. It would indeed seem to be the case that policy-making in modern Liberal democracies has become increasingly sectorized with a different set of actors operating within each sector. We have seen, for instance, that in the environmental sphere, there is an acute problem of integrating an environmental perspective across a range of policy areas each centring on a distinct set of government departments and agencies. To take account of this policy sectorization, political scientists have developed the concept of policy networks which would seem to have considerable explanatory potential at least as far as environmental policy is concerned (Marsh and Rhodes, 1992; Smith, 1993).

Although there has been some dispute about the actual character of policy networks, a useful continuum has been developed based on the degree of openness, complexity and competition (Marsh and Rhodes, 1992, p. 249). At one end is the so-called policy community characterized by regular interaction between a small number of long-standing participants, usually a government agency and certain privileged interest groups, operating within a considerable degree of consensus and closed off both from competing groups not accepting the shared values and from other policy networks. At the other is the so-called issue network, characterized by a considerable degree of openness and flux, with a variety of competing groups able to gain access (Heclo, 1978). These are ideal types and most policy networks will lie between the two extremes. Different networks may, of course, be placed at different positions on the spectrum.

Once a particular network has been characterized, it is then possible to explain why it exists, and what the policy-output consequences and the prospects for change are. Even if we accept that policy is made in distinct networks, a view that has been disputed (Hogwood, 1987), it still does not necessarily result in confirmation of the pluralist position. For, if within a particular policy sphere, one set of unified interests continually gets its own way we are entitled to draw attention to it as an example of a structure which is more in accord with a corporatist or élitist model. Further, if, in the case of environmental policy, the objectives of the environmental lobby are continually thwarted by opponents within the different policy networks impacting on the environment, we are surely also entitled to say that there is a power bloc obstructing change. If this is so, we are able both to pinpoint the reason for the gap between the is and the ought, and to raise questions about the democratic legitimacy of this situation.

Political parties and the environment

One possible determinant of environmental policy is the political party. An examination of the role of political parties is particularly important in Britain where they are peculiarly central to government and politics. Elections are contests between candidates chosen and financed by the parties, Parliament is organized along party lines and, of course, single-party governments, supported by a majority in the House of Commons, are the norm (Garner and Kelly, 1993, ch.1).

It is certainly the case that since the late 1970s, and particularly after 1983, all of the main parties in Britain have become increasingly interested in the environment (Carter, 1992a, pp. 121–7; Robinson, 1992, pp. 25–6). The catalyst was Thatcher's dramatic volte-face in the late 1980s when she replaced her previous hostility to environmentalism with a keen enthusiasm (Flynn and Lowe, 1992, p. 12; McCormick, 1991, pp. 58–60). The Conservative government's subsequent actions were to firmly place the environment on the political agenda, and the other parties were forced to respond, doing so by producing lengthy policy statements of their own (the Liberal Democrat document was called *What Price our Planet?* and Labour's was titled *An Earthly Chance*) (Carter, 1992a, pp. 126–30). Despite this, however, it also needs to be explained why the environment has not figured prominently in any general election. In the 1992 and 1997 election campaigns, despite the Liberal Democrats' attempt to turn it into a major election issue, both they and the Green Party were submerged as the big parties fought the campaign on the traditional economic issues (Carter, 1992b; Carter, 1997, pp. 192–205). Thus, 'the sacred cow of economic growth has not been sacrificed' by the main parties and, indeed, remains their 'clarion call' (Robinson, 1992, p. 217).

Pressure and intentional explanations

Establishing the major parties' growing interest in environmental issues is one thing, explaining its significance is much more difficult. Robinson (1992) usefully suggests two opposing viewpoints here which we can utilize. One the one hand, the greening of the major parties can be explained in terms of a reaction to external pressure applied by the environmental movement, the media, public opinion, and supranational institutions. This is consistent with an 'economic' approach to political competition which sees parties merely as vote maximizers who, just like producers in a market economy, will shift their position in order to attract votes (Downs, 1959). Alternatively, we can explain the existence and character of the major parties' environmental commitments in terms of 'internal factors relating to the actions and positions of key personalities, and to ideological developments within the parties' (Robinson, 1992, p. 4).

Establishing the validity of the internal explanation is important because it would reveal political parties as an important determinant of environmental policy. Such a position, however, is difficult to prove. Thatcher's 'conversion', for instance, might be explained in terms of her recognition, as a trained scientist, that severe environmental problems existed. Equally, external pressures, in particular the threat posed by the Green Party – particularly after their success in the 1989 European elections – and the Green credentials of the new Liberal Democratic Party might be regarded as significant (Flynn and Lowe, 1989, pp. 25–9).

Within all of the mainstream British parties, there have been internal factors encouraging or limiting the development of environmental policy. The Liberal Democrats and, prior to 1988, the Liberal Party have usually been regarded as the greenest of the mainstream parties. The old Liberal Party was particularly oriented towards environmental concerns, with a radical faction constantly seeking to move the party towards an anti-nuclear position and an emphasis on local community politics where the quality of the environment was often a issue. The radicals, however, were constrained by the party's more restrained leadership and, after the merger with the newly-formed Social Democratic Party in the early 1980s, the Liberals' inherent radicalism was submerged (Garner and Kelly, 1993, ch.8).

The Liberal Democrats remain 'greener' than the other two main parties. In the 1997 election campaign, for example, the party's environmental promises included a larger cut in CO_2 emissions than the other parties (30 per cent to Labour's 20 per cent and the Conservative's 10 per cent), and more radical proposals, including a carbon tax on fossil fuels and a radical overhaul of car excise duty, to achieve this target (*Independent*, 2 April 1992). Two factors go a long way towards explaining this greater environmental awareness. First, the party's distance from power means that it can recommend the adoption of radical environmental policies knowing full well it is not going to have the responsibility of carrying them out after an election. The two main parties, on the other hand, have to ensure they maximize their vote and this encourages a bland and vague approach to policy in case important sections of the electorate are offended. Secondly, unlike the Labour and Conservative parties, the Liberals have never been associated with economic interests which may place constraints on the development of environmental policy. These two points are related in the sense that the electoral dominance of the two parties is a product of their links with important social and economic groupings. It also leads to the conclusion that there is an environmental case for electoral reform, involving the introduction of a system of proportional representation and the state funding of political parties.

Internal factors have also been present in the Conservative party. In the first place, it might be suggested that there are natural limits to the stringency of environmental policy within the Conservative party. Clearly, the party's financial reliance on business interests including energy suppliers, farmers and house builders has obvious, if unquantifiable, consequences for environmental policy (Robinson, 1992, pp. 193–7). Within the boundaries of these constraints, the ideological balance within the party can determine the nature of environmental policy. In the 1980s, for instance, debates about Conservative countryside policy was fought out on ideological grounds. Throughout much of the 1980s, the traditional paternalistic or 'wet' tradition within the Conservative party stood opposed to the free-market rational individualism represented by Thatcher, and this traditional Conservatism was invoked by those interested in protecting Britain's national heritage from the ravages of urban expansion. This was the main influence, for instance, behind the Conservative Ecology Group set up in 1977, and the conservation credentials claimed for the Conservatives from such 'wet' factions as the Bow Group (Flynn and Lowe, 1992, p. 20).

This ideological division is graphically illustrated if one compares Nicholas Ridley with Chris Patten, successive Environment Secretaries in the 1980s. While Nicholas Ridley's ideological guide had been Adam Smith, Chris Patten invoked Edmund Burke, the father-figure of traditional Toryism, in his first conference speech as Environment Secretary. Burke, he argued, reminds 'us of our duties as trustees for the nation, as good stewards of its traditions, its values and its riches' (Flynn and Lowe, 1992, p. 31). William Waldegrave, the Minister for Environment, Countryside and Planning up to the 1987 election, also came from the wet wing of the Tory Party, and the Burkean language in his comment that 'Most environmental disasters are the result of grand plans that somebody has imposed on others' is unmistakable (Porritt and Winner, 1988, p. 83).

In general, then, it might be argued that at times when the free-market brand of Conservatism, with its antipathy to the regulatory framework most environmentalists regard as essential, plays a leading role in the party, environmental policy is likely, at best, to be neglected. This may well explain why the environment has not played a significant role in the Hague-led Conservative party. Indeed, the one noticeable foray into environmental policy by the Conservatives under Hague has been an attack on Labour's transport policy (see Chapter 8). Significantly, this focused, not on the need for greater investment on public transport or the failure of the Labour government to implement the transport White Paper in full, but rather on the issue of the personal freedom of motorists and the need to pander to their interests.

The internal and external constraints operating on the Labour party are particularly significant, not only because the party now forms the government, but also because there have been important ideological developments within the party which, potentially at least, have an impact on the nature of environmental policy. Labour's environmentalism has traditionally been filtered through its ideological and organizational commitment to the urban working class. This has coloured the party's environmental policy focus. Thus, the desire to improve the quality of life for the ordinary working-class family and the disadvantaged in general – through cleaning up the inner cities, promoting public transport, improving access to the countryside and tackling Third World debt – has traditionally been paramount (see, for instance, Labour Party, 1992, pp. 21, 22, 27).

While there is a strong case for saying that the objectives of environmental policy are not necessarily anathema to the interests of the working class (see Chapter 10), Labour's traditional organizational and financial ties with the trade unions has been a potentially crucial, limiting factor on the development of a comprehensive environmental programme. Within the party, there has been a presumption in favour of maximizing economic growth in order to maximize employment opportunities, and an assumption that this goal will be hindered by the adoption of more stringent environmental policy. In the past, at least, there was a general suspicion in the Labour party and the labour movement, that environmentalism was a preoccupation of the middle classes (Carter, 1992a, pp. 119–20) and this explains, for instance, why the Socialist Environment and Resources Association, formed within the party in 1973, has had relatively little impact.

Important changes to Labour's organization and ideology in the past decade arguably make the party much more likely to embrace environmentalism. The party is no longer (or at least nowhere near as) organizationally dependent on the organized working class and is largely shorn of, not only any last vestiges of the 'hard' left variety of socialism, but also, under Blair, of even moderate social democracy. As a consequence, the potential for the adoption of environmental protection as a key part of Labour's programme would seem to be significantly enhanced. Anthony Giddens (1998, pp. 54–68), regarded as one of Blair's most important intellectual influences, certainly regards ecology as one of the key pillars of the so-called 'Third Way' that Labour is apparently gravitating towards.

We saw in Chapter 8 that the Labour government's environmental record so far leaves something to be desired. One of the problems may relate to an important characteristic of Labour's new ruling ideology. It is clear that the Labour government has perceived there to be conflict between its pursuit of economic growth, low levels of taxation and personal prosperity and autonomy on the one hand, and protecting the environment on the other. This perception would be problematic for any government but it is particularly so for one that prides itself on pursuing the politics of inclusivity and the end of adversarial conflict. In practice, as we have seen, the Labour government has not been prepared to sacrifice the needs of business and the economy when, as in the case of a radical transport policy or more far-reaching green taxes, these needs are perceived to be threatened. Rather, as Roger Cowe (*Guardian*, 4 November 1998) points out, the government's, ultimately unrealistic, desire to build consensus means they are 'obsessed with consideration and consultation'.

The adoption by the Labour government of ecological modernization principles would enable at least a partial reconciliation between the objectives of environmental protection on the one hand, and on the other, the belief in consensus and inclusion enshrined in the Third Way. Economic growth does not necessarily have to be sacrificed for the sake of a cleaner, safer environment and, as a result, environmentalists can sit round the same table as economic interests with the hope that a common set of policies will emerge. To some degree, and particularly in transport policy, decision-makers have grasped this idea. It would be wrong, however, to assume that there are no economic costs, at least in the short term, to be borne in return for the protection of the environment (see Chapter 10). Some sectors of the economy, and particularly those involved in the use of fossil-fuel combustion, cannot be left untouched if internationally agreed targets are to be met. Moreover, tackling transport problems will surely necessitate considerable disruption to many of Blair's natural supporters in 'Middle England'. Whether the Labour government is prepared to ride out the protests that are bound to be the result of effective environmental policies is a moot point, although evidence that failure to act may also be a vote loser (see Chapter 8) may produce the necessary impetus.

Although it is difficult to demonstrate conclusively, it is surely the case that the ideological disposition of political parties, and the individuals within them, plays a relatively small part in an explanation of the nature of environmental policy and politics. External influences, provided by organized interests, the electorate in general, and international treaty obligations would seem to be more important. Indeed, political parties have looked increasingly redundant, failing to be the focus of environmental concerns and unable to offer resolutions to these concerns.

The limited role played by parties is revealed below in our two case studies, on agricultural and countryside policy and on pollution control policy. For now, it should be noted that a classic instance of the irrelevance of parties was the live exports controversy which erupted in 1995. This issue emerged as a result of protest action which did not involve any of the parties. Moreover, no party has been able to implement its policy goal in the face of the growing supranational authority of the EU. Thus, as the Conservative government of the time regularly, and perhaps conveniently, explained, it is illegal under European law for Britain to ban the live export of animals to other member states just as it would be to prohibit the import of veal meat produced by the crate system which is banned in Britain. Despite Labour's claim that it would ban live exports, it has, since being elected in 1997, conformed to the reality of policy-making by merely calling for a European-wide ban, an objective which will be very difficult to achieve.

Agriculture, the countryside and the environment

The first of the case studies in this chapter considers the relationship between agriculture and the environment. It is hardly surprising that a study of countryside politics should focus on agriculture. Over 80 per cent of rural land is managed by farmers and, as McCormick (1991, p. 69) points out, the threat to the countryside by modern farming methods is 'the most controversial and widely debated environmental issue of the post-war years – and perhaps of the twentieth century'. We shall consider the issue in four parts corresponding to four specific questions:

(1) Why is agriculture an important environmental issue?
(2) How has agricultural policy traditionally been made, and by whom?
(3) Why have the effects of agriculture on the countryside become a political issue?
(4) How far has the respective influence of the National Farmers Union (NFU) and the environmental lobby changed?

The consequences of modern farming

Agriculture has become an environmental issue partly at least because there are now more people concerned about the condition of the countryside who do not have a vested interest in exploiting it. Without the objectively measured increase in environmental problems in the countryside, though, it is unlikely there would be a political dimension to the issue. When we consider the damage that has been done, farming methods are held to be largely responsible.

The countryside has been exploited for centuries and very little true wilderness in Britain now remains. For some deep ecologists this, by itself, would lead to condemnation even though human impacts need not necessarily be destructive. The problem is that much modern farming *is* environmentally destructive. These modern agricultural practices date back to the Second World War when the development of intensive farming methods coincided with the desire for Britain to be self-sufficient in food. From this point on, the priority for most farmers was to increase the output and efficiency of their land. This was done with remarkable success. Prior to the Second World War, nearly 70 per cent of Britain's food requirements were imported. By the mid-1980s, the position had been reversed with about two-thirds being provided by British agriculture to a population which had grown from 47 to 56 million (Lowe *et al.*, 1986, p. 21). This increase has involved arable and livestock farming. To take the latter case, increasing use of 'factory' farming methods has massively increased the availability, and therefore reduced the price, of meat and poultry, turning some products, such as chicken, from a luxury item into a common purchase.

The environmental costs of this increase in efficiency, though, were considerable (Body, 1982; Shoard, 1982; Lowe *et al.*, 1986 pp. 64–80). The result was a disregard for ecologically important parts of the countryside such as hedgerows, forests and wetlands. Between 1946 and 1974, 25 per cent of the hedgerows in England and Wales disappeared and in a similar period half of the ancient woodlands in Britain were felled (McCormick, 1991, p. 71). Likewise, in the past 30 years 95 per cent of lowland herb-rich grassland, 60 per cent of lowland heaths, and 50 per cent of lowland fens and marshes have been lost (Lowe *et al.*, 1986, p. 55).

Not only has this damage meant a loss of amenity for people to enjoy, it has also resulted in the extinction of a number of plant and animal species. Otters, badgers and bats have become so rare that it required legislation to protect them. Moreover, the application of fertilisers and pesticides used to increase yields, has had consequences not only for animal and plant species but also for human health (Carson, 1962). Finally, quite apart from the animal welfare implications of factory farming, the water requirements of intensive units can be phenomenal and, in addition, serious waste disposal problems occur, particularly as increasing specialization has resulted in the separation of arable and livestock farming and therefore, for many farming units, a natural outlet for animal wastes has been lost (Mason and Singer, 1990).

The agricultural policy community

So how has this come about? Why were farmers allowed to damage the countryside with so few apparent controls on their activities? In attempting to answer these questions, the policy network concept would appear to have a great deal of relevance. Indeed, agriculture would appear to be a classic case of a policy community with the NFU having a privileged position within the Ministry of Agriculture, Fisheries and Food (MAFF). This dated back to the period immediately after the Second World War. The Agriculture Act 1947 gave the NFU a statutory right to be consulted over agricultural policy and, since then, the NFU has had a very close relationship with the MAFF so that the department's and the farmers' interests have become indivisible.

As Smith (1990, pp. 124–31) points out, the ideological glue which held the agricultural policy community together was based on a shared belief in agricultural expansion – that farmers should be encouraged to produce as much as possible as efficiently as possible. Any group of people, such as environmentalists or consumers, who did not concur with this were excluded from the policy community. So, for much of the post-war period, the environmental effects of intensive agriculture were excluded from the primary decision-making arena – a classic case of non-decision-making.

Indeed, for a large part of the post-war period, the expansionist ideology was so widely held that very few voices could be raised against it. Originally, there was a widespread assumption that farmers were the guardians of the countryside, so that there was no thought of protecting the countryside against them (Lowe *et al.*, 1986, pp. 15–17). Crucially, though, even when the opposition to intensive farming became more vocal, not least through the activities of environmental groups, the closed agricultural policy community still prevented those issues from being part of the mainstream policy agenda. In a classic instance of this, only the RSPB of the conservation community had any input into the Wildlife and Countryside Bill before it was put before Parliament in the early 1980s. Even the state conservation agencies were excluded. Numerous amendments were proposed during the bill's passage through Parliament but none of the successful amendments was opposed by the NFU (Cox and Lowe, 1983).

The assumption in the policy network literature is that the type of network will influence policy outcomes. In the case of the agricultural policy community, this would seem to be the case, with policies serving the NFU's interests predominating. Thus, the Agriculture Act 1947 introduced a system of guaranteed prices for all major agricultural produce. Since then, the farming industry has had subsidies far in excess of any other industry. Britain's entry into the European Union in 1973 changed the nature of the way these subsidies were paid to farmers – from consumers through guaranteed prices to taxpayers through direct subsidies – but the existence of substantial financial assistance remained (Smith, 1990, pp. 147–7). In addition, as we saw in Chapter 8, the Town and Country Planning Act 1947 largely excluded farming from planning controls and farms were also exempt from paying rates.

Some scholars (Self and Storing, 1962; Wilson, 1977) have argued that the NFU's influence can be exaggerated, that the resources they can muster are not exceptional and that close contact with the MAFF produces the risk of imprisonment so that the NFU becomes fearful of openly criticizing government policy in case the MAFF turns against them. The evidence, however, does not really support this position and it might be the case that an analysis along these lines misunderstands the reasons why the NFU was incorporated into government in the first place. Two alternative explanations are pertinent here. The first is more consistent with pluralist methodology in that it suggests that the NFU became powerful because of the resources it could muster. These would include factors such as its all-inclusive membership, its considerable financial resources enabling it to lobby institutions in Britain and the European Union, its links with land-owning interests in Parliament and the executive, the agricultural vote it can call upon, and support from elsewhere in the industrial and financial community (Lowe *et al.*, 1986, pp. 85–91; Grant, 1989, p. 102, 139; Smith, 1990, pp. 147–77). This resource-based explanation is pluralist not because the role of the NFU fits the pluralist model: indeed, exactly the opposite since the NFU/MAFF relationship is corporatist or élitist in nature (Cox *et al.*, 1987). Rather, it is pluralist because it assigns to government a largely passive role. Government, according to this view, is merely reacting to the power of a particular group.

The alternative explanation emphasizes not the resources of the NFU but the historical, ideological and structural context within which the government and the NFU were operating. According to this view (associated, most notably, with Smith, 1990), the state itself played a positive role. Here, it is argued that the NFU was invited into government because it was functional for the government to do so. During and after the Second World War the major problem facing the government was the need to ensure a regular supply of food. This was the structural factor which established 'the limits of possibility' (Smith, 1990, p. 38) within which governments and pressure groups had to operate. Once established in government, the dominant position of the NFU was maintained by the institutional framework which excluded other interests from emerging and the ideological promotion of expansionism which prevented alternative scenarios being raised. Thus, while the first resource-based explanation suggests that the close relationship between MAFF and the NFU is the *cause* of the adopted policy, the second, state autonomy, explanation suggests that the close relationship is the *result* of the policy adopted.

The politicization of agriculture

In recent years, the effects of intensive agriculture on the countryside has become a political issue and, as a result, the agricultural policy community is under threat. Why has this come about? There are a number of possible reasons. First, there is the increasing financial costs of agricultural policy which British people have become much more aware of since Britain joined the EU, and the negotiations over the Common Agricultural Policy have taken place in a glare of publicity (Grant, 1989, p. 146). The emergency action to introduce milk quotas in the 1980s to forestall the bankruptcy of the EU is regarded here as a particularly crucial event (Lowe *et al.*, 1986, p. 52). Coupled with this was the free-market ideology of the Thatcher governments. The privileged position of the farmers was bound to sit uneasily with the antipathy of these governments both to subsidies and to corporatist relationships with interest groups. As a result, the NFU became much more vulnerable (Grant, 1989, p. 146). Added to these factors were the campaigns of environmental groups which disseminated information about the environmental and animal welfare consequences of intensive agriculture.

Greater public awareness of, and concern for, the deteriorating state of the countryside was also a product of social and demographic changes (Grant, 1989, p. 147; McCormick, 1991, pp. 82–3). In particular, the mass ownership of cars has made the countryside more accessible. Further, many people have moved to rural areas taking advantage of changing work patterns and, as a result, farmers are being out-numbered by middle-class escapees from the cities who have no vested interest in farming and many of whom may indeed be concerned about the protection of the countryside.

As a consequence, it should be seen that the original problem – lack of self-sufficiency in food – which gave rise to the policy community has disappeared. Food shortages have become a thing of the past and the expansionary ethos has been successfully challenged. By the 1980s, new problems – food safety, healthy foods, animal welfare and the effects of intensive agriculture on the environment – had emerged to which government had to find solutions. Far from being a solution to the problem, the farmers had become a problem themselves (Smith, 1990, p. 212).

The break-up of the policy community?

How far, then, has the agricultural policy community begun to fragment, as one would expect if we accept the state-autonomy explanation for its formation? The short answer here is: not very much. Clearly, the very fact that the impact of agriculture on the environment has become a political issue demonstrates some weakening of the NFU's position. Farmers have lost their ideological privilege and, because of this, they may be in danger of losing their institutional privilege (Smith, 1990, p. 190). As a result, the NFU has to engage in much more conventional pressure group lobbying in order to justify its activities to a more sceptical public. The NFU now emphasizes conservation as an important concern of farmers (Lowe *et al.*, 1986, p. 102). Likewise, MAFF has at least to appear to reconcile the interests of farmers with the interests of consumers, those concerned about the countryside and the welfare of animals. Compare, for instance, the 1975 White Paper *Food From Our Own Resources* (HMSO, 1975) which emphasizes the expansionist ethos and has little to say about the environment, with MAFF's *Our Farming Future* (MAFF, 1991) which devotes almost half of its 40 pages to countryside, animal welfare and food consumer issues.

Legislation seeking to intervene in farming activities has also been forthcoming. The Agricultural (Miscellaneous Provisions) Act 1968 dealt with farm animal welfare, and the Wildlife and Countryside Act 1981, the Agricultural Acts 1986 and 1988 and parts of the Environmental Protection Act 1990 focused on countryside issues. There is no doubt, too, that environmental groups now find it easier to get their voices heard within MAFF (Smith, 1990, pp. 200–1). Some conservation groups, such as the RSNC and the RSPB, were formally incorporated within the MAFF in the Farming and Wildlife Advisory Group founded in 1969 where, together with Ministry and NFU officials, conservation issues are discussed (Grant, 1989, p. 149; McCormick, 1991, p. 81).

Despite all this, however, it is doubtful if the changes represent the death throes of the MAFF/NFU policy community. One only has to contrast MAFF's responses to the Bovine Spongiform Encephalopathy (BSE) crisis with the live exports issue to realize that the department's primary motivation is to support the producers rather than protesters or consumers. Not only was BSE probably caused by the cost-cutting which is fundamental to intensive agriculture (the use of cheap recycled sheep protein in cattle feed is widely thought to be the most likely cause), but it is also alleged that MAFF did its utmost to suppress or belittle any evidence which hinted at the possibility of a link between BSE and the human equivalent Creutzfeldt Jakob Disease (*Guardian*, 23 March 1996; Gellatley, 1996, pp. 187–93). Moreover, MAFF and the British government went to considerable lengths to get the EU beef ban reversed, seemingly irrespective of the dangers faced by consuming BSE-infected products. By contrast, MAFF passively accepted that it could not take unilateral action to ban the export of live animals from Britain, despite the opposition of the British public to the practice, and despite the legal case which, however unlikely to succeed, could have been made.

It is true that while environmental groups have greater access to the MAFF now, the NFU's access is still quantitatively and qualitatively greater. Furthermore, it tends to be the moderate conservation groups who have been co-opted and not the more radical groups such as Friends of the Earth. The intention here is to give the impression that MAFF is listening to conservation interests. To some extent this may be true, but the more moderate conservation groups are less likely to challenge the prevailing ideology within the policy community – that there is no fundamental incompatibility between conservation and intensive agriculture and that farmers should not be penalized for good conservation practice.

The legislation supports this interpretation since the measures introduced have essentially protected the interests of farmers. Thus, with the exception of the banning of stubble burning introduced in the Environmental Protection Act 1990, all of the conservation schemes are voluntary and allow for compensation to be paid to farmers for carrying them out (Smith, 1990, p. 193; Pearce *et al.*, 1993, pp. 119–20). The Wildlife and Countryside Act, for instance, does not plug the planning gap as conservationists wanted (see Chapter 8). Likewise, the Environmentally Sensitive Areas scheme, introduced in the Agriculture Act 1988, pays farmers for managing landscapes for environmental purposes rather than maximizing food production (Young, 1993, p. 62). In addition, it is hardly a sacrifice for farmers not to use land for food production when subsidies for production are diminishing anyway. In 1994 alone, English farmers were paid £124 million to allow their land to remain idle under the EU set-aside scheme (*Guardian*, 23 May 1994).

It has often been claimed that Britain's membership of the EU has had the effect of opening up policy-making to a wider array of interests, thereby reducing the power of policy community actors. While this may be the case in some policy areas, it is not the case in agriculture. In the EU, agribusiness interests are extremely influential, and the policy community label is equally applicable to the European, as it is to the British level (Garner, 1998, pp. 158–60). It is indeed an irony that during the BSE crisis the EU was looked on by some as the champion of the consumer. In reality, though, the EU has traditionally been the leading promoter of intensive methods which, as we saw, was the primary cause of the outbreak in the first place. The Common Agricultural Policy, with its system of massive financial incentives for intensive production, remains a symbol of the dominance of agribusiness interests within the EU.

What we have, then, is a classic case of a policy community protecting its interests by managing change in directions which it can control. By itself, this represents some weakening of the MAFF/NFU relationship. The biggest threat to the policy community, however, is the creation of a new institutional framework which removes significant powers from MAFF. The politicization of agricultural policy, resulting primarily from the BSE outbreak, other food safety issues and the live exports controversy, may herald such an institutional shake-up. One important proposal is the Labour government's planned new independent Food Standards Agency with powers to enforce hygiene standards from the 'plough to the plate', which is to report to the Department of Health rather than MAFF (*Guardian*, 28 January 1999). Another is the potentially more important proposal, presently under consideration, to create a separate ministry for rural affairs with responsibilities taken from both MAFF and DETR (*Independent*, 30 July 1999).

Agriculture is not the only constituent element of countryside politics. Another element is hunting. Hunting has traditionally been regarded as a moral issue to which a free vote in the Commons can be attached, and the absence of direct executive involvement would seem to indicate the existence of an issue network where a wide variety of groups compete on a reasonably equal footing for the ear of MPs. Traditionally, though, the hunting lobby, consisting mainly of the British Field Sports Society, has had enormous influence within Parliament. Many MPs and Peers are landowners themselves, and others represent rural constituencies where the support for hunting among farmers is crucial.

In addition, pro-hunters have skilfully adapted their strategy to maximum effect. First, they cleverly changed the focus of their argument, from justifying hunting on the grounds that it is an effective means of pest control (an argument popular with many farmers) to justifying it on conservation grounds – that without the hunting community there would be no incentive for landowners to preserve the habitats which the hunted animals rely on. This switch causes problems for the anti-hunting lobby because it potentially divides the animal welfarists and rightists from many environmentalists whose ideological emphasis is on preserving endangered species and not protecting individual animals against cruelty (see Chapter 3). The very existence of a group calling itself the British Society for Shooting and Conservation is totally incomprehensible from an animal protection perspective but is less so from an environmentalist one.

Secondly, faced with increasing public opposition to hunting, and the election of a seemingly unsympathetic Labour government in 1997, the British Field Sports Society, originally formed in 1930, has sought to mobilize wider rural support for hunting. It played a leading role in the creation of the so-called Countryside Alliance which has organized two major demonstrations in London. The second of these, on March 1 1998, attracted an estimated quarter of a million people. While the demonstration was supposedly concerned with a whole range of rural issues such as farming, the right to roam, the development of the green belt and the state of the rural infrastructure, opposition to Michael Foster's anti-hunting bill (see below) was the primary objective (*Guardian*, 21 February 1998; 28 February 1998; 2 March 1998). As Janet George, the Countryside Alliance's then press office commented, the strategy was to 'wrap hunting up in the wider rural fabric. Because everyone loves the country and hates hunting' (*Guardian*, 13 August 1998). A Labour government has also enabled the hunting community to emphasize what they see as the illiberalism of an interventionist policy designed to infringe the rights of a persecuted minority (Young, 1999).

There are signs, though, that the previously strong position of the hunting lobby is waning. Fewer MPs now represent rural constituencies and those that still do have to take into account the large number of new middle-class rural dwellers who are more hostile to hunting. As a result, recent votes on the issue have been much closer. For the first time, in March 1995, an anti-hunting bill was given a second reading in the Commons although it was later emasculated in the committee stage. The Labour party promised a free vote on an anti-hunting bill in its 1997 general election manifesto, and Foster, a Labour backbencher, duly introduced such a bill in November 1997. Despite receiving a massive 260 vote majority at second reading (a vote which followed party lines), the bill subsequently, and predictably, ran out of time as a result of filibustering by its opponents. The issue came to prominence again in July 1999, when Blair, allegedly as a result of the Labour party's poor showing in the European Parliament elections and the perceived need to offer something for the party's core supporters, announced that the government would, after all, provide time for an anti-hunting bill as soon as possible. Given the support for such a bill among Labour backbenchers, and reforms to the House of Lords which removes some of the most fervent supporters of hunting, one would expect such a bill to become law.

The politics of pollution

We saw in Chapter 8 that pollution control policy in Britain has gone through a period of change in recent years. The purpose of this section is to seek to explain why changes have occurred and, equally importantly, to explain their limitations. Providing the context here is the notion of integrated pollution control (IPC) in its internal and external manifestations (see Chapter 8). It is widely recognized that IPC provides the most appropriate mechanism for environmental protection and, as such, it provides a benchmark against which we can measure the depth of the changes introduced.

Explaining pollution control reform

When examining the changing nature of British pollution control policy, it becomes apparent that a number of factors were at work. In the case of the creation of Her Majesty's Inspectorate of Pollution (HMIP), for instance, an important determining factor was the role of ideas. For example, the case for integrating the various pollution control agencies had been advocated in the 1970s by the Royal Commission on Environmental Pollution and, by the 1980s, the necessity for internal integration had become the accepted view among environmental experts (Weale, 1992, pp. 96–7, 102–3). This would support the 'policy discourse idiom' identified by Weale since it suggests that problem-solving and the role of research, argument and discussion was, in this case, an important determinant of policy outcomes.

Equally, the creation of HMIP and the move towards IPC can be explained by reference to the policy network approach. As Smith (1997) documents, the original air pollution regime was 'the domain of a policy community of inspectors and operators' (*ibid.*, p. 207), which was subject to external pressures from an emerging issue network in the 1970s and 1980s consisting, in part, of the environmental movement and the RCEP. Government, though, took a long time to be persuaded of the value of an integrated inspectorate. Indeed, it took the British government six years even to reply to the RCEP's proposal, and then it was rejected (Weale, 1992, p. 104). The RCEP called again in 1986 for the creation of HMIP but its eventual creation in 1987 owed more to additional factors.

Most importantly, there was pressure from the EU which, as we saw in Chapter 6, had enhanced authority in environmental matters from the mid-1980s. An additional factor was the embarrassment caused by the revelations that the existing regulatory machinery had failed to prevent discharges from Sellafield; also important was the support for the reform from the Environment Minister William Waldegrave (*ibid.*, p. 105). It was the environmental movement which drew attention to the problems at Sellafield but, other than that, it played little part in this central environmental reform.

Likewise, the environmental movement was only partly responsible for the creation of the NRA. Indeed, the debate about water pollution in general, and the quality of Britain's drinking water in particular, came about largely as an unintended consequence of water privatization (McCormick, 1991, pp. 96–8). In the original White Paper published in 1986, the government announced its intention of transferring environmental responsibilities from the Regional Water Authorities to the private water companies. The European Commission was made aware of this plan, largely due to the scrutiny of the CPRE, and informed the government that it was illegal under EU law to place pollution controls into the hands of private companies. As a result, the White Paper was discarded and, after the 1987 election, plans to create an independent NRA with pollution control responsibilities were announced (Richardson, 1992).

The privatization of electricity had environmental consequences too. As a result of pressure from the environmental lobby, it led, first, to the creation of a new Office of Electricity Regulation (OFFER) which has responsibilities for environmental oversight of the electricity supply industry (McCormick, 1991, p. 102). More importantly, electricity privatization has had severe consequences for the nuclear industry which for the vast majority of environmentalists has been a positive step.

In the early days of the first Thatcher government, there was considerable commitment to nuclear power and the plan was to build one reactor per year for a ten-year period beginning in 1982. This was not just a technical matter but reflected a political strategy designed to weaken the position of the miners who had all but brought down Heath's Conservative administration in 1974 (Greenaway *et al.*, 1992, p. 130). By the end of the decade, however, this programme had been scrapped and there are now no future plans to build nuclear power stations in Britain.

It is difficult to pinpoint exactly why this turnaround occurred. The atmospheric and political fall-out from the Chernobyl disaster was clearly one factor and nuclear power was obviously opposed vigorously by the anti-nuclear movement (who did their best to publicize safety problems in the nuclear industry) and also (not so predictably) by the House of Commons Select Committee on Energy (Greenaway *et al.*, 1992, p. 130). Thus, Michael Saward (1992) traces the development of the nuclear energy policy network and claims that it was transformed in the mid to late 1970s from a closed policy community, dominated by the Atomic Energy Authority and its scientific experts, into a much more open issue network in which the competing manufacturers of nuclear reactors, the Central Electricity Generating Board and the anti-nuclear movement played an important role.

There is a suspicion that Saward's interpretation accords too much influence to the anti-nuclear lobby here. In general terms, as we intimated in Chapter 7, the anti-nuclear movement in Britain has been relatively weak. Saward (1992, pp. 93–5) bases much of his claim on the participation of the anti-nuclear movement in the Windscale, Sizewell and Hinkley Point public inquiries. As Ward (1983) indicates, though, Friends of the Earth, who were heavily involved in the inquiries, could not compete with the resources of the nuclear industry (see above) and, despite marshalling a good case, their claims were largely ignored in the final reports. As for Chernobyl, the nuclear industry could, somewhat plausibly, explain it away by focusing on particular problems in the Soviet Union while denying claims about the inherent safety problems of nuclear power in general.

At the most, then, we can say that the anti-nuclear lobby has raised the issue of nuclear safety in particular and the wider issue of energy needs in general, thereby putting the nuclear industry and the government, which for so long had supported it, on the defensive. It still remains the case, however, that, ultimately, the role played by electricity privatization (coupled with the emergence of gas as a preferred source of relatively clean energy) has been a crucial factor in weakening the case for nuclear power. The major effect of privatization was to reveal the true costs of nuclear power (and the alternatives) by subjecting it to what, for true Thatcherites at least, is the real test of value – the market.

The original intention, outlined in the 1988 White Paper on electricity privatization, was to divide the publicly-owned Central Electricity Generating Board generators between two private companies – PowerGen and National Power – with the latter being given responsibility for nuclear power generation. It soon became apparent, however, that nuclear power, when thoroughly accounted for separately from other sources of energy, was much more expensive than previously thought. Realizing that nuclear power constituted a poor investment, it was eventually removed from the public sale and put into the hands of a new public body, Nuclear Electric. British Energy (a company created after the merger of Nuclear Electric and Scottish Nuclear) was eventually privatized in 1996, but it only has responsibility for the eight most modern plants, with the older Magnox reactors (together with a significant proportion of the reprocessing and decommissioning costs of the eight plants sold off) remaining in public hands (see *Sunday Times*, 17 December 1995; *Guardian*, 10 June 1996; 20 May, 11 June 1998). As Greenaway (1992, p. 138) points out, then, 'Both the public and its representatives in Parliament play a peripheral role in the story of nuclear power'.

Explaining the limits to British pollution control

So far, we have attempted to explain why changes occurred in the character of pollution politics in Britain. In Chapter 8, we also noted that these changes have only gone so far down the road towards IPC. One possible explanation for this focuses on policy styles and, in particular, on the disjointed way in which decisions tend to be made in all Liberal democracies and Britain in particular (Richardson, 1982). This theory of 'disjointed incrementalism' or, as Charles Lindblom (1959) famously calls it, the 'science of muddling through', holds that the normal pattern of policy-making involves regular small and cautious adjustments to the existing framework. These adjustments are often accompanied by a low level of understanding and are more often than not reactions to events that unexpectedly arise.

For Lindblom, at least at the time, this was not just a description of the way in which policy was usually made, it was also in his view a prescription about how it *ought* to be made. Certainly, it is consistent with the pluralist framework, emphasizing the diffuse nature of power with a wide variety of actors able to influence policy outcomes leading to an outcome which satisfies at least some of the demands of the participants. In terms of pollution control policy, however, it arguably militates against the integrated approach which most environmentalists regard as crucial (Dryzek, 1990, pp. 70,122–3; Weale, 1992, p. 100). For this to be achieved, a synoptic approach to policy-making is necessary, one which takes large steps, is proactive and involves a high degree of understanding.

An alternative explanation focuses not on the style of decision-making but on the power of those interests who oppose IPC. This power-based form of explanation, it seems to me, is more able to explain the fact that only limited steps have been taken towards IPC. As with agricultural policy, the notion of policy communities is particularly useful here. From this perspective, it can be argued that the major obstacle to integration is the power exercised by economic interests occupying a privileged status within environmental decision-making arenas.

Both internal and external integration has been constrained by the influence of economic interests operating in policy communities. In the case of internal integration, the delays in the creation of HMIP was undoubtedly partly a product of the suspicions industrial interests harboured over its precise powers. Moreover, as Smith (1997) demonstrates, HMIP abandoned the arm's-length regulatory approach it initially adopted (see Chapter 8) because industry was unwilling to provide the information and expertize such a policy required. The return 'to site-specific flexibility and the participation of operators in standard setting' that occurred, therefore, meant that the members of the original policy community retained control of the regulatory process (*ibid.*, pp. 210–11). Finally, there were 'intense Whitehall battles over' the 'size, structure and remit' of the Environment Agency (Connelly and Smith, 1999, p. 259). In particular, as we saw in Chapter 8, at the behest of the DTI and the Treasury the EA has to explicitly justify its actions through a cost-benefit analysis which may result in pollution authorizations being more lenient they than might otherwise have been (*Guardian*, 10 October 1994).

In the case of external integration, as we saw in Chapter 8, the key White Paper *This Common Inheritance* was far less stringent than Chris Patten wanted, in particular failing to include his preference for a carbon tax, and a convincing explanation for this is the pressure applied by development-oriented interests. To establish the exact nature of the relationships between economic interests and state actors requires detailed research for each policy network within which they are involved. We have already considered in some detail, for instance, the influence exercised by the NFU within the agricultural policy community. Equally, if not more privileged are the constituent parts of the road lobby (originally within the Department of Transport and now within DETR), the power generators and suppliers (within the energy policy community) and a variety of business interests (operating within the DTI).

The policy community centring on transport is a particularly pertinent area for study. For, despite the politicization of the transport issue – as the environmental consequences of more cars, more heavy goods vehicles and more roads have become well known – the policy emphasis of the transport policy community (at least until recently) did not change. All forms of road traffic have grown as governments in the 1980s neglected public transport in favour of major road-building programmes (Pearce *et al.*, 1993, pp. 150–1). As recently as May 1989, the government announced a more than doubling of expenditure on road building, from £5 billion to £12 billion, over a ten year period (Ward, 1990, pp. 232–3). This policy emphasis is clearly related to the influence of the road lobby. One only has to examine its constituent elements to recognize how formidable this lobby is. The umbrella organization is the British Road Federation, within which is contained the motor industry, the bus operators, road haulage firms, motorists' organizations, the road construction industry and the oil industry (Hamer, 1974; Pearce, 1993, p. 191).

The recent cuts in the road-building programme do reflect a weakening of the roads lobby and, in part, a victory for the various parts of the environmental lobby, which has campaigned and protested hard on this issue in recent years. Other factors have been equally if not more important, though. The government's desire to cut public spending is one. In addition, a growing consensus, accepted at least partly even by the road lobby, has emerged that building new roads is not the answer to road congestion and other methods, such as road pricing and greater resources being directed at maintaining existing roads, need to be considered (*Guardian*, 26 October 1994; O'Riordan and Jordan, 1995, p. 243). This would seem to be an example of the importance of ideas in explaining policy outcomes, and therefore provides some additional support for Weale's 'policy discourse idiom'.

* * *

Our analysis of environmental policy-making in general, and agricultural and pollution control policy-making in particular, indicates that explaining the nature of the environmental crisis and attempted resolutions of it involves above all a consideration of competing interests and the exercise of power. What is most revealing is that the evidence does not seem to support a pluralist interpretation of policy-making. Not only do the internal politics of political parties appear to play a relatively insignificant role in determining the character of environmental policy, but the environmental lobby too does not seem to have had much of an impact. Since 1945, agricultural policy has been made by a small group of actors seeking to defend the interests of farmers. Even when the environmental effects of agriculture became a political issue and a matter of public concern, environmentalists still failed to break into the policy community and, although attempts have been made to take account of the environmental damage agriculture has done to the countryside, policy is still geared to protecting the interests of farmers. In the case of pollution politics, the moves towards IPC did not occur primarily as a result of the environmental lobby's influence. Rather, change came about as a result of a variety of other factors – the technical case for IPC, the dynamic role played by state actors, the unintended by-products of government policy and the impact of the EU. Likewise, the limited character of the move towards IPC can best be explained in terms of the veto exercised by powerful economic interests and their departmental allies.

The caveat we ought to introduce here is that it is by no means clear whether the decision-making structures described in our account of countryside and pollution politics can be said to challenge notions of democratic legitimacy. It might be argued, for instance, that more stringent controls on the sources of environmental problems would result in outcomes which most people would find difficult to swallow, and governments, when making environmental policy, are taking account of this as much as the pressure applied by vested economic interests. According to this argument, then, until the public are prepared to sacrifice their cars and use public transport, pay more for food and for products manufactured by companies shackled by more stringent environmental legislation, the present patchy response to environmental problems will continue. For environmentalists, and particularly those of a radical disposition, this suggests that the route to a sustainable society must not merely focus on traditional lobbying in the hope that governments will take their ideas on board. Rather, it must explore a wide variety of strategies designed to overcome the wider societal obstacles to change. These we consider in the final chapter.

Further reading

General studies of policy-making approaches which might be applied to environmental issues are Greenaway *et al.* (1992), Ham and Hill (1984), Richardson (1982), Marsh and Rhodes (1992), Dunleavy and O'Leary (1987), Lukes (1974) and Smith (1993). There have been a number of attempts to apply theories of decision-making to environmental issues. The most important are Matthew Crenson's study of pollution (1971), Blowers' (1984) study of a Bedfordshire brickworks, Sandbach's (1980) attempt to apply Marxist theory and Smith's (1997) account of the politics of integrated pollution control. Weale (1992) also seeks to apply a number of theories in his study of pollution politics.

The reaction of the main parties to the rise of environmentalism is dealt with admirably in Robinson (1992). On the Labour party, see Carter (1992a). On the Conservatives, see McCormick (1991) and Flynn and Lowe (1992). On the agricultural policy case study, McCormick (1991) and Grant (1989) provide useful introductions. Essential book-length studies are Lowe *et al.* (1986) and Smith (1990). Essential to a study of pollution politics is Weale (1992) and Smith (1997). McCormick (1991) also has a useful chapter which goes beyond mere institutional description. E. Richardson (1992) provides details about the political context surrounding the creation of the NRA and Greenaway (1992), Saward (1992) and Ward (1983) are useful sources for the politics of nuclear power. Transport policy is covered in Hamer (1974) although this is now somewhat dated. See Pearce (1993) for more up-to-date information.

10
Conclusion: Towards a Sustainable Future

It is clear that the environmental record of governments across the world falls hopelessly short of radical Green objectives, and arguably, at least in public, environmentalists should stop expecting governments to achieve them. As Barry (1999, p. 27) points out: 'The problem with deep ecology is that it brings green politics into irresolvable conflict with settled convictions, giving it a "fundamentalist" complexion which is a hindrance to convincing non-believers to support its political aims'. However, it should also be recognized that until relatively recently, many countries, including Britain, were governed according to a cornucopian ideology, which accepted the validity of unrestrained economic growth and an instrumental attitude towards the exploitation of the natural world, and was naively optimistic about science and technology's ability to come up with solutions to environmental problems (Pearce, 1993, pp. 18–19). It is a mark of how far the world has come that, in rhetoric at least, few governments would now subscribe to this ideology.

Environmentalism in one country: faltering steps

We have suggested that Britain, like many other developed countries, has begun to adopt a more sustainable approach, but that the steps taken so far have been short and faltering. Indeed, even from a very lightish green perspective, Britain's environmental record leaves a great deal to be desired. Whether because of the limitations of incremental decision-making, the power of economic interests or the perceived electoral consequences of more stringent environmental

regulations, the governmental machinery in Britain remains fragmented and the main policy focus is reactive and voluntary,
persuasion and compromise being preferred to compulsion. Making
policy as a reaction to environmental problems is particularly
constraining. It leads to a reliance on conclusive scientific evidence
– described by Porritt and Winner (1988, p. 144) as the '"Where is the
pile of bodies?" school of environmental management' – which is
rarely forthcoming.

   Of course, the picture is not all bad. As John Gray (1993, p. 155)
points out: 'If time travel were possible, a visitor from an earlier
period of industrial society ... would most likely be astonished by the
cleanliness and integrity of our environment, which early industrialism ravaged'. The key message of this book is that environmental
protection largely depends on agreements reached at a supranational
level. Here, we saw that British decision-makers have, at the very
least, been reconciled to the enhanced environmental role of the EU,
and have ensured that Britain was a key participant in the negotiations leading to the, largely successful, treaty to reduce the production
and use of ozone-destroying chemicals, and the Rio agreement which
started the process of tackling global warming and maintaining
biological diversity.

   Achieving the goals set at such international gatherings depends to
a large degree on the extent to which environmental objectives are
integrated into general policy-making. We saw, however, that the
institutional structure for internal integration in Britain took a long
time to emerge and the resources and powers available to HMIP and
its successor the Environment Agency have been limited. Furthermore, there is little evidence that the attempts to integrate environmental policy externally have been much more than cosmetic. At the
very least, departmental secrecy makes it difficult to assess how far
environmental costs and benefits have been taken into account in
policy development. The examples of agriculture and transport policy
do not suggest that much has changed. In the former case, the
continuing exclusion of agriculture from planning controls and the
lack of protection accorded to designated areas has resulted in the
'continual erosion of the UK's biological diversity' (Pearce, 1993,
p. 113). The environmental damage caused by present transport
policies is even more stark, and this can only continue while there
remains a bias in favour of private cars and road freight and against
public transport.

Ecological modernization, sustainability and democracy

The reliance on conclusive scientific evidence of the causes and consequences of environmental problems is predicated, of course, on the assumption that action to protect the environment will have negative economic consequences. In this context, the theory of ecological modernization seems to offer an important way forward since its central argument, as we saw in Chapter 3, is that conflict between economic and environmental objectives is illusory. We have seen that a key obstacle to effective environmental policy-making is the lack of integration across a range of governmental activities. This, it was suggested, is primarily a product of departmental policy communities within which development-oriented interests have a dominating role. It might be thought that an acceptance of the ecological modernization ideology would remove the problem since if economic interests accepted that tougher environmental measures were not going to damage them, they have no reason to object. Of course, it is not as simple as that. The argument is that, *overall*, the economy will not suffer from the adoption of sustainable policies. Some individual industries, however, will suffer from such policies, at least in the short term, and some of these (those, for instance, with a vested interest in the continuation of existing transport policy) are well placed within the decision-making machinery to fight their corner.

This situation clearly requires an effective political strategy, something which environmentalists have not been particularly good at developing. There has tended to be an assumption that once the public are informed about the seriousness of environmental problems, they will eventually come round to accepting the need to act (Dobson, 1990, pp. 130–1). Such an assumption is naive, not least because it fails to recognize the power relations central to an understanding of decision-making. Environmental reformism along the lines suggested, therefore, would seem to require substantial changes to the values and institutions of existing liberal democratic regimes (see the versions in Dryzek, 1997, pp. 143–50; and Barry, 1999, pp. 118–37).

A strategy to promote ecological modernization requires a number of elements (see Pearce, 1993, pp. 12–13). First, industries that profit from environmental regulation should be encouraged, and the fact, that the benefits of environmental regulation are economic in nature as well as connected with a general improvement in the quality of life, should be promoted. More importantly, perhaps, the dominance of certain vested economic interests, which do stand to lose out through stricter regulatory regimes, can only be countered if there is a climate favourably inclined towards environmental protection. It is here that environmental reformists can learn from the radical Green claim that environmentalism goes hand in hand with an active citizenry (see Dryzek, 1990). Thus, the move towards a sustainable future requires more than a top-down government response but also a major cultural transformation. Following Dobson (1990, ch.4), we can discuss the possible dimensions of this transformation in terms of lifestyle, communities and class.

Lifestyle changes

One seemingly effective way of promoting active environmentally-aware citizens is in terms of encouraging individuals to adopt sustainable lifestyles. This can be in terms of our behaviour as consumers, as investors, as commuters and in the way we treat the animals we directly encounter. Encouraging green consumerism has been the major component of this strategy. Conserving energy and water through actions such as better insulation and a more discriminate use of the toilet flush, is one form of this, as is the recycling of products bought – a practice which some local authorities have done a great deal to promote. The use of lead-free petrol, a product given a favourable tax regime, is another example as are the local exchange trading systems (LETS) which now exist in over 100 cities in Britain (*Guardian*, 19 November 1997).

Most attention, though, has been placed on the green dimension of regular shopping. Superficially, at least, this strategy – 'shopping for a better world' as it has been called (Porritt and Winner, 1988, p. 193) – has been very successful. In the late 1980s, there was a huge increase in products claiming to be environmentally friendly – CFC-free aerosols, cruelty-free cosmetics, minimal and biodegradable packaging, 'dolphin-friendly' tuna and free-range eggs – as companies sought to compete with each other to satisfy the new green demands of the consumer. A book directing consumers to the best green products became a best seller (Elkington and Hailes, 1988), and retailers specializing in providing such products, most notably the Body Shop and Beauty Without Cruelty, massively increased their market shares. Industry has more generally recognized the marketability of environmental concern: witness Shell's 'Better Britain' campaign and the Heinz's 'Guardians of the Countryside' programme. Industry too has contributed significantly to the funds of environmental groups, with 20 per cent of the WWF's income in 1987 coming from corporate contributions (Simpson, 1990, p. 31).

The main advantage of the lifestyle strategy in general, and Green consumerism in particular, is that it focuses on what individuals can do, thereby encouraging participation which in turn may lead to an increased consciousness about wider environmental issues. Without wishing to belittle the importance of the consumer strategy, however, it should be noted that there are a number of problems with it. In the first place, the 'Green' claims made by some manufacturers are dubious and it is difficult, at least without legislative intervention, for consumers to interpret the competing claims made. This lack of information provides an incentive for manufacturers to make misleading, or just bogus, statements. An infamous example here is the claim made by many manufacturers of washing-up liquids that their products are 'phosphate-free'. True enough, but what they forgot to add was that phosphates had never been added to washing-up liquids in the first place! (Yearley, 1992, p. 98). Similarly, what is a 'cruelty-free' cosmetic can vary from one manufacturer to another. For some companies, it is justifiable to make this claim if they themselves have not done any animal testing (even if the manufacturers of the ingredients have). For others, the label can be applied if products have not been tested for a five-year period. This problem can and has started to be overcome with the introduction of eco-labelling schemes, but this requires governmental action, which may not be forthcoming.

Secondly, it is doubtful if enough consumers can be persuaded to adopt Green lifestyles, particularly if not doing so is more convenient and/or less expensive. It is a strategy that appeals in particular to those who can afford to engage in substantial consumption. For those who cannot, the options are often limited to buying cheaper but more environmentally damaging products or, in other cases, not consuming at all. In both cases, the individual is locked out of the strategy completely, thus undermining its educative and consciousness-raising purpose. There is also a classic collective-action problem here in that the environmental benefits of green consumerism will be available to all, irrespective of whether any one individual seeks to participate in achieving them. Thirdly, the consumer strategy focuses on the finished product and not the nature of the whole production process. Important environmental questions, such as how the product was manufactured and how it is transported to retailers, are thereby avoided (Yearley, 1992, p. 101).

While the consumer-oriented strategy is acceptable from a reformist perspective, from a dark Green perspective, of course, it is inadequate because even though it encourages green growth, it is growth all the same. Radical Greens emphasize the need to reduce consumption, whether it is environmentally-friendly consumption or not (Dobson, 1990, pp. 141–2). It is argued, therefore, that Greens would do far better to focus their attention on the spiritual dimension of what it is to be Green rather than seeking to promote 'grubby' materialism whether or not it has a green tint to it (Young, 1993, pp. 105–6).

Communities and class

Another strategy to increase environmental consciousness is based on the creation of alternative communities working outside of the dominant industrial and materialist paradigm (Dobson, 1990, pp. 147–51). These communities, in the words of the German Green Rudolf Bahro, are 'liberated from the industrial system ... liberated from nuclear weapons and from supermarkets. What we are talking about is a new social formation and a different civilisation' (quoted in Dobson, 1990, p. 146). Examples here would include self-sufficiency farms, some squats and workers' co-operatives and, in particular, mention should be made of the Centre for Alternative Technology at Machynlleth in Wales, the Findhorn community in Scotland and the Earth Centre educational project in South Yorkshire.

We can applaud the existence of such communities, but as an agent of social and political change they are surely very limited. Their success in this context will depend upon how far they are able to persuade others to adopt similar lifestyles. Here, they have been a complete failure. This is partly because such communities tend to be 'outsiders' rather than 'oppositional' in that they represent opting out of society as opposed to deliberately setting themselves in a confrontational sense against the norms and values of industrial society (Dobson, 1990, p. 147). Whatever the reason, while laudable by themselves, they do not represent a convincing strategy for achieving a widespread raising of environmental consciousness.

A more promising strategy is the identification of a particular group or class in society who can be mobilized on behalf of environmental objectives. We saw earlier that the assumption of a simple link between a greater awareness of environmental problems and a desire to have them dealt with is inadequate. David Pepper (1986, pp. 215–25) describes this as education *about* the environment in that it is a science-based response to the environmental predicament. Equally fallacious for Pepper is what he calls education *from* the environment. Although this approach introduces values to the debate by asking why we ought to protect the environment – something which, as Chapter 3 of this volume revealed, Greens have not been shy about – it is still inadequate because it assumes that environmental problems represent a common threat against which we should all pull together. The point here then is that environmentalists regularly fail to take into account the socio-political realities of environmentalism. It is important therefore, to identify and mobilize a collectivity in society who are more likely to lead a cultural transformation in favour of environmental protection.

For Pepper, writing from a socialist perspective, it is the class-based power structure which has to be tackled if environmental degradation is to be reversed. The logic of this argument is that the working class are the obvious agents of any social transformation, not least because there is much evidence to suggest that 'the processes of environmental degradation almost always impact most devastatingly on the poorest and least powerful communities, both within countries and globally' (Benton, 1997, p. 43; see also Huby, 1998; and Monbiot, 1999). By contrast, the middle classes are not affected by environmental degradation to the same degree as the less affluent. As we have seen, the more affluent are able to escape from the grime of the inner cities and, when encamped in more salubrious locations, they can exercise considerable political clout through the party system and, moreover, are articulate enough to influence the planning system. As a result, they can ensure that their immediate environment remains reasonably good.

The converse view is that, precisely because of this political leverage and the desire for a protected environment, the middle class or at least a section of it, might be an effective green agency. This claim is reinforced by Inglehart's claim, discussed in Chapter 2, that post-material values are a product of affluence; further evidence is the Green Party's support which, as we saw in Chapter 7, tends to be drawn from the more affluent sections of society. As Porritt (1984,

p. 116) points out: 'the post-industrial revolution is likely to be pioneered by middle-class people ... such people not only have more chance of working out where their own *genuine* self-interest lies, but they also have the flexibility and security to act upon such insights'. On the other hand, the middle classes have, despite Hirsch's identification of the positional economy, benefited from (sometimes unsustainable) economic growth. Moreover, their adoption of a suburban or rural lifestyle is essentially shallow since it is based upon material convenience and, in so far as the middle classes do engage in environmental campaigns, it is more often than not designed to protect their own privileges against encroachment by others.

If the middle class is not a particularly likely agent for environmental change, does the working class fair any better? Arguably not. For one thing, in Britain at least, the working class has fragmented in recent years and it can no longer be regarded as an homogeneous block. The new, more-affluent sections of the working class were seduced by the materialistic promises by the Thatcher governments in the 1980s, and are therefore unlikely to be a vehicle for environmental protection (Garner and Kelly, 1993, ch.9). Furthermore, the organized labour movement in Britain has always been 'labourist' in character, concerned, despite the strain of ethical socialism associated with such luminaries as William Morris and R.H. Tawney, with gaining for itself a larger slice of the capitalist pie rather than seeking to change the acquisitive and materialist nature of the system (Garner and Kelly, 1993, ch.6). It was noted in Chapter 9 that the trade unions have often provided a constraint on Labour adopting more radical environmental policies and, while their role in the Labour party has been reduced, they still represent a significant obstacle to a Labour prime minister intent on carrying out more radical environmental policies.

Two other social groupings suggest themselves as Green agents. The first is the women's movement. As we saw in Chapter 4, there has been an attempt to develop a feminist strand of ecology and part of this is concerned with explaining why women might be more likely than men to identify with environmental concerns. To talk about women as a homogenous group, though, is problematic since, by virtue of their class position, they experience different life-chances. Furthermore, as Chapter 2 revealed, the empirical evidence suggests that affluence and occupation, rather than gender, provide important influences upon the adoption of post-material values. On the other hand, support for environmental reforms is not dependent on holding such values and the life position of women (as, for instance, carers of children) may make them more likely than men to support some environmental initiatives, such as those relating to transport policy.

The final possibility is the unemployed, a social grouping which Andrew Dobson (1990, pp. 163–9) suggests offers great potential as an agent of environmentalism (a view also advanced by Gorz, 1985). This is a group, he argues, which is 'not only relatively "disengaged"' from industrial society but which 'also is already inclined towards the foundations of sustainable living'. Thus, in so far as 'the capacity of any group in society for Green social change' is determined by its 'distance from the process of consumption and the degree of permanence of this isolation', the unemployed would seem to fit the bill. In particular, the long-term unemployed have little stake in society and their predicament can be explained by the limits to growth, in that unemployment is at least partly a product of the increasing price of scarce resources necessitating cuts in labour costs.

There are problems with according to the unemployed a role as the agents of social change, some of which are recognized by Dobson himself (1990, pp. 167–9). Crucially, there is little evidence that the unemployed perceive their role as agents of such a change. The Green movement could attempt to make them more aware of their marginalized status and how it relates to the environmental crisis but, in the past, it has been notoriously difficult to mobilize the unemployed to campaign against their predicament. This is associated with the point that there is no necessary link between the marginalization of the unemployed and their rejection of the social and political institutions of unsustainable industrial society. Indeed, British political history demonstrates that it was the non-unionized part of the working class, those at the bottom of the social scale working in casual jobs or not at all, who were more likely to be deferential towards the established order. This is why, historians argue, the Labour party was not greatly concerned, before 1918, to achieve universal suffrage, since it would introduce into the electorate many of the poorest members of society who were more likely to vote Conservative (Pugh, 1982, ch.7).

The point, then, is that marginalization is just as likely, without the introduction of any evidence to the contrary, to lead to a desire for inclusion rather than the development of an oppositional mentality. Moreover, it is doubtful if the number of unemployed, and the poor in general, constitute a large enough group to make a significant impact. The Labour party, for instance, recognized that it needed to focus on attracting the votes of the better-off sections of the working class as well as middle-class white-collar workers, if it was to win a general election again. Finally, although there is evidence that the unemployed have played a significant role in environmental protest, there is a problem of causation. It seems likely that it is not unemployment which leads to the development of an environmental consciousness, but a concern for the environment and a wish to pursue a life untainted by material excesses, that makes unemployment attractive (Taylor, 1999).

Global change

The cultural transformation required to break the hold that certain economic interests have over environmental policy-making has a long way to go. The promotion of radical Green values which challenge the dominant materialism of industrial society obviously have an important role to play in the development of a greater environmental consciousness. Equally if not more important is the ecological modernization claim that environmental protection and economic advancement can co-exist. Pursuing such an approach may not answer all of the questions posed by radical Greens but it is politically realistic and might just be enough to provide a viable future for the human species and the natural environment we depend upon.

Pursuing environmental protection in the developed world is also a prerequisite for persuading the developing world to act. Without the participation of the latter in a global effort, there is little chance of a sustainable future. While the peoples of the rich North may be prepared to accept some economic sacrifice in return for environmental protection, in the developing world, as Brundtland recognized, only a strategy which promotes the long-term economic benefits of sustainability will succeed, and, in the interests of justice, deserves to succeed.

This book has, above all, sought to demonstrate the dichotomy between, on the one hand, the widespread recognition of environmental problems and an environmental movement bristling with both scientific expertize and moral indignation at the present state of affairs and, on the other, the very slow progress that has been made towards changing people's attitudes and persuading public authorities to introduce more sustainable environmental measures. The spark that seemed to ignite widespread concern for the environment in the mid to late 1980s has failed to keep the fire alight as we enter a new century, and yet the problems remain acute. As an important political issue and a subject worthy of study by natural and social scientists, however, the environment is here to stay. Those who despair at the absence of fundamental change should remember the old adage that the perfect should not be allowed to be the enemy of the good.

Bibliography

Abramovitz, J. (1997) 'Valuing nature's services' in L.R. Brown *et al.* (eds) *State of the World 1997* (New York: Norton) pp. 95–114.

Adams, C. (1990) *The Sexual Politics of Meat* (New York: Continuum).

Allaby, M. (1986) *Green Facts* (London: Hamlyn).

Ashford, N. (1989) 'Market liberalism and the environment: A response to Hay', *Politics* 9 (1), pp. 43–4.

Atkinson, A. (1991) *Principles of Political Ecology* (London: Belhaven Press).

Attfield, R. (1983) *The Ethics of Environmental Concern* (Oxford: Blackwells).

Axelrod, A. and Phillips, C. (1993) *The Environmentalists: A Biographical Dictionary from the 17th Century to the Present* (New York: Facts on File Inc.).

Bachrach, P. (1969) *The Theory of Democratic Elitism: A Critique* (London: University of London).

Bachrach, P. and Baratz, M. (1962) 'The two faces of power', *American Political Science Review*, 56, pp. 947–52.

Bahro, R. (1986) *Building the Green Movement* (London: Heretic).

Baker, S. (1997) 'The evolution of European Union environmental policy: From growth to sustainable development?' in S. Baker, M. Kousis, D. Richardson and S. Young (eds), *The Politics of Sustainable Development: Theory, Policy and Practice Within the European Union* (London: Routledge) pp. 91–106.

Baker, S., Kousis, M, Richardson, D. and Young, S. (eds) (1997) *The Politics of Sustainable Development: Theory, Policy and Practice Within the European Union* (London: Routledge).

Barry, J. (1994) 'The limits of the shallow and the deep: Green politics, philosophy and praxis', *Environmental Politics*, 3 (3), pp. 369–94.

Barry, J. (1999) *Rethinking Green Politics: Nature, Virtue and Progress* (London: Sage).

Beck, U. (1992) *Risk Society: Towards a New Modernity* (London: Sage).

Beckerman, W. (1974) *In Defence of Economic Growth* (London: Cape).

Beckerman, W. (1992) 'Global warming and international action: An economic perspective' in A. Hurrell and B. Kingsbury (eds), *The International Politics of the Environment* (Oxford: Clarendon Press) pp. 253–89.

Beckerman, W. (1995) *Small is Stupid: Blowing the Whistle on the Greens* (London: Duckworth).

Beder, S., Brown, P. and Vidal, J. (1997), 'Who killed Kyoto', *Guardian*, October 29.

Benedick, R. (1991) *Ozone Diplomacy: New Directions in Safeguarding the Planet* (Cambridge: Mass: Harvard University Press).

Bennie, L. (1998) 'Brent Spar, Atlantic oil and Greenpeace' in F.F. Ridley and G. Jordan (eds), *Protest Politics: Cause Groups and Campaigns* (Oxford: Oxford University Press), pp. 89–102.

Benton, T. (1993) *Natural Relations: Ecology, Animal Rights and Social Justice* (London: Verso).

Benton, T. (1997) 'Beyond left and right? Ecological politics, capitalism and modernity' in M. Jacobs, *Greening the Millennium: The New Politics of the Environment* (Oxford: Blackwell), pp. 34–46.

Blowers, A. (1984) *Something in the Air: Corporate Power and the Environment* (London: Harper and Row).

Blowers, A. (1987) 'Transition or transformation? Environmental policy under Thatcher', *Public Administration*, 65, pp. 227–94.

Boardman, R. (1981) *International Organisations and the Conservation of Nature* (London: Macmillan).

Body, R. (1982) Agriculture: The Triumph and the Share (London: Maurice Temple Smith).

Boehmer-Christiansen, S. (1996) 'The international research enterprise and global environmental change: Climate change policy as a research process' in J. Vogler and M. Imber (eds), *The Environment and International Relations* (London: Routledge), pp. 171–95.

Bomberg, E. (1998) *Green Parties and Politics in the European Union* (London: Routledge).

Bookchin, M. (1962) *Our Synthetic Environment* (New York: Knopf).

Bookchin, M. (1971) *Post Scarcity Anarchism* (Berkeley: Ramparts).

Boons, F. (1992) 'Product-oriented environmental policy and networks: Ecological aspects of economic internationalism', *Environmental Politics* 1 (4), pp. 84–105.

Booth, N. (1994) *How Soon is Now? The Truth about the Ozone Layer* (Hemel Hempstead: Simon & Schuster).

Bostock, S. (1993) *Zoos and Animal Rights: the ethics of keeping animals* (London: Routledge).

Bradbeer, J. (1994) 'Environmental policy: past and future agendas' in P. Savage, R. Atkinson, and L. Robins (eds), *Public Policy in Britain* (London: Macmillan), pp. 116–36.

Bramwell, A. (1989) *Ecology in the Twentieth Century* (New Haven: Yale University Press).

Brenton, T. (1994) *The Greening of Machiavelli: The Evolution of International Environmental Politics* (London: Earthscan).

Bretherton, C. (1996) 'Gender and environmental change: Are women the key to safeguarding the planet?' in J. Vogler and M. Imber (eds), *The Environment and International Relations* (London: Routledge), pp. 99–119.

Brown, L.R. *et al.* (eds) (1997) *State of the World 1997* (New York: Norton).

Brown, L.R. *et al.* (eds) (1998) *State of the World 1998* (New York: Norton).

Brown, L.R. (1998) 'The future of growth' in L.R. Brown *et al.* (eds), *State of the World 1998* (New York: Norton), pp. 3–20.

Brown, L.R. *et al.* (eds) (1999) *State of the World 1999* (New York: Norton).

Brown, P. (1997) 'Man's greed fuels global bonfire', *Guardian*, December 17.

Brown, P. (1998) 'Setting the world ablaze', *Guardian*, March 20.

Brown, P. and Cowe, R. (1997) 'For sale: The right not to use this factory', *Guardian*, December 11.

Callaghan, J. (1990) 'The greening of British politics', *Contemporary Record*, 4 (2), pp. 2–5.

Callicott, J.B. (1995) 'Animal Liberation: A Triangular Affair' in R. Elliot (ed), *Environmental Ethics* (Oxford: Oxford University Press), pp. 29–59.

Carson, R. (1962) *Silent Spring* (New York: Fawcett Crest).

Carter, A. (1993) 'Towards a green political theory' in A. Dobson and P. Lucardie (eds) *The Politics of Nature: Explorations in Green Political Theory* (London: Routledge).

Carter, N. (1992a) 'The "greening" of Labour' in M.J. Smith, and J. Spear (eds), *The Changing Labour Party* (London: Routledge).

Carter, N. (1992b) 'Whatever happened to the environment? The British general election of 1992' *Environmental Politics*, 1 (3), pp. 442–8.

Carter, N. (1997) 'Prospects: The parties and the environment in the UK' in M. Jacobs, *Greening the Millennium: The New Politics of the Environment* (Oxford: Blackwell), pp. 192–205.

Carter N. and Lowe, P. (1995) The Establishment of a cross-sector Environment Agency in Gray, T. (ed.) UK Environmental Policy in the 1990s (Basingstoke: Macmillan) pp. 38–56.

Chatterjee, P. and Finger, M. (1994) *The Earth Brokers* (London: Routledge).

Cherfas, J. (1988) *The Hunting of the Whale* (London:The Bodley Head).

Clarke, P. and Linzey, A. (eds) (1990) *Political Theory and Animal Rights* (London: Pluto Press).

Clayton, P.H. (1998) *Connection on the Ice: Environmental Ethics in Theory and Practice* (Philadephia: Temple University Press).

Collard, A. (1988) *Rape of the Wild* (London:The Women's Press).

Collier, U. (1997) 'Sustainability, subsidiarity and deregulation: New directions in EU environmental policy', *Environmental Politics*, 2 (6), pp. 1–23.

Collins, K. and Earnshaw, D. (1992) 'The implementation and enforcement of European Community environment legislation' *Environmental Politics*, 1 (4), pp. 213–49.

Connelly, J. and Smith, G. (1999) *Politics and the Environment: From Theory to Practice* (London: Routledge).

Connolly, J. and Norris, P. (1991) 'Making green policy: A guide to the politics of the environment', *Talking Politics*, 4 (2), pp. 96–100.

Cooper, M. E. (1987) *An Introduction to Animal Law* (London: Academic Press).

Cotgrove, S. and Duff, A. (1980) 'Environmentalism, middle class radicalism and politics', *Sociological Review*, 28, pp. 333–51.

Cotgrove, S. and Duff, A. (1981) 'Environmentalism, values and social change', *British Journal of Sociology*, 32, pp. 92–110.

Cox, G. and Lowe, P. (1983) 'Countryside politics: goodbye to goodwill', *Political Quarterly*, 54, pp. 268–82.

Cox, G, Lowe, P. and Winter, M. (1987) 'Farmers and the state: A crisis for corporatism', *Political Quarterly*, 58, pp. 73–81.

Crace, J. (1997) 'Smoke gets in your eyes', *Guardian*, October 14.

Crenson, M. A. (1971) *The Unpolitics of Air Pollution* (Baltimore: The Johns Hopkins Press).

Curtice, J. (1989) 'The 1989 European elections: Protest or green tide? *Electoral Studies,* 8, pp. 217–30.

Dahl, R. (1961) *Who Governs?* (New Haven: Yale University Press).

Dahl, R. (1971) *Polyarchy* (New Haven: Yale University Press).

Dasgupta, P. (1989) 'Exhaustible resources' in L. Friday, and R. Laskey (eds) *The Fragile Environment* (Cambridge: Cambridge University Press), pp. 107–26.

Dearlove, J. and Saunders, P. (1984) *Introduction to British Politics: Analysing a Capitalist Democracy* (Cambridge: Polity Press).

Department of the Environment (1990) *This Common Inheritance: Britain's Environmental Strategy,* Cmnd1200 (London: HMSO).

Department of the Environment (1994) *Sustainable Development: The UK Strategy* (London: HMSO).

Department of Environment, Transport and the Regions (1998) *A New Deal for Transport: Better for Everyone* (London: HMSO).

Dickson, L and McCulloch, A. (1996) 'Shell, the Brent Spar and Greenpeace: A Doomed Tryst?, *Environmental Politics,* 5, (1), Spring 1996, pp. 122–9.

Dobson, A. (1990) *Green Political Thought* (London: Unwin Hyman).

Dobson, A. (ed.) (1991) *The Green Reader* (London: Andre Deutsch).

Dobson, A. (1995) *Green Political Thought,* 2nd edn (London: Unwin Hyman).

Dobson, A. (1996) 'Democratising green theory: Preconditions and principles' in B. Doherty and M. de Geus (eds), *Democracy and Green Political Thought* (London: Routledge), pp. 132–48.

Dobson, A. (1998) *Justice and the Environment: Conceptions of Environmental Sustainability and Theories of Distributive Justice* (Oxford: Oxford University Press).

Dobson, A. and Lucardie P. (eds) (1993) *The Politics of Nature: Explorations in Green Political Theory* (London: Routledge).

Dodds, F. (ed.) (1989) *Into the 21st Century* (London: Green Print).

Dodds, F. and Bigg, T. (1995) *The United Nations Commission on Sustainable Development: Three Years Since the Rio Summit* (London: UNED-UK).

Doherty, B. (1992a) 'The autumn 1991 conference of the UK Green party', *Environmental Politics,* 1 (2), pp. 292–8.

Doherty, B. (1992b) 'The fundi-realo controversy: An analysis of four European Green parties', *Environmental Politics,* 1 (1), pp. 95–120.

Doherty, B. (1998) 'Opposition to road building' in F.F. Ridley and G. Jordan (eds), *Protest Politics: Cause Groups and Campaigns* (Oxford: Oxford University Press), pp. 62–75.

Doherty, B. (1999) 'Paving the way: The rise of direct action against road building and the changing character of British environmentalism', *Political Studies,* 42, pp. 275–91.

Doherty, B. and de Geus, M. (eds) (1996) *Democracy and Green Political Thought* (London: Routledge).

Downs, A. (1959) *An Economic Theory of Democracy* (New York: Harper & Row).

Dryzek, J. (1987) *Rational Ecology* (Oxford: Blackwells).

Dryzek, J. (1990) *Discursive Democracy: Politics, Policy and Political Science* (Cambridge: Cambridge University Press).

Dryzek, J. (1997) *The Politics of the Earth: Environmental Discourses* (Oxford: Oxford University Press).

Dryzek, J. and Schlosberg, D. (eds) (1998) *Debating the Earth: The Environmental Politics Reader* (Oxford: Oxford University Press).

Duff, A. (ed.) (1997) *The Treaty of Amsterdam* (London: Federal Trust).

Dunleavy, P. and O'Leary, B. (1987) *Theories of the State* (London: Macmillan).

Eckersley, R. (1989) 'Green politics and the new class: Selfishness or virtue?', *Political Studies*, 2 (37), pp. 205–23.

Eckersley, R. (1992) *Environmentalism and Political Theory* (London: UCL).

Eckersley, R. (1993) 'Free market environmentalism: friend or foe?', *Environmental Politics*, 2 (1), pp. 1–19.

Eckersley, R. (1995) 'Liberal Democracy and the rights of nature: The struggle for inclusion' in F. Matthews (ed.) *Ecology and Democracy*, special edition of *Environmental Politics*, 4 (4), pp. 169–98.

Eckersley, R. (1996) 'Greening liberal democracy: The rights discourse revisted' in B. Doherty and M. de Geus, M (eds), *Democracy and Green Political Thought* (London: Routledge), pp. 212–36.

Ehrlich, P. (1972) *The Population Bomb* (London: Pan).

Elkington, J. and Hailes, J. (1988) *The Green Consumer Guide* (London: Gollancz).

Elliot, L. (1998) *The Global Politics of the Environment* (Basingstoke: Macmillan).

Elliot, R. (ed.) (1995) *Environmental Ethics* (Oxford: Oxford University Press).

Elliot, R. (1995) 'Introduction' in R. Elliot (ed.), *Environmental Ethics* (Oxford: Oxford University Press), pp. 1–20

Enzensberger, H. (1974) 'A critique of political ecology', *New Left Review*, 84, pp. 3–31.

Evans, D. (1991) *A History of Nature Conservation in Britain* (London: Routledge).

Evans, J. (1993) 'Ecofeminism and the politics of the gendered self' in A. Dobson and P. Lucardie (eds), *The Politics of Nature: Explorations in Green Political Theory* (London: Routledge), pp. 177–89.

Flynn, A. and Lowe, P. (1992) 'The greening of the Tories: The Conservative party and the environment' in W. Rudig (ed.), *Green Politics Two*, (Edinburgh: Edinburgh University Press), pp. 9–36.

Fox, W. (1984) 'Deep ecology: A new philosophy of our times', *The Ecologist*, 14 (5), pp. 199–200.

Fox, W. (1995) *Toward a Transpersonal Ecology: Developing New Foundations for Environmentalism* (Totnes: Resurgence).

Frey, R. K. (1983) *Rights, Killing and Suffering* (Oxford: Clarendon Press).

Friday, L. and Laskey, R. (eds) (1989) *The Fragile Environment* (Cambridge: Cambridge University Press).

Gallatley, J. (1996) *The Silent Ark* (London: Thorsons).

Gamble, A. (1981) *An Introduction to Modern Social and Political Thought* (London: Macmillan).

Gamson, W. (1975) *The Strategy of Social Protest* (Illinois: The Dorsey Press).

Garner, R. (1993a) *Animals, Politics and Morality* (Manchester: Manchester University Press).

Garner, R. (1993b) 'Political animals: A survey of the animal protection movement in Britain', *Parliamentary Affairs*, 46 (3), pp. 333–52.

Garner, R. (1994) 'Wildlife conservation and the moral status of animals', *Environmental Politics*, 3 (1), pp. 114–9.

Garner, R. (1995) 'The politics of animal protection: A research agenda', *Society and Animals*, 3 (1), pp. 43–60.

Garner, R. (ed.) (1996) *Animal Rights: The Changing Debate* (Basingstoke, Macmillan).

Garner, R. (1998) *Political Animals: Animal Protection Politics in Britain and the United States* (Basingstoke: Macmillan).

Garner, R. and Kelly R.N. (1993) *British Political Parties Today* (Manchester: Manchester University Press).

Georgescu-Roegen (1973) 'The entropy law and the economic problem' in Daly, H.E. (ed.), *Towards a Steady State Economy* (San Francisco: Freeman), pp. 37–49.

Giddens, A. (1998) *The Third Way: The Renewal of Social Democracy* (Cambridge: Polity).

Goddard Svendsen, R. (1996) 'Animal welfare and the European Union' in R. Garner (ed.), *Animal Rights: The Changing Debate* (Basingstoke, Macmillan), pp. 143–65.

Goldsmith, E.; Allen, R.; Allaby, M; Davoll, J. and Lawrence, S. (1972) *Blueprint for Survival* (Harmondsworth: Penguin).

Golub, J. (1996a) 'Sovereignty and subsidiarity in EU environmental policy', *Political Studies*, 4 (44), pp. 686–703.

Golub, J. (1996b) 'British sovereignty and the development of EC environmental policy', *Environmental Politics*, 4 (5), pp. 700–28.

Goodin, R. E. (1992a) *Green Political Theory* (Cambridge: Polity Press).

Goodin, R. E. (1992b) 'The high ground is green', *Environmental Politics*, 1 (1), pp. 1–8.

Goodwin, B. (1997) *Using Political Ideas*, 4th edn (Chichester: John Wiley & Sons).

Gorz, A. (1982) *Fairwell to the Working Class:An Essay in Post-Industrial Socialism* (London: Pluto).

Gorz, A. (1985) *Paths to Paradise: On the Liberation from Work* (London: Pluto).

Goudie, A. (1989) 'The changing human impact' in L. Friday and R. Laskey (eds) *The Fragile Environment* (Cambridge: Cambridge University Press), pp. 1–21.

Grant, W. (1989) *Pressure Groups, Politics and Democracy in Britain* (Hemel Hempstead: Philip Allan).

Gray, J. (1993) *Beyond the New Right: Markets, Government and the Common Environment* (Cambridge: Cambridge University Press).

Gray, J. (1999) 'Misguided man', *Guardian*, July 31.

Gray T. (ed.) (1995) *UK Environmental Policy in the 1990s* (Basingstoke: Macmillan).

Greenaway, J.; Smith, S. and Street, J. (1992) *Deciding Factors in British Politics: A Case Study Approach* (London: Routledge).

Gribben, J. (1988) *The Hole in the Sky* (London: Corgi).

Griffin, S. (1978) *Woman and Nature: The Roaring Inside Her* (New York: Harper & Row).

Griggs, S., Howarth, D. and Jacobs, B. (1998) 'Second runway at Manchester' in F.F. Ridley and G. Jordan (eds), *Protest Politics: Cause Groups and Campaigns* (Oxford: Oxford University Press), pp. 50–61.

Haigh, N. (1986) 'Developed responsibility and centralization: effects of EEC environmental policy', *Public Administration*, 64, pp. 197–207.

Haigh, N. (1990) *EEC Environmental Policy and Britain*, 2nd edn (London: Longman).

Haigh, N. (1992) 'The European Community and international environmental policy' in A. Hurrell and B. Kingsbury (eds), *The International Politics of the Environment* (Oxford: Clarendon Press), pp. 228–49.

Haigh, N. and Lanigan, C. (1995) 'Impact of the European Union on UK environmental policy making' in T. Gray (ed.), *UK Environmental Policy in the 1990s* (Basingstoke: Macmillan), pp. 11–17.

Hajer, M. (1997) *The Politics of Environmental Discourse: Ecological Modernization and the Policy Process* (Oxford: Clarendon Press).

Ham, C. and Hill, M. (1984) *The Policy Process in the Modern Capitalist State* (Hemel Hempstead: Harvester Wheatsheaf).

Hamer, M. (1974) *Wheels Within Wheels* (London: Friends of the Earth).

Hansen, A. (ed.) (1993) *The Mass Media and Environmental Issues* (Leicester: Leicester University Press), pp. 143–65.

Hardin, G. (1968) 'The tragedy of the commons', *Science*, 162, pp. 1243–8.

Hardin, G. (1977) 'Living on a lifeboat' in G. Hardin and J. Baden (eds), *Managing the Commons* (San Francisco: Freeman).

Harvey, B. and Hallett, J. D. (1977) *Environment and Society: An Introductory Analysis* (London: Macmillan).

Hawkins, K. (1984) *Environment and Enforcement* (Oxford: Clarendon Press).

Hay, P. R. (1988) 'Ecological values and western political traditions: From anarchism to fascism', *Politics*, 8 (2), pp. 22–9.

Hayward, T. (1995) *Ecological Thought: An Introduction* (Cambridge: Polity).

Hayward, T. (1998) *Political Theory and Ecological Values* (Cambridge: Polity).

Heclo, H. (1978) 'Issue networks and the executive establishment' in A. King (ed.), *The New American Political System* (Washington DC: American Enterprise Institute).

Heilbroner, R. L. (1974) *An Inquiry into the Human Prospect* (New York: Norton).

Held, D. and McGrew, A. (1993) 'Globalization and the liberal democratic state', *Government and Opposition*, 2 (28), pp. 261–88.

Hewett, C. (1997) 'Environment: The undisputed European issue' in E. Barrett and S. Tindale (eds), *Britain in Europe. Initiatives for the 1998 Presidency* (London, Institute for Public Policy Research).

Heywood, A. (1992) *Political Ideologies: An Introduction* (Basingstoke: Macmillan).

Hildebrand, P. M. (1993) 'The European Community's environmental policy,1957 to 1992: From incidental measures to an international Regime?', *Environmental Politics*, 1 (4), pp. 13–44.

Hirsch, F. (1977) *Social Limits to Growth* (London: Routledge & Kegan Paul).

HMSO (1975) *Food From Our Own Resources*, Cmnd 5254.

HMSO (1998) *Modern Public Services for Britain: Investing in Reform. Comprehensive Spending Review*. Cmnd 4011.

Hogwood, B. (1987) *From Crisis to Complacency? Shaping Public Policy in Britain* (Oxford: Oxford University Press).

Huby, M. (1998) *Social Policy and the Environment* (Buckingham: Open University Press).

Hulsberg, W. (1987) *The West German Greens* (London: Verso).

Humphreys, D. (1996), 'The Global politics of forest conservation since the UNCED', *Environmental Politics*, 2 (5), pp. 231–56.

Hurrell, A. (1992) 'The 1992 Earth Summit: Funding mechanisms and environmental institutions', *Environmental Politics*, 4 (1), pp. 273–8.

Hurrell, A. (1995) 'International Political Theory and the Global Enviroment' in K. Booth and S. Smith (eds), International Relations Theory Today (Cambridge: Polity Press), pp. 129–53.

Hurrell, A and Kingsbury, B. (eds) (1992a) *The International Politics of the Environment* (Oxford: Clarendon Press).

Hurrell, A and Kingsbury, B. (1992b) 'The international politics of the environment: An introduction' in A. Hurrell and B. Kingsbury (eds), *The International Politics of the Environment* (Oxford, Clarendon Press).

Inglehart, R. (1977) *The Silent Revolution:Changing Values and Political Styles Among Western Publics* (Princeton: Princeton University Press).

Inglehart (1990) 'Values, ideology and cognitive mobilization in new social movements' in R. Dalton and M. Kuechler (eds), *Challenging the Political Order: New Social and Political Movements in Western Democracies* (Cambridge: Polity Press), pp. 43–66.

Inglehart, R. and Rabier, J.R., (1986) 'Political realignment in advanced industrial society: From class based politics to quality of life politics', *Government and Opposition*, 21, 4, pp. 456–79.

Jacobs, M. (1996) *The Politics of the Real World* (London: Earthscan).

Jacobs, M. (1997) *Greening the Millennium: The New Politics of the Environment* (Oxford: Blackwell).

Johnson, L. E. (1991) *A Morally Deep World* (Cambridge: Cambridge University Press).

Jones, B. (1989) 'Green thinking', *Talking Politics*, 2 (2), pp. 50–4.

Jordan, A. (1993) 'Integrated pollution control and the evolving style and structure of environmental regulation in the UK', *Environmental Politics*, 2 (3), pp. 405–27.

Jordan, A. (1998) 'The Impact on UK environmental administration', in P. Lowe and S. Ward (eds), British Environmental Policy and Europe: Politics and policy in transition (London: Routledge), pp. 173–94.

Jordan, G. and Maloney, W. (1997) *The Protest Business* (Manchester: Manchester University Press).

Jordan, T. and Lent, A. (eds) (1999) *Storming the Millennium: The New Politics of Change* (London: Lawrence & Wishart).

Judge, D. (1993) '"Predestined to save the earth": The environment committee of the European Parliament', *Environmental Politics*, 1 (4), pp. 186–212.

Keohane, R.O. (1989) *International Institutionms and State Power* (Boulder, CO: Westview).

Kimber, R. and Richardson, J. J. (eds) (1974) *Campaigning for the Environment* (London: Routledge & Kegan Paul).

Kitsuse, J. I. and Spector, M. (1981) 'The labelling of social problems' in E. Rubington and M.S. Weinberg, (eds), *The Study of Social Problems* (New York: Oxford University Press), pp. 198–206.

Labour Party (1992) *It's Time to Get Britain Working Again* (London: Labour Party election manifesto).

Labour Party (1997) *New Labour Because Britain Deserves Better* (London: Labour Party election manifesto).

Lauber, V. (1978) 'Ecology politics and liberal democracy', *Government and Opposition*, 13 (2), pp. 199–217.

Lear, L. (1998) *Rachel Carson: Witness for Nature* (London: Penguin).

Leopold, A. (1949) *A Sand County Almanac* (Oxford: Oxford University Press).

Liberatore, A. (1997) 'The integration of sustainable development objectives into EU policy making: Barriers and prospects' in S. Baker, M. Kousis, D. Richardson and S. Young (eds), *The Politics of Sustainable Development: Theory, Policy and Practice Within the European Union* (London: Routledge), pp. 107–26.

Liefferink, D.; Lowe, P and Mol, T. (eds) (1993) *European Integration and Environmental Policy* (London: Belhaven).

Liefferink, D.; Lowe, P and Mol, T. (1993) 'The environment and the European Community: The analysis of political integration' in D. Liefferink, P. Lowe and T. Mol (eds) *European Integration and Environmental Policy* (London: Belhaven), pp. 1–13.

Liefferink, D. and Skou Andersen, M., (1998) 'Greening the EU: National positions in the run-up to the Amsterdam Treaty', *Environmental Politics*, 3 (7), pp. 66–93.

Lindblom, C. (1959) 'The science of "muddling through"', *Public Administration Review*, 19, pp. 79–88.

Lindblom, C. (1977) *Politics and Markets* (New York: Basic Books).

List, M. and Rittberger, V (1992) 'Regime theory and international environmental management' in A. Hurrell and B. Kingsbury (eds), *The International Politics of the Environment* (Oxford: Clarendon Press), pp. 85–109.

Lively, J. (1975) *Democracy* (Oxford: Basil Blackwell).

Long, T. (1998) 'The environmental lobby' in P. Lowe and S. Ward (eds), *British Environmental Policy and Europe: Politics and Policy in Transition* (London: Routledge), pp. 105–18.

Lovelock, J. (1979) *Gaia* (Oxford: Oxford University Press).

Lowe, P. *et al.* (1986) *Countryside Conflicts: The Politics of Farming, Forestry and Conservation* (Aldershot: Gower).

Lowe, P. and Flynn, A. (1989) 'Environmental politics and policy in the 1980s' in J. Moham, *The Political Geography of Contemporary Britain* (Basingstoke: Macmillan), pp. 255–279.

Lowe, P. and Goyder, J. (1983) *Environmental Groups in Politics* (London: Allen & Unwin).

Lowe, P. and Rudig, W. (1986) 'Review article: Political ecology and the social sciences – The state of the art', *British Journal of Political Science*, 16, pp. 513–50.

Lowe, P. and Ward, S. (eds) (1998a) *British Environmental Policy and Europe: Politics and Policy in Transition* (London: Routledge).

Lowe, P. and Ward, S. (1998b) 'Britain and Europe: Themes and issues in national environmental policy' in P. Lowe and S. Ward (eds) *British Environmental Policy and Europe: Politics and Policy in Transition* (London: Routledge) pp. 3–30.

Lowe, P. and Ward, S. (1998c) 'Domestic winners and losers' in P. Lowe and S. Ward (eds), *British Environmental Policy and Europe: Politics and Policy in Transition* (London: Routledge), pp. 87–104.

Lowe, P. and Ward, S. (1998d) 'Lessons and prospects: The prospects for the UK environment in Europe' in P. Lowe and S. Ward (eds) *British Environmental Policy and Europe: Politics and Policy in Transition* (London: Routledge), pp. 285–99.

Lukes, S. (1974) *Power: A Radical View* (London: Macmillan).

Lyster, S. (1985) *International Wildlife Law* (Cambridge: Grotius).

MacNeil, J.;Winsemius, P. and Yakushiji, T (1991) *Beyond Independence: The Meshing of the World's Economy and the Earth's Ecology* (Oxford: Oxford University Press).

Maddison, D. and Pearce, D. (1995) 'The UK and global warming policy' in T. Gray (ed.), *UK Environmental Policy in the 1990s* (Basingstoke: Macmillan), pp. 123–43.

Maddox, J. (1972) *The Doomesday Syndrome* (London: Maddox Editorial Ltd).

MAFF (1991) *Our Farming Future* (London: Central Office of Information).

Mannion, A. M. (1991) *Global Environmental Change: A Natural and Cultural Environmental History* (London: Longman).

Marsh, D. (ed.) (1983) *Pressure Politics: Interest Groups in Britain* (London: Junction Books).

Marsh, D. and Rhodes, R. (eds) (1992) *Policy Networks in British Politics* (Oxford: Oxford University Press).

Martell, L. (1994) *Ecology and Society* (Cambridge: Polity).

Maslow, A. H. (1954) *Motivation and Personality* (New York: Harper).

Mason, J. and Singer, P. (1990) *Animal Factories*, 2nd edn (New York: Harmony).

Matthews, F. (1991) *The Ecological Self* (London: Routledge).

Matthews, F. (ed.) (1995) *Ecology and Democracy*, special edition of *Environmental Politics*, 4, (4).

May, R. (1989) 'How many species?' in L. Friday and R. Laskey (eds), *The Fragile Environment* (Cambridge: Cambridge University Press), pp. 61–81.

Mazey, S. and Richardson, J. (1993) 'Environmental groups and the EC: Challenges and opportunities', *Environmental Politics*, 1 (4), pp. 109–28.

McCarthy, J. D. and Zald, M. N. (1977) 'Resource mobilization and social movements', *American Journal of Sociology*, 82, pp. 1212–41.

McCleod, R. (1998) 'Calf Exports at Brightlingsea' in F.F. Ridley and G. Jordan (eds), *Protest Politics: Cause Groups and Campaigns* (Oxford: Oxford University Press), pp. 37–49.

McCormick, J. (1989) *Acid Earth: The Global Threat of Acid Pollution* (London: Earthscan).

McCormick, J. (1991) *British Politics and the Environment* (London: Earthscan).

McCormick J. (1992) *The Global Environmental Movement* (London: Belhaven).

McCormick J. (1993) 'Environmental Politics', in P. Dunleavy, A. Gamble and G. Peele (eds), Developments in British Politics 4 (Basingstoke: Macmillan), pp. 267–84.

McCulloch, A. (1988a) 'Shades of green: Ideas in the British Green Movement', *Teaching Politics*, 17 (2), pp. 186–207.

McCulloch, A. (1988b) 'Politics and the environment', *Talking Politics*, 1 (1), pp. 14–19.

McCulloch, A. (1991) 'Green pressure', *Contemporary Record*, 4 (3), pp. 10–12.

McCulloch, A. (1992) 'The Green party in England and Wales: Structure and development: The early Years', *Environmental Politics*, 1 (3), pp. 418–36.

McKay, G. (1996) *Senseless Acts of Beauty: Cultures of Resistance Since the Sixties* (London: Verso).

McTaggart, D. (1978) *Greenpeace III. Journey into the Bomb* (London: Collins).

Meadows, D. H.; Meadows, D. L.; Randers, J. and Behrens III, W. (1972) *The Limits to Growth: A Report for the Club of Rome's Project on the Predicament of Mankind* (New York: Universe).

Meadows, D. H.; Meadows, D. L. and Randers, J. (1992) *Beyond the Limits: Global Collapse or a Sustainable Society: Sequal to the Limits to Growth* (London: Earthscan).

Mellor, M. (1992) 'Ecofeminist, ecofeminine or ecomasculine', *Environmental Politics*, 1 (2), pp. 229–51.

Mellor, M. (1997) *Feminism and Ecology* (Cambridge: Polity).

Merchant, C. (1980) *The Death of Nature: Women, Ecology and the Scientific Revolution* (NewYork: Harper & Row).

Miller, M. (1995) *The Third World in Global Environmental Politics* (Buckingham: Open University Press).

Monbiot, G. (1999) 'Poisoning those who are poor', *Guardian*, May 20.

Morgenthau, H. J. (1962) *Politics in the Twentieth Century* (Chicago: University of Chicago Press).

Myers, N. (1989) 'The future of forests' in L. Friday, L. and R. Laskey (eds), *The Fragile Environment* (Cambridge: Cambridge University Press), pp. 22–40.

Myers, N. and Simon, J. (1994) *Scarcity or Abundance: A Debate on the Environment* (New York: Norton).

Naess, A. (1973) 'The shallow and the deep, long range ecology movement. A summary', *Inquiry*, 16, pp. 95–100.

Newby, H. (1988) *The Countryside in Question* (London: Hutchinson).

Nordliner, E. (1981) *On the Autonomy of the Democratic State* (Cambridge, Mass: Harvard University Press).

North, P. (1998) '"Save our Solsbury!"': The anatomy of an anti-roads protest', *Environmental Politics*, 3 (7), pp. 1–25.

North, R. (1995) *Life on a Modern Planet: A Manifesto for Progress* (Manchester: Manchester University Press).

Norton, B. (1991) *Toward Unity Among Environmentalists* (Oxford: Oxford University Press).

Nyhagen Predelli, L. (1995) 'Ideological conflict in the radical environmental group Earth First!', *Environmental Politics*, 1 (4), pp. 123–9.

Olson, M. (1965) *The Logic of Collective Action* (Cambridge, Mass.: Harvard University Press).

O'Neil, J. (1993) *Ecology, Policy and Politics: Human Well-Being and the Natural World* (London: Routledge).

Ophuls, W. (1973) 'Leviathan or oblivion?' in H.E. Daly (ed.), *Toward a Steady State Economy* (San Francisco: Freeman), pp. 215–30.

Ophuls, W. (1977) *Ecology and the Politics of Scarcity* (San Francisco: W.H. Freeman & Co).

O'Riordan, T. (1976) *Environmentalism* (London: Pion).

O'Riordan, T. and Jager, J. (eds) (1996) *Politics of Climate Change: A European Perspective* (London: Routledge).

O'Riordan, T. and Weale, A. (1989) 'Administrative reorganisation and policy change: The case of Her Majesty's Inspectorate of Pollution', *Public Administration,* 67, pp. 277–95.

O'Riordan, T and Jordan, A. (1995) 'British environmental politics in the 1990s', *Environmental Politics*, 4 (4), pp. 237–46.

Paehlke, R.C. (1989) *Environmentalism and the Future of Progressive Politics* (New Haven: Yale University Press).

Parkin, S. (1989) *Green Parties:An International Guide* (London: Heretic Books).

Parsons, H. (1978) *Marx and Engels on Ecology* (Westport, Conn.: Greenwood).

Passmore, J. (1980) *Man's Responsibility for Nature*, 2nd edn (London: Duckworth).

Pateman, C. (1970) *Participation and Democratic Theory* (Cambridge: Cambridge University Press).

Paterson, M. (1992) 'The Convention on Climate Change agreed at the Rio conference', *Environmental Politics*, 4 (1), pp 267–72.

Paterson, M. (1996) *Global Warming and Global Politics* (London: Routledge).

Pearce, D.; Markandya, A. and Barbier, E. B. (1989) *Blueprint For a Green Economy* (London: Earthscan).

Pearce, D. *et al.* (1993) *Blueprint 3: Measuring Sustainable Development* (London: Earthscan).

Pennington, M. (1997) 'Budgets, bureaucrats and the containment of urban England', *Environmental Politics*, 4, (6), pp. 76–107.

Pepper, D. (1986) *The Roots of Modern Environmentalism* (London: Routledge).

Pepper, D. (1993a) *Eco-Socialism:From Deep Ecology to Social Justice* (London: Routledge).

Pepper, D. (1993b) 'Anthropocentrism, humanism and eco-socialism: A blueprint for the survival of ecological politics', *Environmental Politics*, 2 (3), pp. 428–52.

Pickering, K. T. and Owen, A. O. (1994) *An Introduction to Global Environmental Issues* (London: Routledge).

Piddington, K. (1992) 'The role of the World Bank' in A. Hurrell and B. Kingsbury (eds), *The International Politics of the Environment* (Oxford: Clarendon Press), pp. 212–27.

Porritt, J. (1984) *Seeing Green* (Oxford: Basil Blackwell).

Porritt, J. and Winner, D. (1988) *The Coming of the Greens* (London: Fontana).

Porter, G. and Brown, J. (1996) *Global Environmental Politics*, 2nd edn (Boulder, CO: Westview).

Pugh, M. (1982) *The Making of Modern British Politics 1867–1939* (Oxford: Basil Blackwell).

Rachels, J. (1990) *Created From Animals: The Moral Implications of Darwinism* (Oxford: Oxford University Press).

Rainbow, S. L. (1992) 'Why did New Zealand and Tasmania spawn the world's first Green parties?', *Environmental Politics*, 1 (3), pp. 321–46.

Redclift, M. (1984) *Development and the Environmental Crisis: Red or Green?* (London: Methuen).

Regan, T. (1988) *The Case for Animal Rights* (London: Routledge).

Regan, T. (1991) *The Thee Generation: Reflections on the Coming Revolution* (Philadelphia: Temple University Press).

Regenstein, L. (1985) 'Animal rights, endangered species and human survival' in P. Singer (ed.), *In Defence of Animals* (Oxford: Blackwell).

Rich, B. (1994) *Mortgaging the Earth: The World Bank, Environmental Impoverishment and the Crisis of Development* (London: Earthscan).

Richardson, D. (1997) 'The politics of susutainable development' in S. Baker,M. Kousis, D. Richardson and S. Young (eds), *The Politics of Sustainable Development: Theory, Policy and Practice Within the European Union* (London: Routledge), pp. 43–60.

Richardson, E. L. (1992) 'Climate change: Problems of law making' in A. Hurrell and B. Kingsbury (eds), *The International Politics of the Environment* (Oxford: Clarendon Press), pp. 166–79.

Richardson, J. (ed.) (1982) *Policy Styles in Western Europe* (London: Allen & Unwin).

Richardson, J. *et al.* (1992) 'The dynamics of policy change: lobbying and water privatisation', *Public Administration*, 70, pp. 157–75.

Ridley, F.F. and Jordan, G. (eds) (1998) *Protest Politics: Cause Groups and Campaigns* (Oxford: Oxford University Press).

Ritvo, H. (1987) *The Animal Estate: The English and Other Creatures in the Victorian Age* (Cambridge, Mass.: Harvard University Press).

Robinson, M. (1992) *The Greening of British Party Politics* (Manchester: Manchester University Press).

Rodman, J. (1983) 'Four forms of ecological consciousness reconsidered' in D. Scherer and T. Attig (eds), *Ethics and the Environment* (Englewood Cliffs, N.J: Prentice-Hall), pp. 82–92.

Rootes, C. A. (1991) 'Environmentalism and political competition: The British Greens in the 1989 elections to the European Parliament', *Politics*, 11 (2), pp. 39–44.

Rose, C. (1990) *The Dirty Man of Europe* (London: Simon & Schuster).

Rowbotham, E. (1996) 'Legal obligations and uncertainties in the climate change convention' in T. O'Riordan and J. Jager (eds), *Politics of Climate Change: A European Perspective* (London: Routledge), pp. 32–50.

Rowell, A. (1996) *Green Backlash: Global Subversion of the Environmental Movement* (London: Routledge).

Rudig, W. (1985) 'The Greens in Europe: Ecological parties and the European elections of 1984', *Parliamentary Affairs*, 38 (1), pp. 56–72.

Rudig, W. (ed.) (1991) *Green Politics Two* (Edinburgh: Edinburgh University Press).

Rudig, W. (1993) 'Wilting greenery', *The Times Higher Education Supplement*, September 17.

Rudig, W. and Franklin, M. N. (1991) 'Green prospects: The future of Green parties in Britain, France and Germany' in W. Rudig (ed.), *Green Politics Two* (Edinburgh: Edinburgh University Press), pp. 37–58.

Rudig, W. and Lowe, P. (1986) 'The withered "greening" of British Politics: a study of the Ecology party', *Political Studies*, 34 (2), pp. 262–84.

Ryder, R. (ed.) (1992) *Animal Welfare and the Environment* (London: Duckworth).

Rydin, Y. (1993) *The British Planning System: An Introduction* (Basingstoke: Macmillan).

Rydin, Y. (1997) 'Policy networks, local discourses and the implementation of sustainable development' in S. Baker, M. Kousis, D. Richardson and S. Young (eds), *The Politics of Sustainable Development: Theory, Policy and Practice Within the European Union* (London: Routledge), pp. 152–74.

Ryle, M. (1988) *Ecology and Socialism* (London: Century Hutchinson).

Sagoff, M. (1988) *The Economy of the Earth: Philosophy, Law and the Environment* (Cambridge: Cambridge University Press).

Sale, K. (1980) *Human Scale* (New York: Coward,Cann and Geoghegan).

Sale, K. (1984) 'Bioregionalism – a new way to treat the land', *The Ecologist*, 14, pp. 167–73.

Sandbach, F. (1980) *Environment,Ideology and Policy* (Oxford: Blackwell).

Saward, M. (1992) 'The civil nuclear network in Britain' in D. Marsh and R. Rhodes, (eds), *Policy Networks in British Politics* (Oxford: Oxford University Press), pp. 75–99.

Saward, M. (1993a) 'Green theory', *Environmental Politics*, 2 (3), pp. 509–12.

Saward, M. (1993b) 'Green democracy' in A. Dobson and P. Lucardie (eds), *The Politics of Nature: Explorations in Green Political Theory* (London: Routledge), pp. 63–80.

Saward, M. (1996) 'Must democrats be environmentalists?' in B. Doherty and M. de Geus (eds), *Democracy and Green Political Thought: Sustainability, rights and citizenship* (London: Routledge), pp. 79–96.

Scarrow, H.A. (1961) 'The impact of British domestic air pollution legislation', *British Journal of Political Science*, 2, pp. 261–82.

Schoon, N. 'Acid Rain that earns Britain a black mark', *The Independent*, March 26 1990.

Schumacher, E. F. (1973) *Small is Beautiful: Economics as if People Mattered* (London: Blond and Briggs).

Seager, J. (1993) *Earth Follies: Feminism, Politics and the Environment* (London: Earthscan).

Seel, B. (1997a) 'Strategies of resistance at the Pollok Free State road protest camp', *Environmental Politics*, 4 (6), pp. 108–39.

Seel, B. (1997b) '"If not you, then who?" Earth First! in the UK', *Environmental Politics*, 4 (6), pp. 172–9.

Self, P. and Storing, H. (1962) *The State and the Farmer* (London: Allen & Unwin).

Shoard, M. (1982) *The Theft of the Countryside* (London: Temple Smith).

Shue, H. (1992) 'The unavoidability of justice' in A. Hurrell and B. Kingsbury (eds), *The International Politics of the Environment* (Oxford: Clarendon Press), pp. 373–97.

Simon, J. (1981) *The Ultimate Resource* (Princeton, NJ: Princeton University Press).

Simon, J. and Kahn, H. (eds) (1984) *The Resourceful Earth: A Response to Global 2000* (New York: Basil Blackwell).

Simpson, S. (1990) *The Times Guide to the Environment* (London: Times Books).

Singer, P. (1974) *Democracy and Disobedience* (Oxford: Oxford University Press).

Singer, P. (1983) *The Expanding Circle: Ethics and Sociobiology* (Oxford: Oxford University Press).

Singer, P. (1990) *Animal Liberation* (London: Cape).

Skea, J. and Smith, A. (1998) 'Integrating pollution control' in P. Lowe and S. Ward (eds), *British Environmental Policy and Europe: Politics and Policy in Transition* (London: Routledge), pp. 265–81.

Smith, A. (1997) *Integrated pollution Control: Change and Continuity in the UK Industrial Pollution Policy Network* (Aldershot: Ashgate).

Smith, D. and Blowers, A. (1991) 'Passing the buck – Hazardous waste disposal as an international problem', *Talking Politics*, 4 (1), pp. 44–9.

Smith, M. J. (1990) *The Politics of Agricultural Support in Britain: The Development of the Agricultural Policy Community* (Aldershot: Dartmouth).

Smith, M. J. (1993) *Pressure, Power and Policy:State Autonomy and Policy Networks in Britain and the United States* (Hemel Hempstead: Harvester Wheatsheaf).

Smith, M. (1998) *Ecologism: Towards Ecological Citizenship* (Buckingham: Open University Press).

Stone, C. (1974) *Should Trees Have Standing: Toward Legal Rights for Natural Objects* (Los Altos, California: Kaufmann).

Susskind, L and Ozawa, C. (1992) 'Negotiating more effective international environmental agreements' in A. Hurrell and B. Kingsbury (eds), *The International Politics of the Environment* (Oxford: Clarendon Press).

Sweeney, N. (1990) *Animals and Cruelty and Law* (Bristol: Aliobi).

Taylor, D. (1999) 'Wage slaves, throw off your chains!', *Guardian*, June 23.

Taylor, P.W. (1986) *Respect For Nature: A Theory of Environmental Ethics* (Princeton, NJ: Princeton University Press).

Thacher, P. S. (1992) 'The role of the United Nations' in A. Hurrell and B. Kingsbury (eds), *The International Politics of the Environment* (Oxford: Clarendon Press), pp. 183–211.

Thomas, C. (1992) 'The United Nations Conference on Environment and Development of 1992 in context', *Environmental Politics*, 4 (1), pp. 250–66.

Thomas, C. (1993) 'Beyond UNCED: An introduction', *Environmental Politics*, 2 (4), pp. 1–27.

Thomas, R. (1983) *The Politics of Hunting* (Aldershot: Gower).

Tickell, O (1997) 'Toothless tiger is on the run', *Guardian*, April 23.

Tuxill, J. (1999) 'Appreciating the benefits of plant biodiversity' in L.R. Brown *et al.* (eds), *State of the World 1999* (New York: Norton), pp. 96–114.

Tuxill, J. and Bright, C. (1998) 'Losing strands in the web of life' in L.R. Brown *et al.* (eds), *State of the World 1998* (New York: Norton), pp. 41–58.

Vidal, J. (1997) 'When the earth caught fire', *Guardian Weekend*, November 8.

Vincent, A. (1993) 'The character of ecology', *Environmental Politics*, 2 (2), pp. 248–76.

Vogel, D. (1986) *National Styles of Regulation: Environmental Policing in Great Britain and the United States* (Ithaca: Cornell University Press).

Vogler, J. (1996) 'Introduction' in J. Vogler and M. Imber (eds), *The Environment and International Relations* (London: Routledge), pp. 1–12.

Vogler, J. and Imber, M. (eds) (1996) *The Environment and International Relations* (London: Routledge).

Waltz, K. (1979) *Theory of International Politics* (Reading, Mass: Addison-Wesley).

Ward, B. and Dubos, R. (1972) *Only One Earth: The Care and Maintenance of a Small Planet* (London: Andre Deutsch).

Ward, H. (1983) 'The anti-nuclear lobby: An unequal struggle?' in D. Marsh (ed.), *Pressure Politics: Interest Groups in Britain* (London: Junction Books), pp. 182–211.

Ward, H. (1990) 'Environmental politics and policy' in P. Dunleavy *et al.* (ed.), *Developments in British Politics 3* (Basingstoke: Macmillan), pp. 221–45.

Ward, N., Lowe, P. and Buller, H. (1997) 'Implementing European water quality directives: Lessons for sustainable development' in S. Baker, M. Kousis, D. Richardson and S. Young (eds), *The Politics of Sustainable Development: Theory, Policy and Practice within the European Union* (London: Routledge), pp. 198–216.

Ward, S. (1993) 'Thinking global, acting local? British local authorities and their environmental plans', *Environmental Politics*, 2 (3), pp. 453–78.

Warren, A. and Goldsmith, F. B. (eds) (1983) *Conservation in Perspective* (Chichester: John Wiley & Sons).

Weale, A. (1992) *The New Politics Of Pollution* (Manchester: Manchester University Press).

Weale, A. and Williams, A. (1992) 'Between economy and ecology? The single market and the integration of environmental policy, *Environmental Politics*, 1 (4) pp. 45–64.

Weston, J. (ed.) (1986) *Red and Green: The New Politics of the Environment* (London: Pluto Press).

Williams, M. (1996) 'International political economy and global environmental change' in J. Vogler and M. Imber (eds), *The Environment and International Relations* (London: Routledge), pp. 41–58.

Williams, R. (1986) 'Hesitations before socialism', *New Socialist*, September, pp. 34–6.

Wilson, G. (1977) *Special Interests and Policy Making* (London: John Wiley & Sons).

Wissenburg, M. (1993) 'The idea of nature and the nature of distributive justice' in A. Dobson and P. Lucardie (eds), *The Politics of Nature: Explorations in Green Political Thought* (London: Routledge), pp. 3–20.

Worcester, R. (1997) 'Public opinion and the environment' in M. Jacobs (ed.), *Greening the Millennium: The New Politics of the Environment*, (Oxford: Blackwell), pp. 160–73.

World Commission on Environment and Development (1987) *Our Common Future*,(Oxford: Oxford University Press).

Wurzel, R. (1993) 'Environmental policy' in J. Lodge (ed.) *The European Community and the Challenge of the Future* (London: Pinter), pp. 48–67

Wynne, B. and Waterton, C. (1998) 'Public information on the environment: The role of the European Environment Agency' in P. Lowe and S. Ward (eds), *British Environmental Policy and Europe: Politics and Policy in Transition* (London: Routledge), pp. 119–37.

Yearley, S. (1992) *The Green Case* (London: Routledge).

Young, H. (1999) 'The intolerant in pursuit of political correctness', *Guardian*, July 13.

Young, J. (1990) *Post Environmentalism* (London: Belhaven).

Young, S. C. (1992) 'The different dimensions of green politics', *Environmental Politics*, 1 (1), pp. 9–44.

Young, S. C. (1993) *The Politics of the Environment* (Manchester: Baseline Books).

Young, S. (1997) 'Local Agenda 21: The renewal of local democracy' in M. Jacobs (eds), *Greening the Millennium: The New Politics of the Environment* (Oxford: Blackwell), pp. 138–47.

Selected Web Sites

Council for the Protection of Rural England
www.greenchannel.com/cpre
Countryside Commission
www.countryside.gov.uk
Department of the Environment, Transport and the Regions
www.detr.gov.uk
DGXI of the European Commission
europa.eu.int/comm/dg11/index_en. htm
Earth First
www.kZnet.co.uk/˜savage/ef
English Nature
www.english-nature.org.uk
Environment Agency
www.environment-agency.gov.uk
Environmental Treaties and Resources Indicators
www.sedac.ciesin.org/entri
European Environment Agency
www.eea.dk
Friends of the Earth
www.foe.co.uk

Green Party
www.gn.apc/green party
Greenpeace
www.greenpeace.org.uk
Hunt Saboteurs Association
www.envirolink.org/arrs/HSA
International Fund for Animal Welfare
www.easynet.co.uk/ifaw
Ministry of Agriculture, Fisheries and Food
www.maff.gov.uk
Reclaim the Streets
www.gn.apc.org/rts
Royal Society for the Prevention of Cruelty to Animals
www.rspca.org.uk
Royal Society for the Protection of Birds
www.rspb.org.uk
This Land is Ours
www.envirolink.org/orgs/tlio
United Nations Environment Programme
www.unep.org
WWF Global Network
www.panda.org

Index